AF226058

Figments of Persuasion

Field Guide   by Nancy Vallette

Illustrations by Don Stephenson

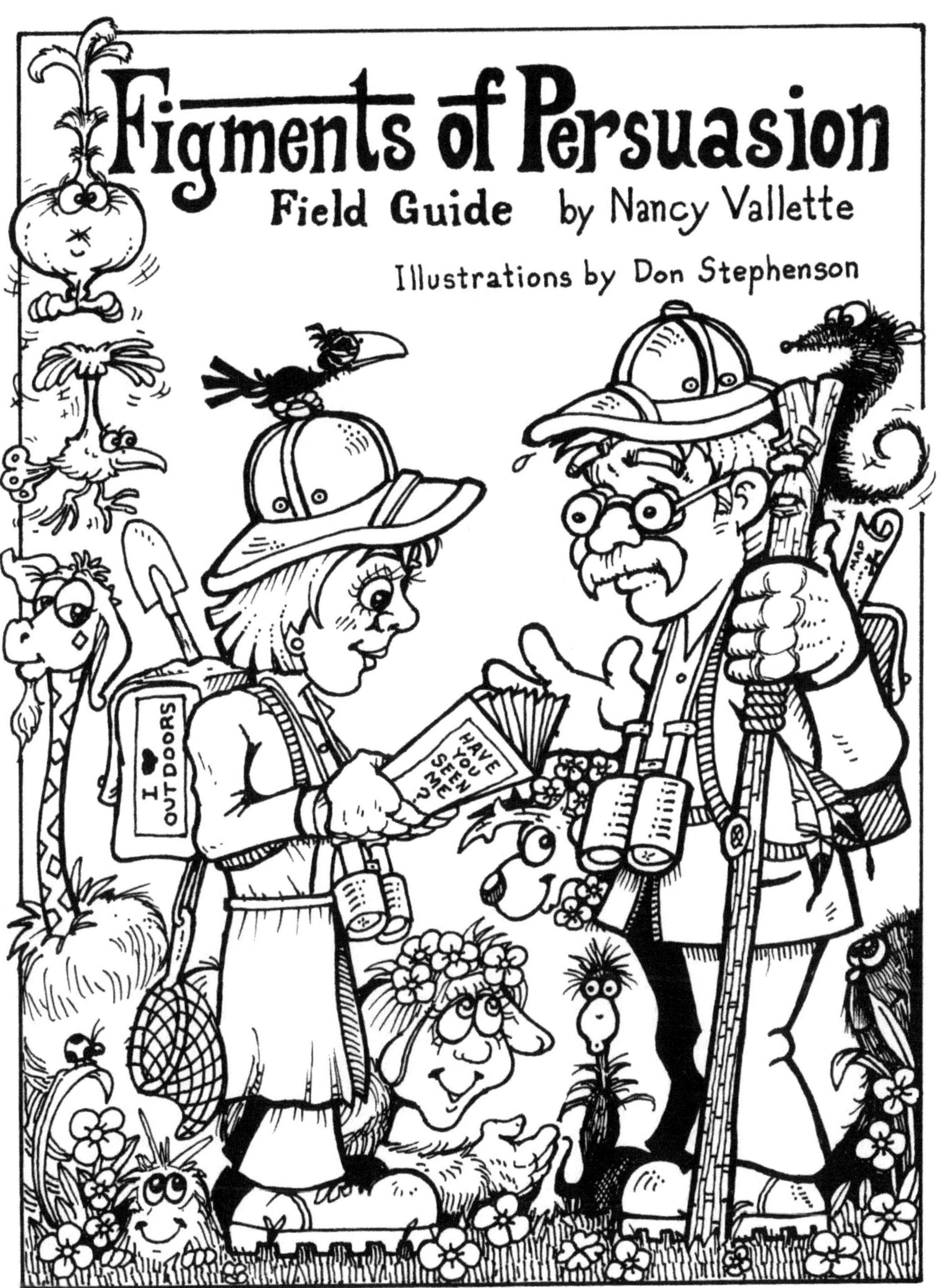

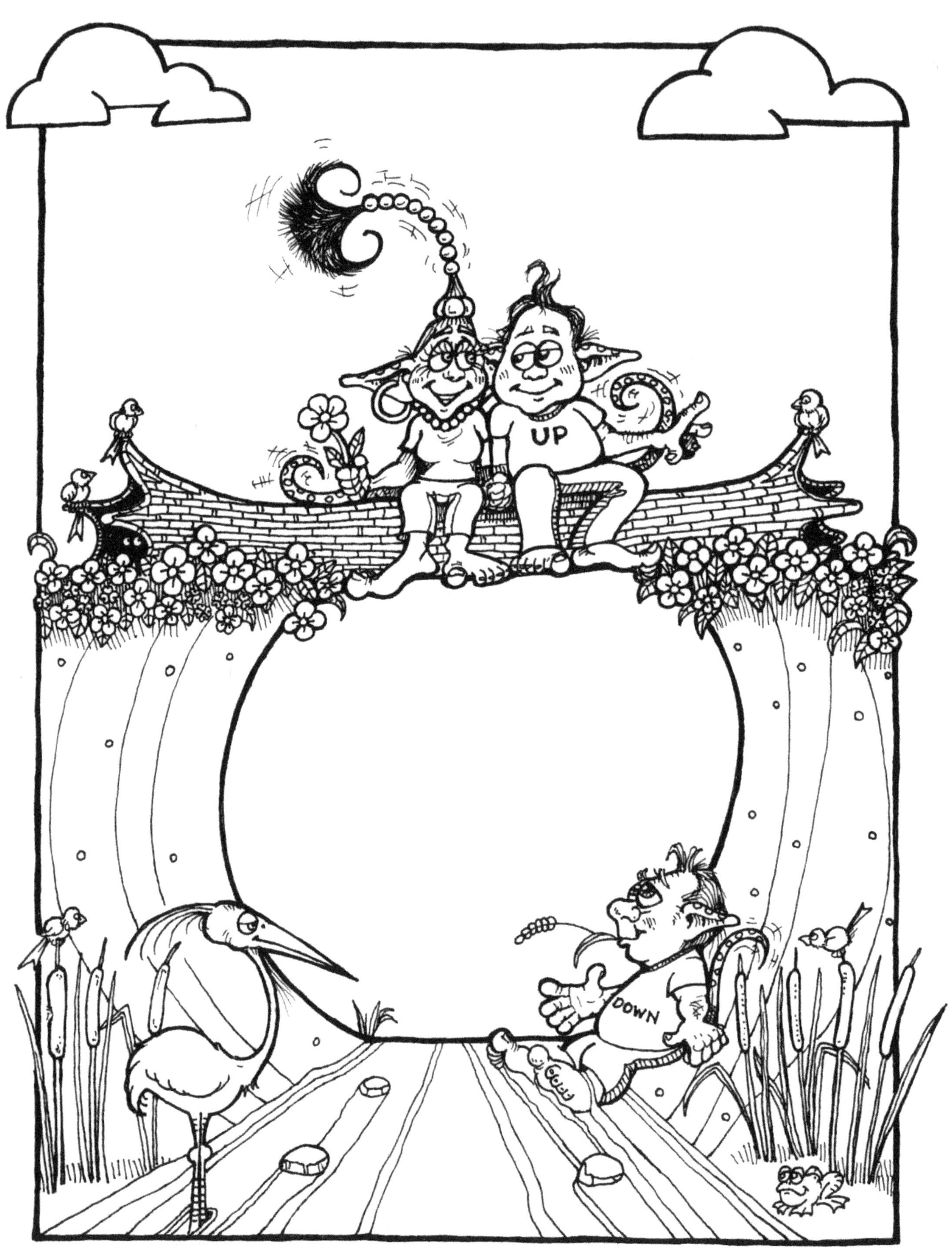

UP
DOWN

Don Stephenson was born and raised in Ohio. He lived in Ohio until joining the Navy in 1974. Don was a photographer for them while stationed in San Diego, California. In 1978 he returned to Ohio, where he went to work for the Yellow Pages as an artist in the Dayton area after a few years. He retired just as the local Yellow Pages were becoming a thing of the past.

He loves to carve wood and do pyrography, wood-burning images into wood. For over five years, he has created comic books for Sparkle and Blood Scream comics: a small independent group locally selling in Dayton and online. He now hopes this will be the first of many collaborations with Nancy. Further, he trusts that all who buy it will enjoy all that went into its creation.

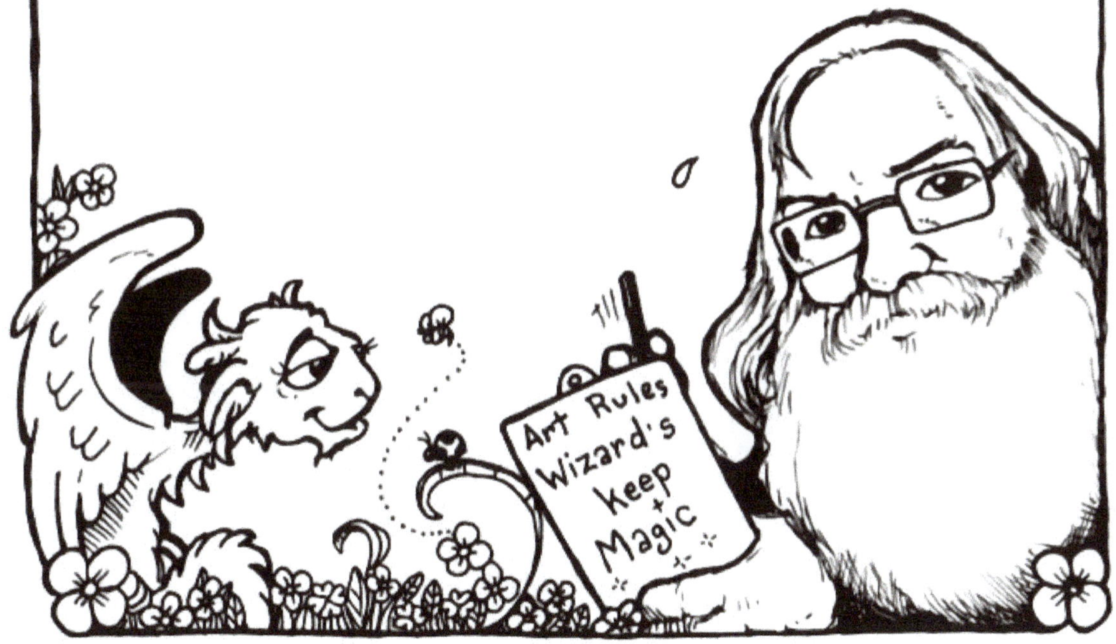

Nancy Vallette is a retired educator of 34 years. She has a master's degree in educational administration, with additional study in Art History, Art Therapy, and Special Education. She taught as an art teacher to kindergarten to 12th graders, adults, and senior citizens. Her specialty was working with students with exceptional special needs. Nancy continued her endeavor in Education Administration as an Assistant Principal for both General and Special Education students in middle and High School settings.

Nancy has also spent much time as a reenactor of Viking culture, bringing her love of history and Education to those endeavors. Those interests lead Nancy and her late husband to cofound what is now the Ashville Viking Festival. This is something she is pretty proud of and has been her heart. Today, she continues to work with The Lost Viking crew, who sees themselves as family and dearly refer to her as their Den-mother.

Nancy finds purpose and love in her writings, identifying various Figments and other things in their world.

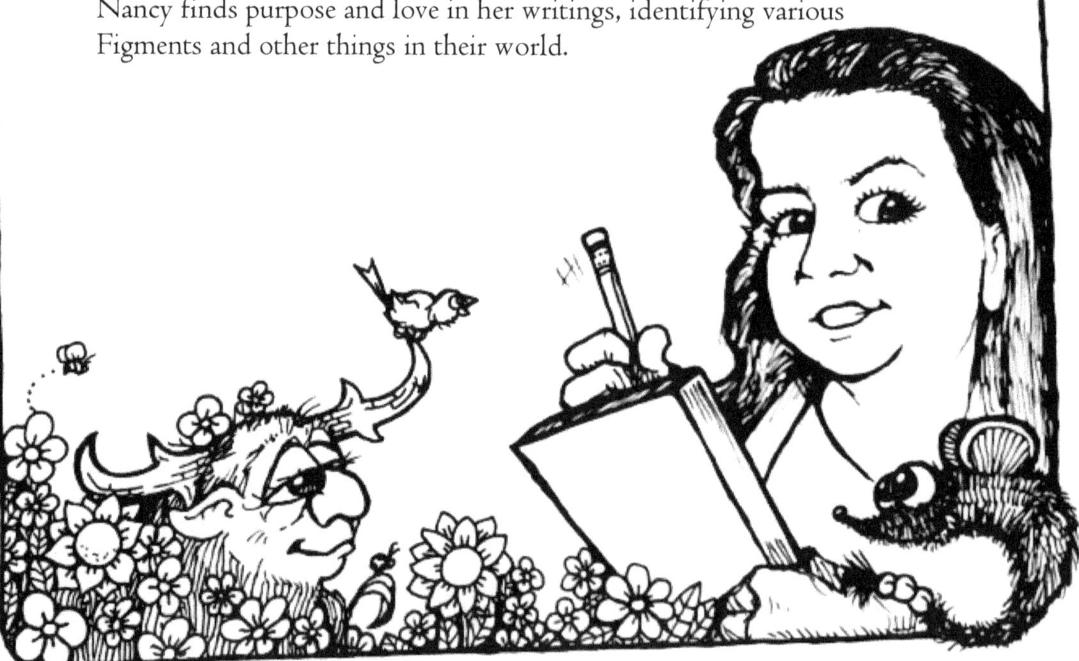

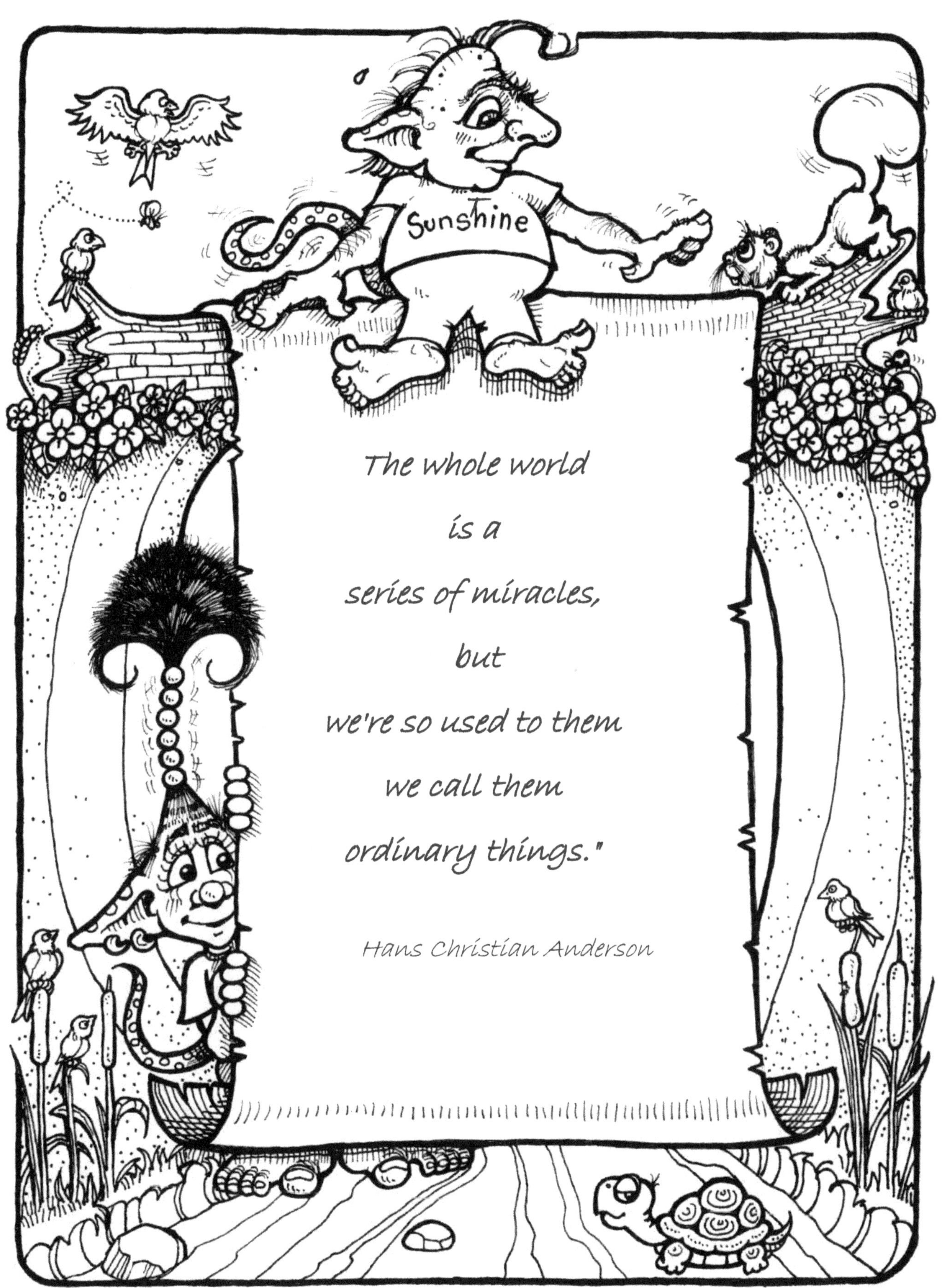

Sunshine
The whole world
is a
series of miracles,
but
we're so used to them
we call them
ordinary things."
Hans Christian Anderson

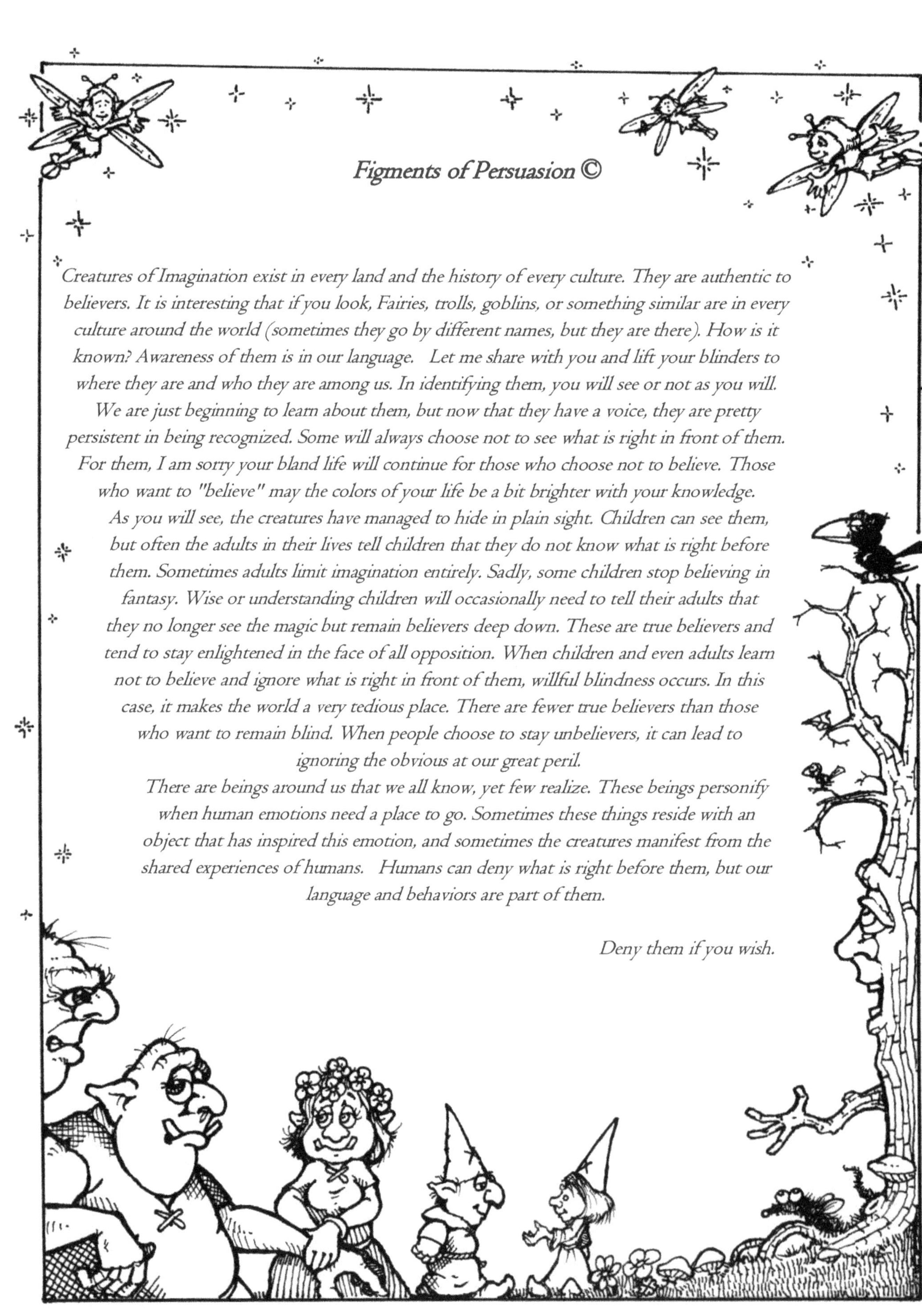

Creatures of Imagination exist in every land and the history of every culture. They are authentic to believers. It is interesting that if you look, Fairies, trolls, goblins, or something similar are in every culture around the world (sometimes they go by different names, but they are there). How is it known? Awareness of them is in our language.   Let me share with you and lift your blinders to where they are and who they are among us. In identifying them, you will see or not as you will.

We are just beginning to learn about them, but now that they have a voice, they are pretty persistent in being recognized. Some will always choose not to see what is right in front of them. For them, I am sorry your bland life will continue for those who choose not to believe. Those who want to "believe" may the colors of your life be a bit brighter with your knowledge.

As you will see, the creatures have managed to hide in plain sight. Children can see them, but often the adults in their lives tell children that they do not know what is right before them. Sometimes adults limit imagination entirely. Sadly, some children stop believing in fantasy. Wise or understanding children will occasionally need to tell their adults that they no longer see the magic but remain believers deep down. These are true believers and tend to stay enlightened in the face of all opposition. When children and even adults learn not to believe and ignore what is right in front of them, willful blindness occurs. In this case, it makes the world a very tedious place. There are fewer true believers than those who want to remain blind. When people choose to stay unbelievers, it can lead to ignoring the obvious at our great peril.

There are beings around us that we all know, yet few realize. These beings personify when human emotions need a place to go. Sometimes these things reside with an object that has inspired this emotion, and sometimes the creatures manifest from the shared experiences of humans.   Humans can deny what is right before them, but our language and behaviors are part of them.

Deny them if you wish.

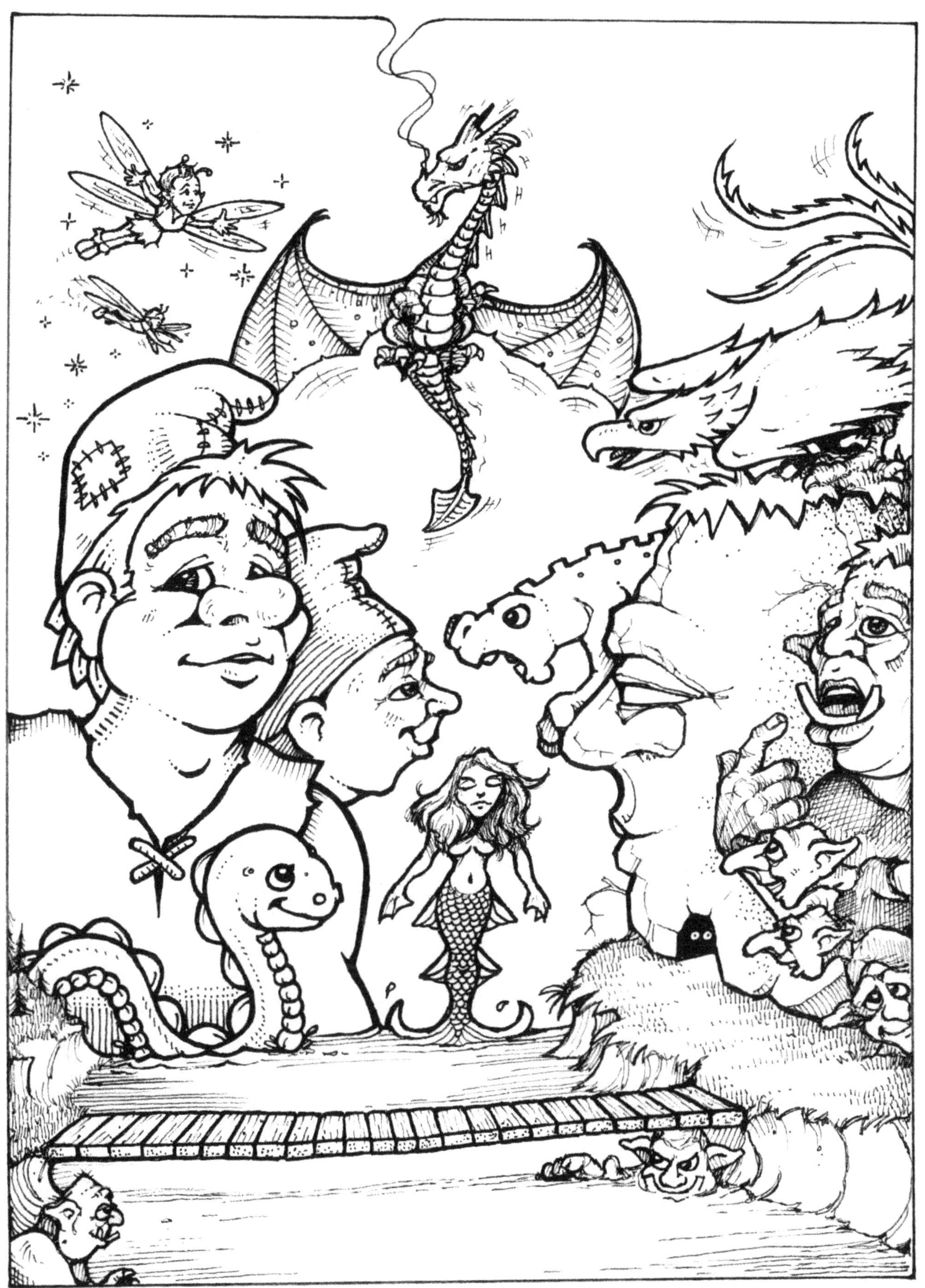

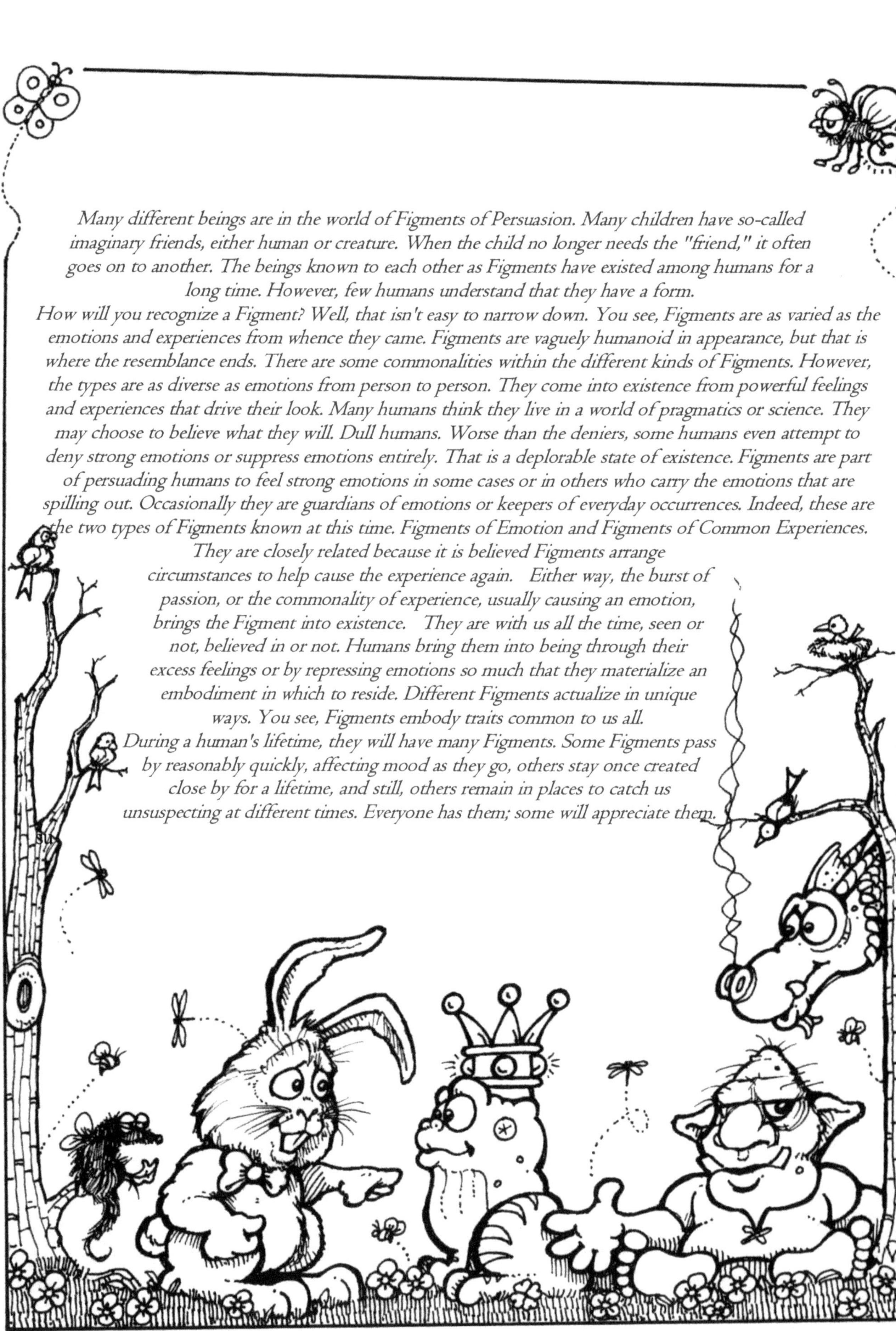

Many different beings are in the world of Figments of Persuasion. Many children have so-called imaginary friends, either human or creature. When the child no longer needs the "friend," it often goes on to another. The beings known to each other as Figments have existed among humans for a long time. However, few humans understand that they have a form.

How will you recognize a Figment? Well, that isn't easy to narrow down. You see, Figments are as varied as the emotions and experiences from whence they came. Figments are vaguely humanoid in appearance, but that is where the resemblance ends. There are some commonalities within the different kinds of Figments. However, the types are as diverse as emotions from person to person. They come into existence from powerful feelings and experiences that drive their look. Many humans think they live in a world of pragmatics or science. They may choose to believe what they will. Dull humans. Worse than the deniers, some humans even attempt to deny strong emotions or suppress emotions entirely. That is a deplorable state of existence. Figments are part of persuading humans to feel strong emotions in some cases or in others who carry the emotions that are spilling out. Occasionally they are guardians of emotions or keepers of everyday occurrences. Indeed, these are the two types of Figments known at this time. Figments of Emotion and Figments of Common Experiences.

They are closely related because it is believed Figments arrange circumstances to help cause the experience again. Either way, the burst of passion, or the commonality of experience, usually causing an emotion, brings the Figment into existence. They are with us all the time, seen or not, believed in or not. Humans bring them into being through their excess feelings or by repressing emotions so much that they materialize an embodiment in which to reside. Different Figments actualize in unique ways. You see, Figments embody traits common to us all.

During a human's lifetime, they will have many Figments. Some Figments pass by reasonably quickly, affecting mood as they go, others stay once created close by for a lifetime, and still, others remain in places to catch us unsuspecting at different times. Everyone has them; some will appreciate them.

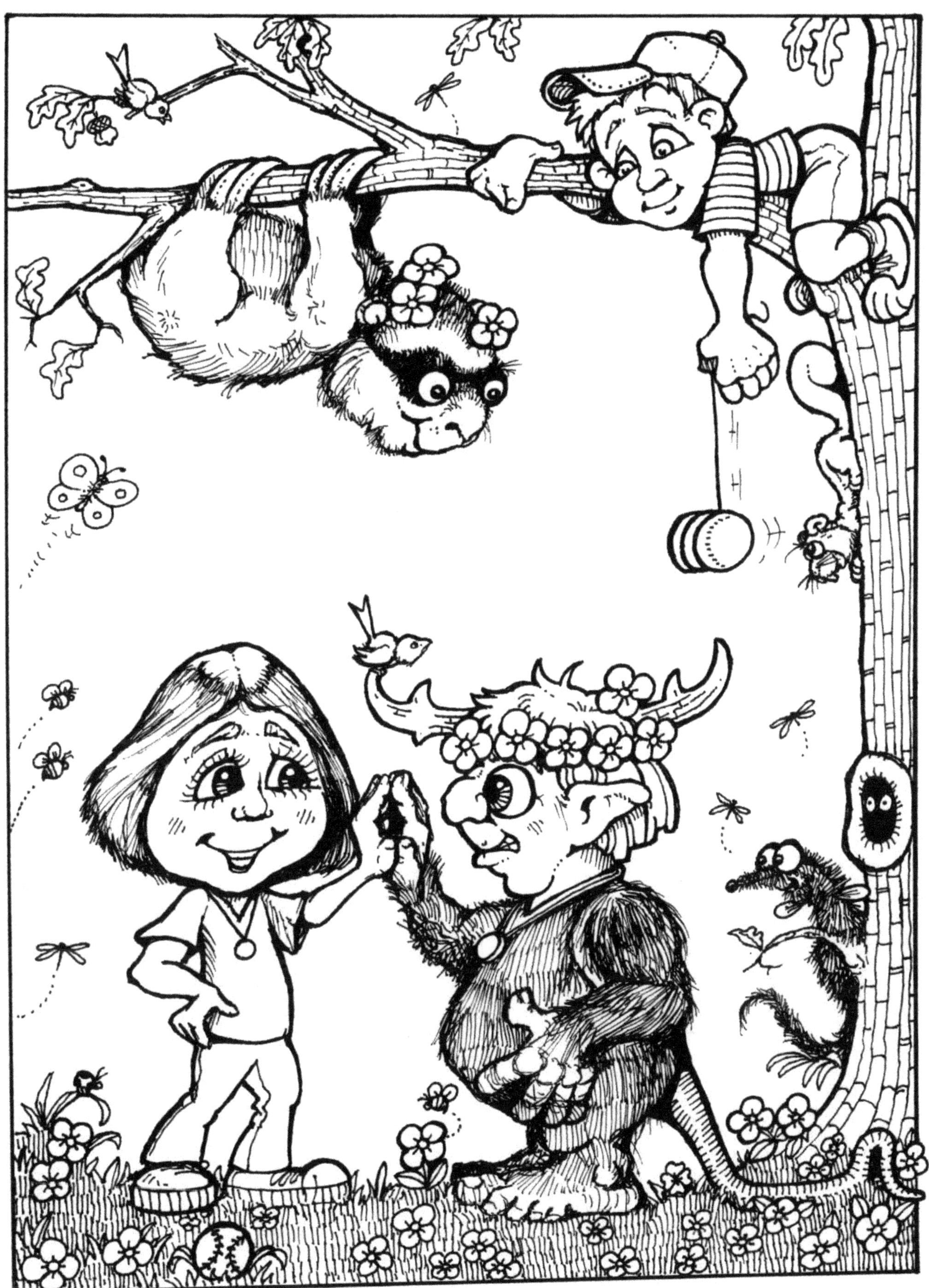

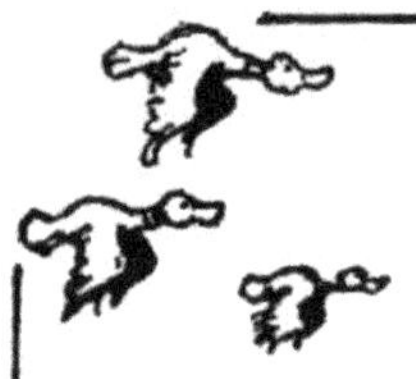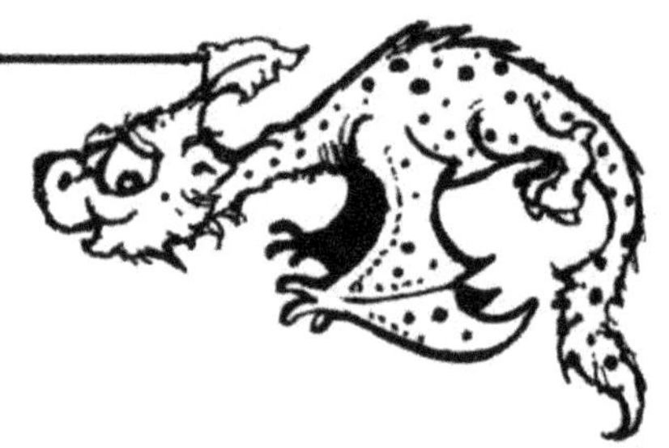

Figments are not afraid of humans; they are amused by them. They accept that they have manifested from human experiences. They sympathize with the fact that a human trait is to resist seeing what is right in front of them.

Figments do tend to find that rather hilarious. And they do love to have fun.   At the same time, Figments believe humans frequently live in extremely humdrum conditions that they find somewhat unsettling. Sometimes that unsettled nature leads to a Sinister. Figments are very wary of Sinisters.

When a Figment is in the vicinity of a human, that person will feel the effects, whether enlightened or not. After all, that intense Energy in one place by its very nature tends to have an impact. Some humans, of course, are more sensitive (or susceptible) than others to different types of Figments. It is observable that appearance, speech, and even customs may differ worldwide, but underneath all hearts feel the same emotions. Figments attach regardless of age or place of dwelling.

Some Figments may come and go throughout a human's lifetime, and some wander away. Some will become more attached as time goes on. Getting rid of a Peeve, for instance, that has become a pet, is challenging. Some Figments are very pleasant to have with you. Others are a bit darker. Other Figments such as Conniptions tend to leave as humans mature and new ones attach. It depends on the nature of the individual Figment.

Remember, just because you don't believe in or acknowledge a thing does not negate its existence.

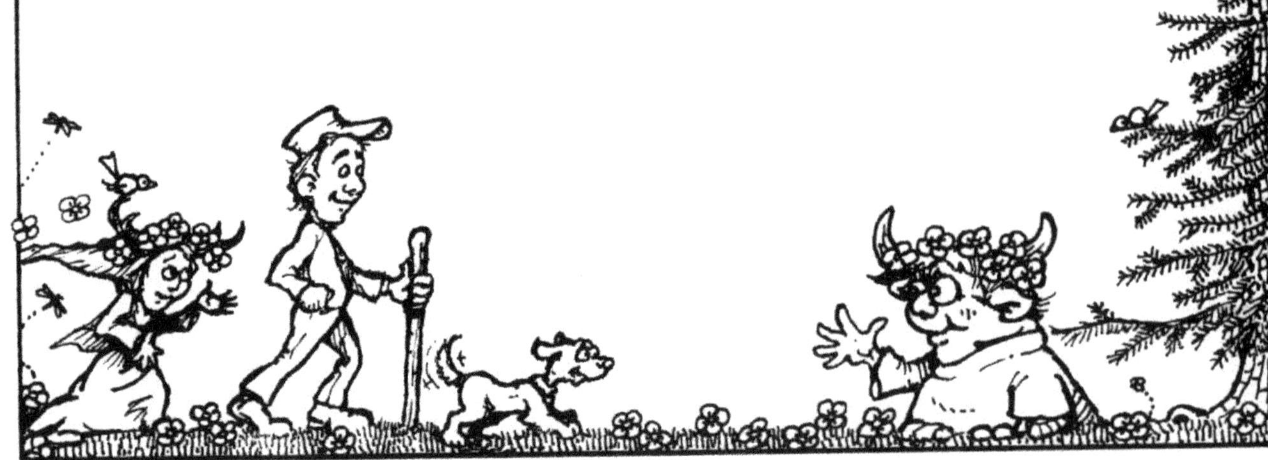

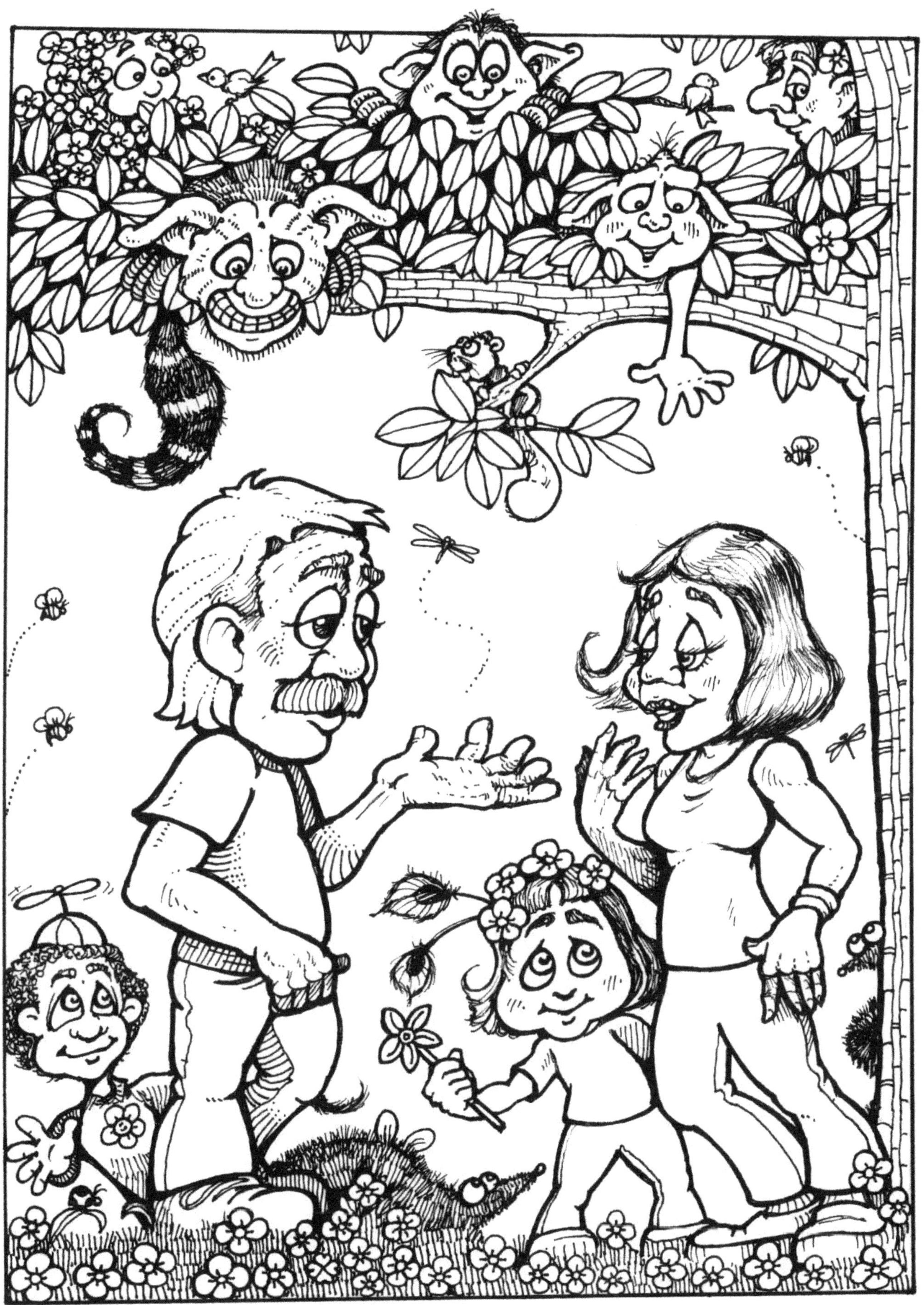

I

s it possible to regain the belief in things creative and unseen if you have lost the ability? Can you return to the wonderment of childhood and "see" once again? It is possible, and some have done it. It is both a relatively simple and yet a challenging thing to accomplish.

First, one must want to believe. Be receptive to the possibilities all around you. Practice finding joy in small things, the smell of rain, or the moss in the cracks between rocks that blooms for a small amount of time. Enjoy the humor in a single stalk of corn defiantly growing in asphalt on the side of the road. Try to experience the joy of the smell of coffee, even when you don't enjoy the taste. Let yourself smile when an older person dances in the rain and splashes in puddles, understanding that there is more to living than existing from day to day, accepting that all the moments of life affect our very nature. Choose to see the magic in the world and celebrate the wonderment of that which is odd and unique. Yet, also embracing those everyday experiences which connect us all. Allow for understanding that miracles are all around us, and science is simply reason. While acknowledging that which does not conform to the typical. If you want to believe, to see beyond the mundane, you must realize and accept that there is much in the world that has no explanation.

If you practice these things and open yourself to the understanding that there is more to experience than the mundane, you allow for magic in your life. Why? To be completely honest, opening yourself to these opportunities encourages creativity in your life and your thinking. It will make you better in all aspects of your life. Being a human, others want to spend time with, or simply being the best version of you. One of the choices of existence is how we live our lives. Belief needs to be practiced to be maintained like all things worth doing.

Find your Figments and enrich your life.

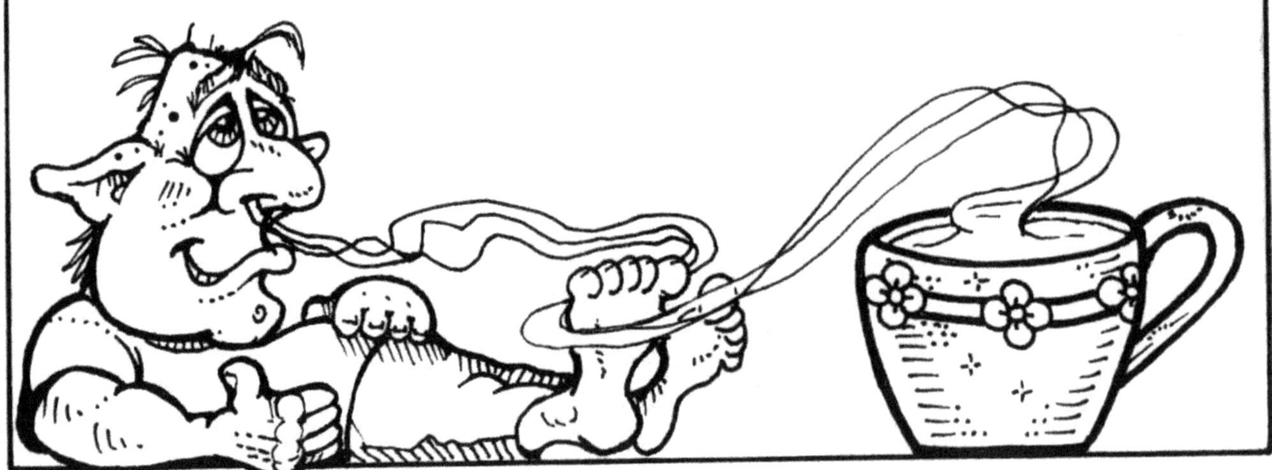

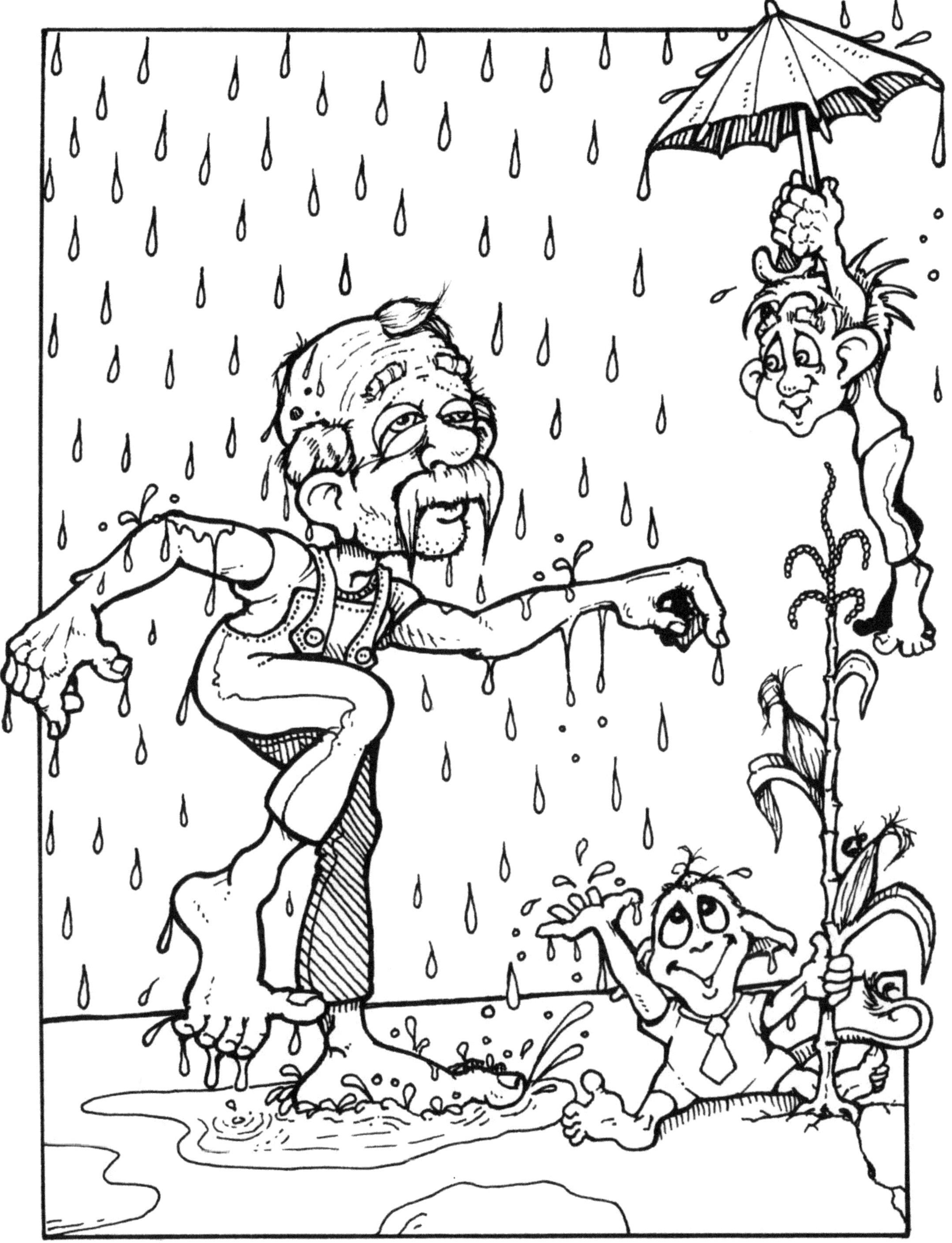

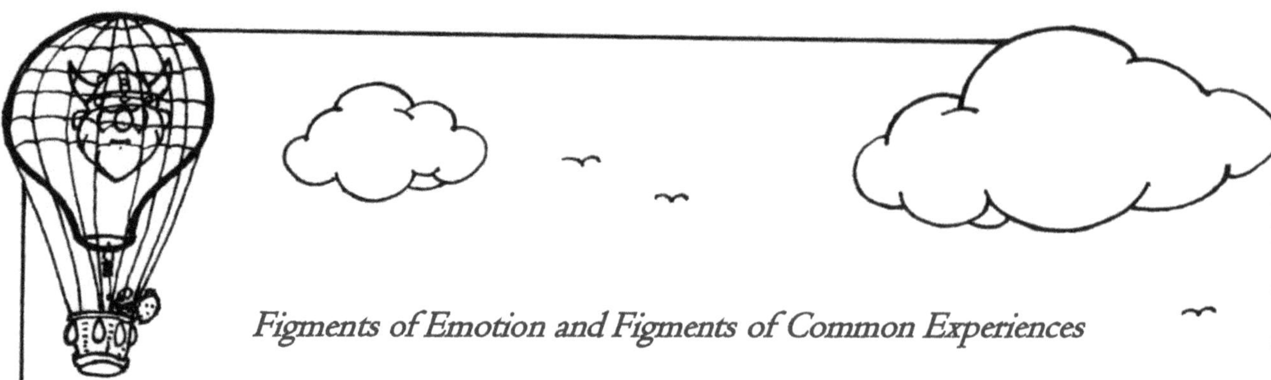

Figments of Emotion and Figments of Common Experiences

Watching Figments over time has become apparent that there are two types of Figments. Those that come from emotions and those that come from the Emotions of Common Experiences.

To detail these things further, The Figments of Emotions manifest when a human has a powerful burst of emotion. That often connects with an object representing the event that caused the emotion. The Figment, now in existence, bonds the sentiment with the object and remains with or near it. When its human is near the object and focuses on it, the Figment seems to amplify the feelings that originated the Figment.

Figments of Common Emotions originate from the powerful feelings generated by shared experiences of humans. They manifest from the connected feelings of humans to experiences that many, if not all, humans share. As you see, the different experiences result in somewhat different types of Figments. Then, of course, the human originated from gives some personality to each individual Figment. Each Figment is unique, sharing simply some general characteristics.

This Field Guide is a book in progress work documenting the known Figments.

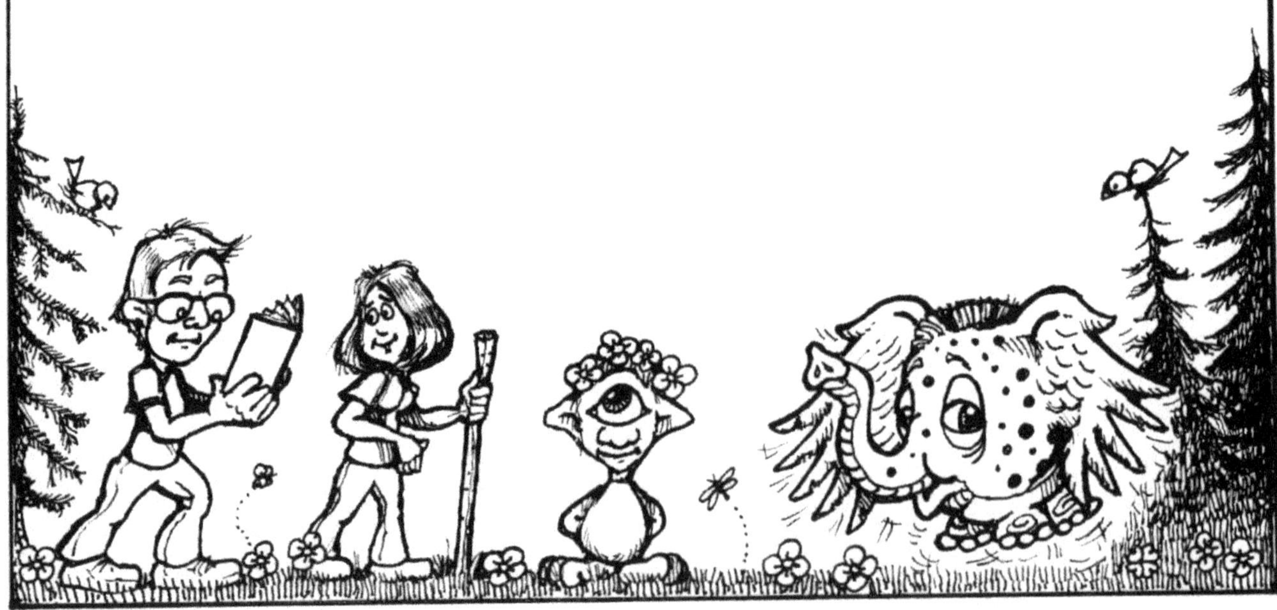

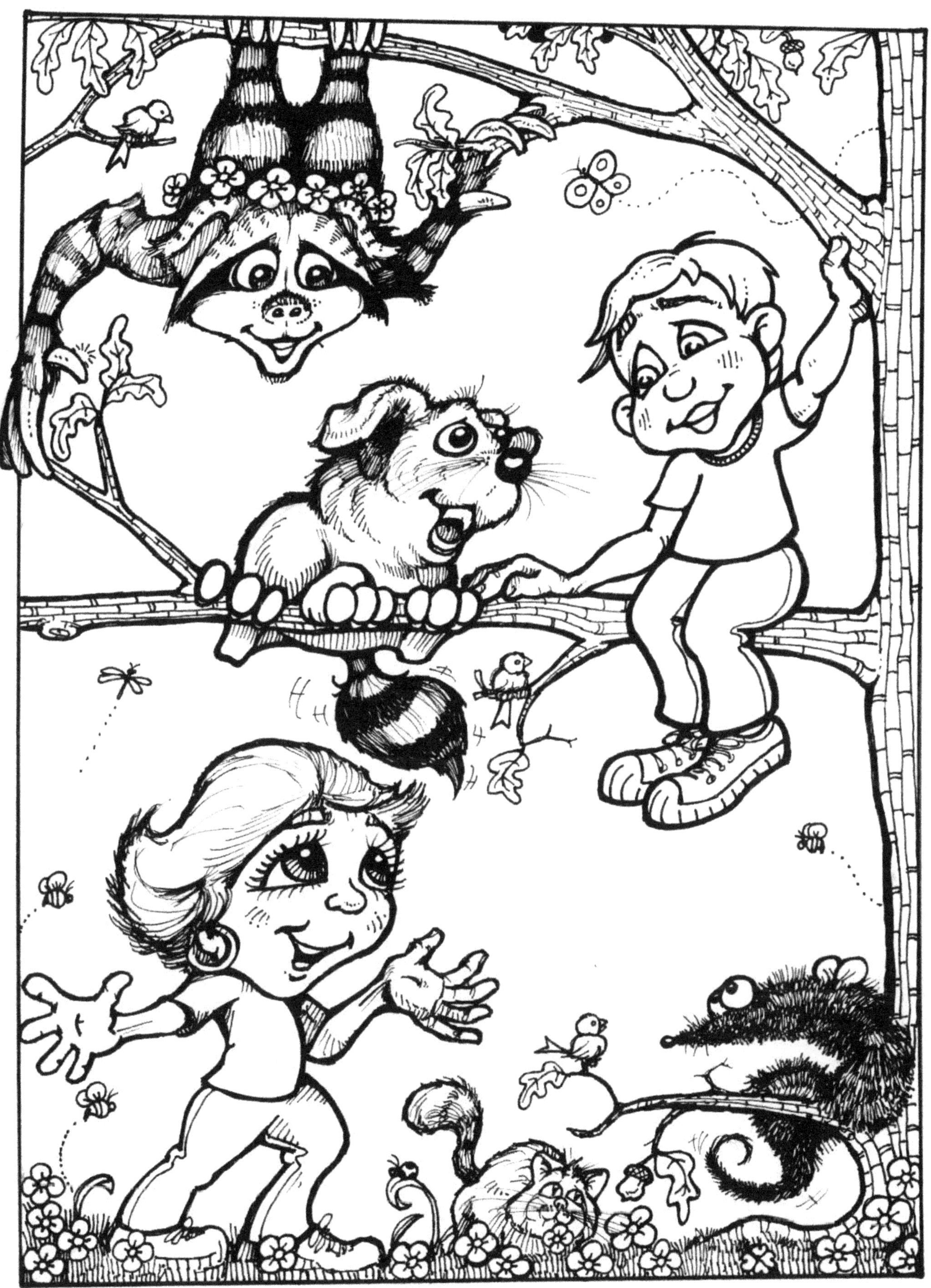

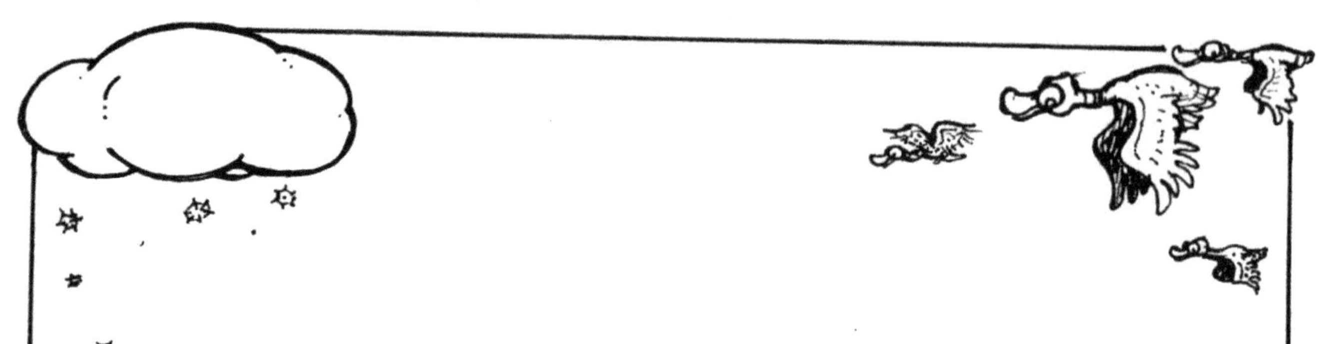

It is not known the first time Figments happened. We do seem to know the first time they were recognized as something other than invisible friends to children when they were too young to be jaded by the world.   Or at least beyond the flits and glimpses often glimpsed out of the corner of one's eye.

It seems that actually to observe Figments you must also believe in them.

It is a human trait to dismiss visual evidence if there is no belief in what you see. The human mind has a vast capacity to ignore the truth. In the inquiry into the nature of Figments, there are some discoveries. One that there is still much unknown. Two, yet they are a part of human reality. Humans seem to be determined in so many ways to deny what part of themselves, yet also cannot seem to dismiss it entirely.   Belief is an advantageous trait.   It is challenging to believe in something you cannot see. However, the reward in opening your mind to a thing more remarkable than what you can see for yourself is compelling.

Everyone has Figments around them; some will appreciate them.

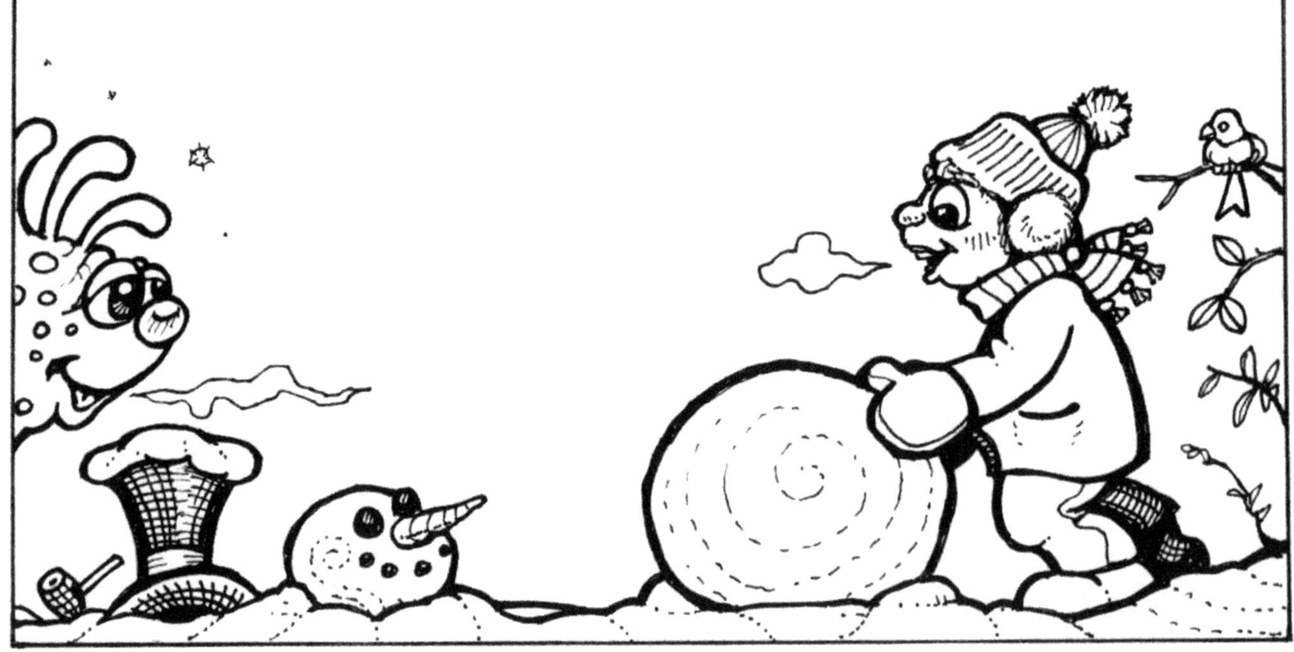

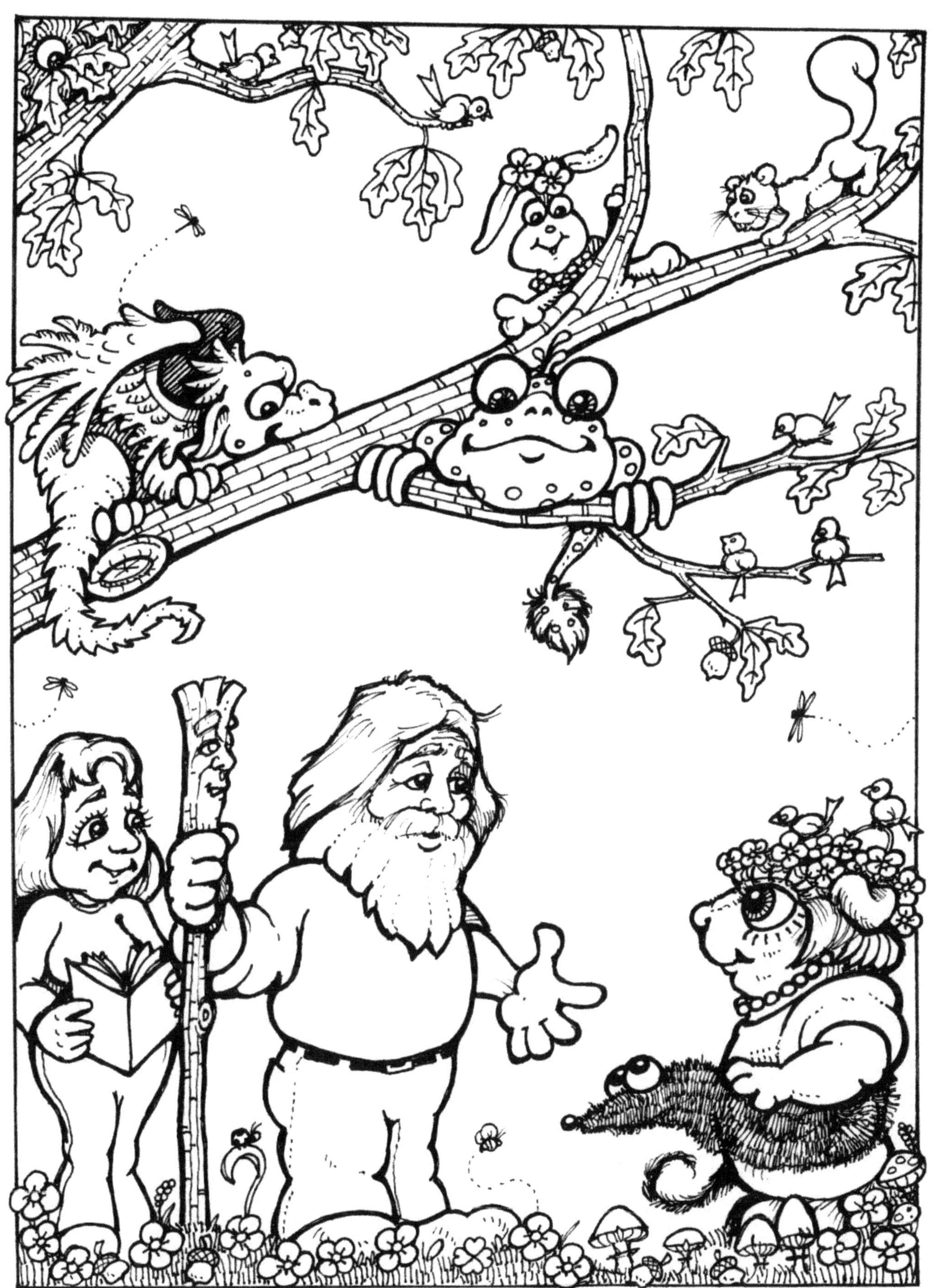

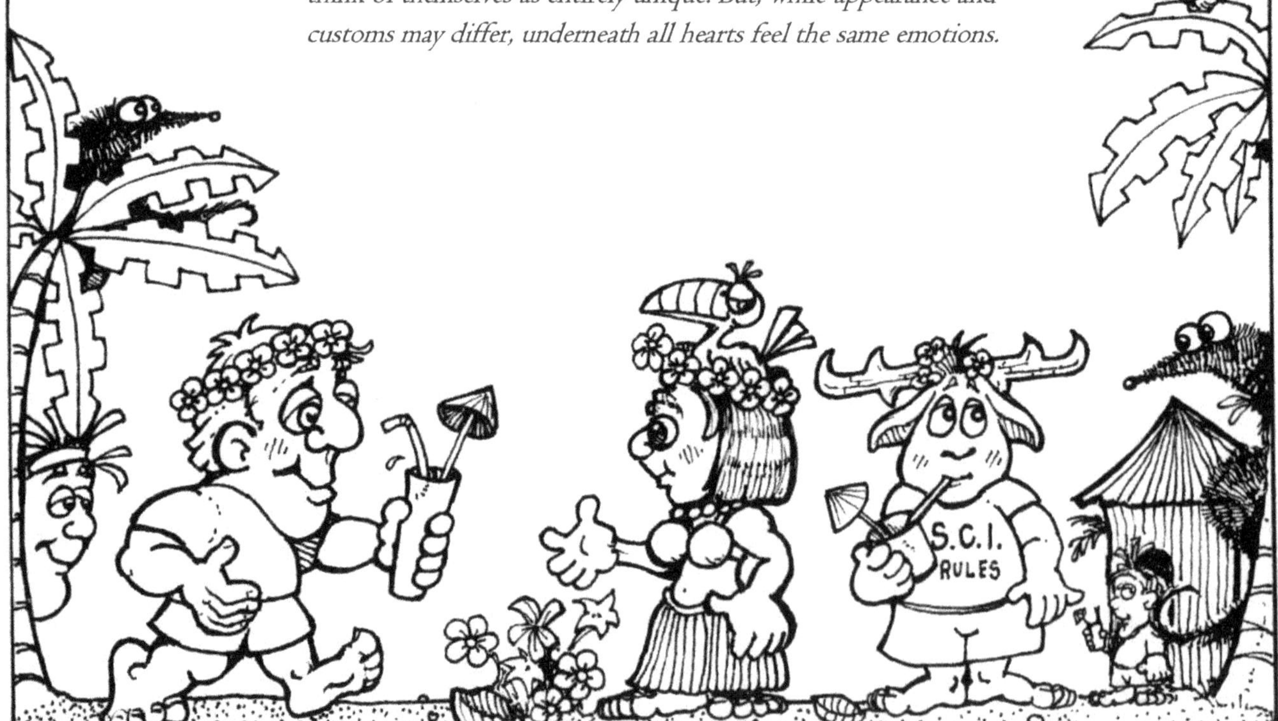

Figment Origins

Let us get to what we know currently about the Figments of Persuasion. It has become apparent that they share Energy from a place on an island known to very few. The island is known to those who inhabit it as Second Chance Island or S.C.I. Why is S.C.I. known to so few? Well, there must be a compelling reason to be there.

Additionally, you must bring something of value as part of your acceptance. While humans have intrinsic value, you will never know it exists if you supply nothing of value to S.C.I. Part of the Energy that is an inherent part of the island means those for whom it is right will find it. If not, your world is secure enough that you will be unable to locate it no matter how hard you look. Although created from excesses in human emotions, Figments sometimes still find themselves in need of a respite from humans. They return to the island to blend their Energy at times.

It is unclear how this works for Figments created off Second Chance, although they seem always to maintain a connection to the Energy of S.C.I. There is much to know if you want to have more information about Second Chance Island, and it is addressed better in its own space.

This tome is about Figments.

One thing that is known around the world and everywhere in it. Humans try very hard to make themselves different. Individuals think of themselves as entirely unique. But, while appearance and customs may differ, underneath all hearts feel the same emotions.

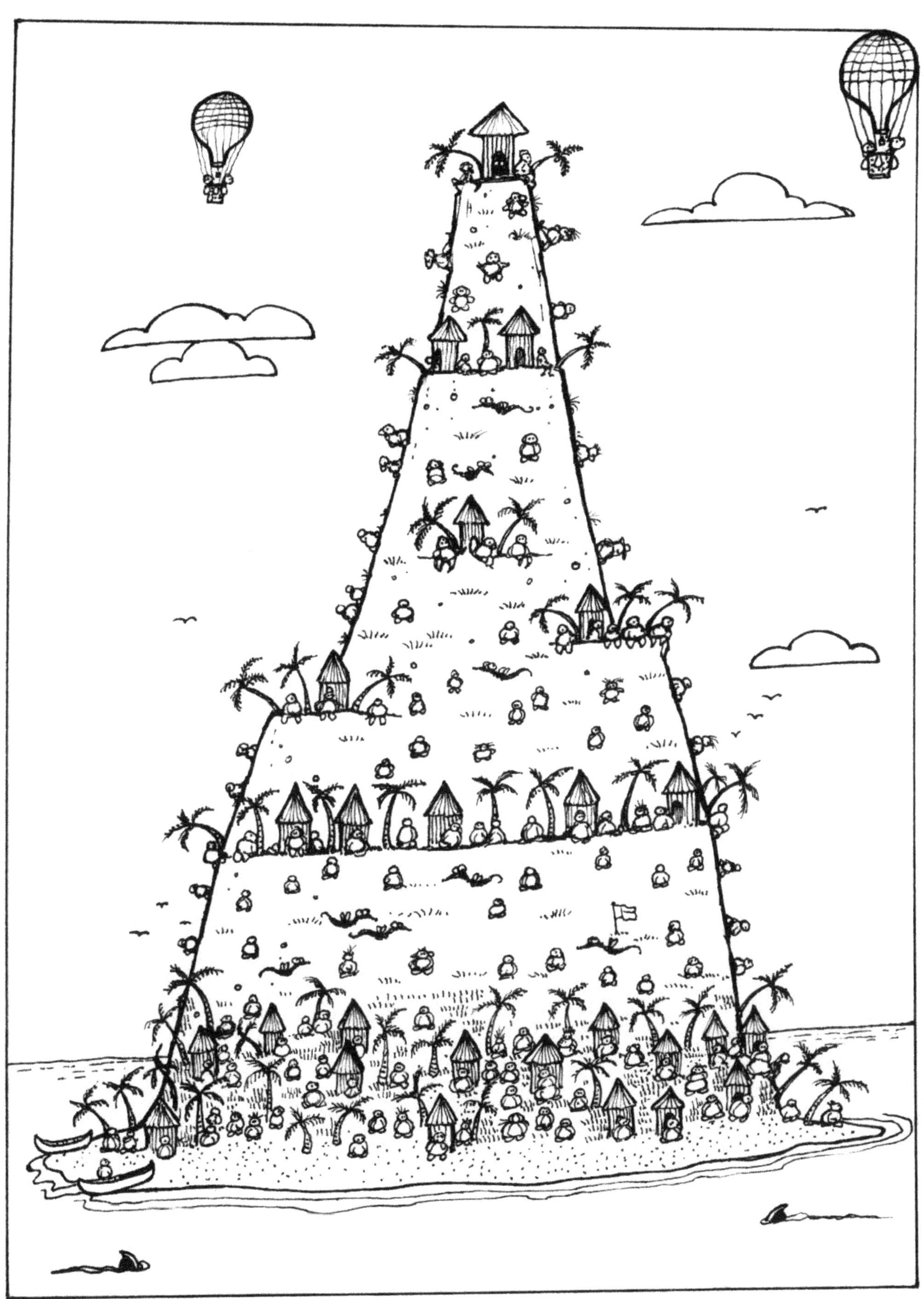

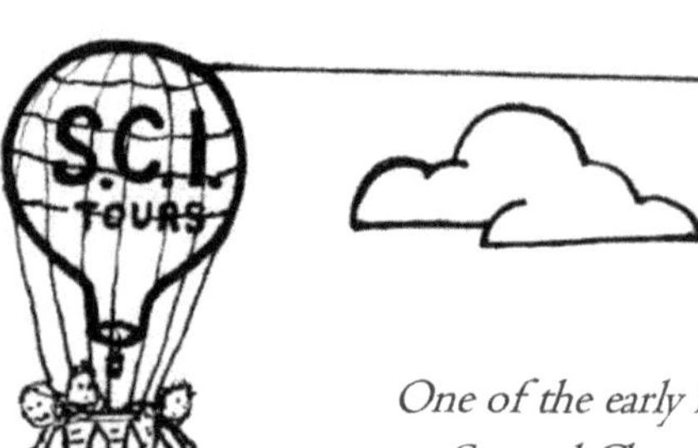
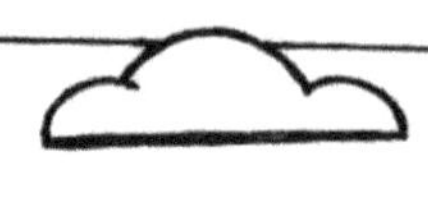
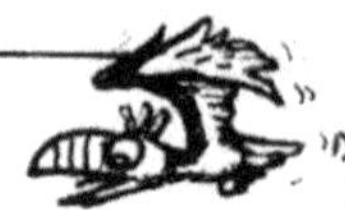

One of the early known sightings of the Figments of Persuasion was on Second Chance Island during the Betadine of a young lady named Kvasthilde. It is essential to understand that she had talked to what her parents called her Unseen Friends like most young people. Many, if not most young people have them. Unlike most children, Kvasthilde never really grew out of this phase as she grew up. When she was serving at the Welcome Center for her Betidinin, she would talk not so much to those arriving but rather to beings no one else was seeing. She was also often seen speaking while walking through a market or strolling along, not seemingly to herself but to something others were not seeing.

The complete story of the beginning of adult human awareness of Figments is covered in-depth in the History of Second Chance. It is too good a story to shortchange it here. It's a lot of fun for enlightened humans who wish to learn more. Those who may have already read that book, let's talk more about the categories of Figments in this endeavor. After all, the author spent a lot of time working with the Figments to write all this down so Humans could understand them better. However, it is essential to note that while Figments of Persuasion are directly from Human Emotions, they are as varied within each of their categories as a Human is within theirs. Need clarification? Red Haired humans are a category, but not all Red-Haired Humans are alike. They have different ways about them. So too are Figments unique within their beings.

It is, however, a start.

So, let's get started!

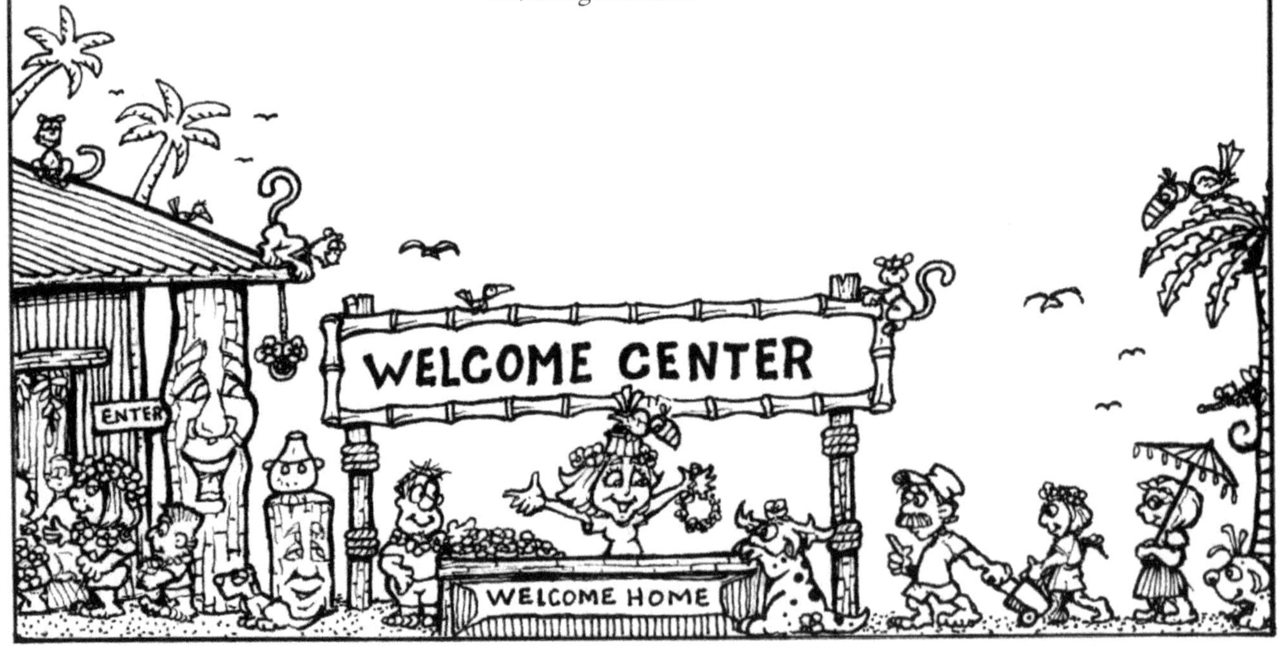

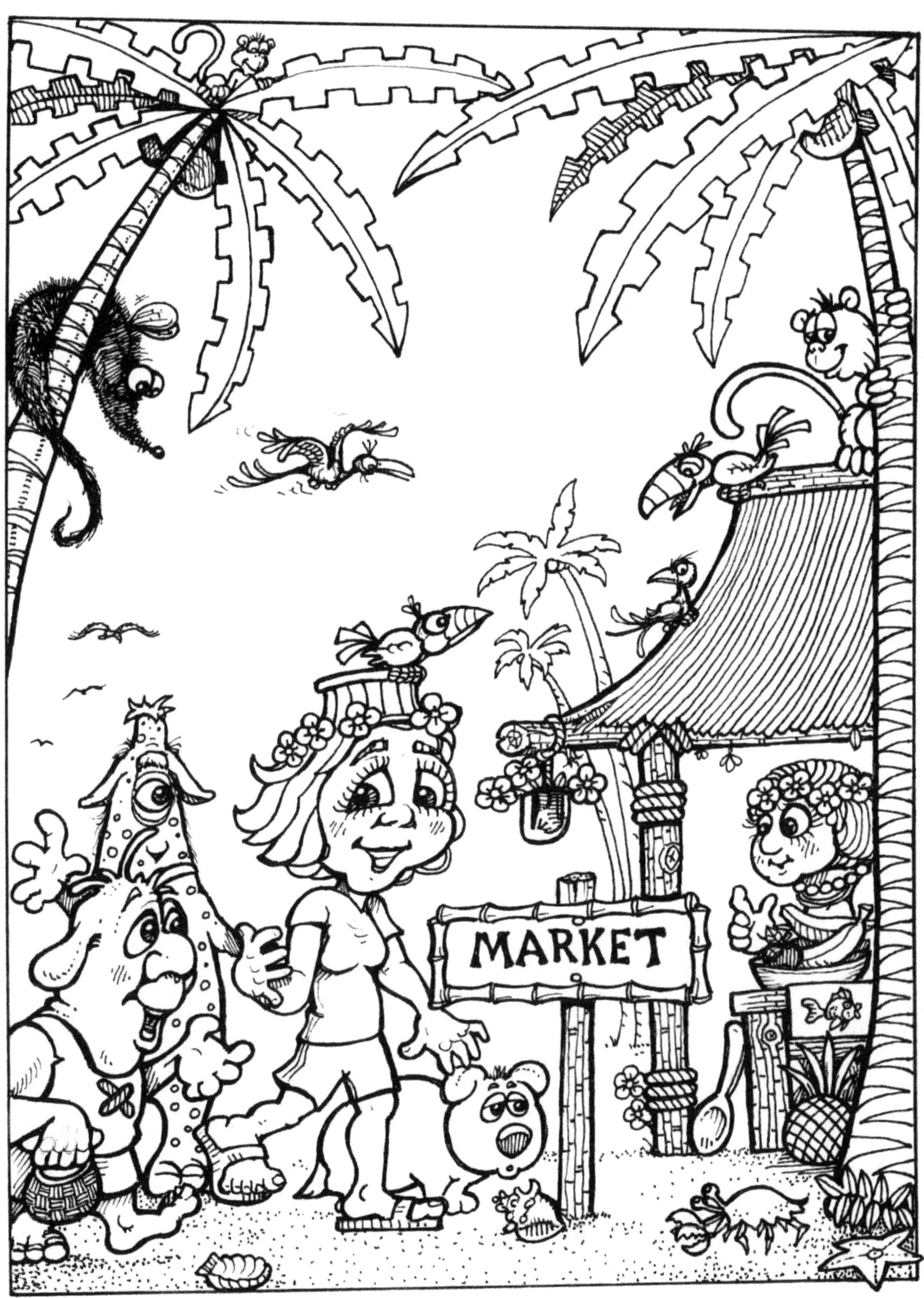
MARKET

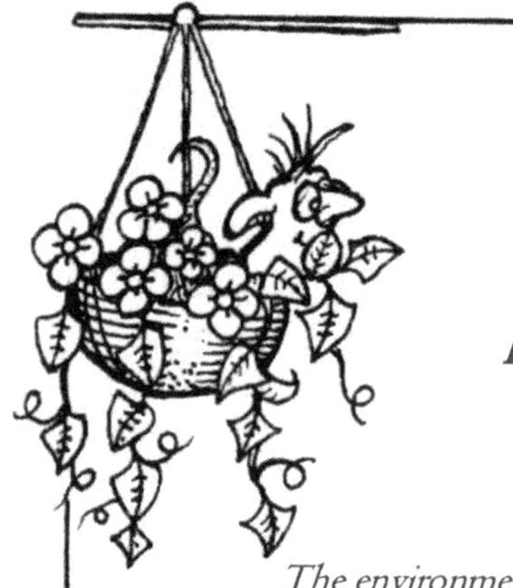

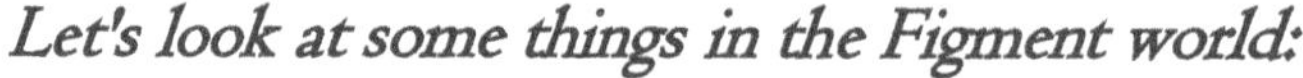

Let's look at some things in the Figment world:

The Environments:

The environments are where the Figments of Persuasion live, play, or exist while with the human. Some live alone, some in small groups, others in large groups. The world of Figments and their unique Environments are vast. When we, as humans, can "see" an environment, it is as the Figment sees it. Non-Believers will see the object and perhaps a vague collection of stuff oddly placed with it.

What you may be privileged to know if you allow yourself is what is there is at this moment in time. In another moment, it may be very different as Figments do as Figments choose. They create an environment to suit themselves. Just as a photograph is a two-dimensional snapshot of a moment in time. The Environments are a moment in three dimensions. Depending on the type of Figments, they may remain in the environment or come and go, returning to the object they have connected to.

Interestingly, both Figments and their items use the exact words. For instance, a Frippery Figment and its fancy item can be considered Fripperies. Especially for those who cannot "see" them. There is much unknown about them. Human conventions do not bind figments, you see. They often make their environments in places humans consider odd, creating spaces for themselves from various found objects. Some like to feel as though they are imitating nature, and others are more like what we think of as living spaces. Some are quite a mess. They tend to make spaces that appeal to the individual Figment.

(Neutral, not a Figment)

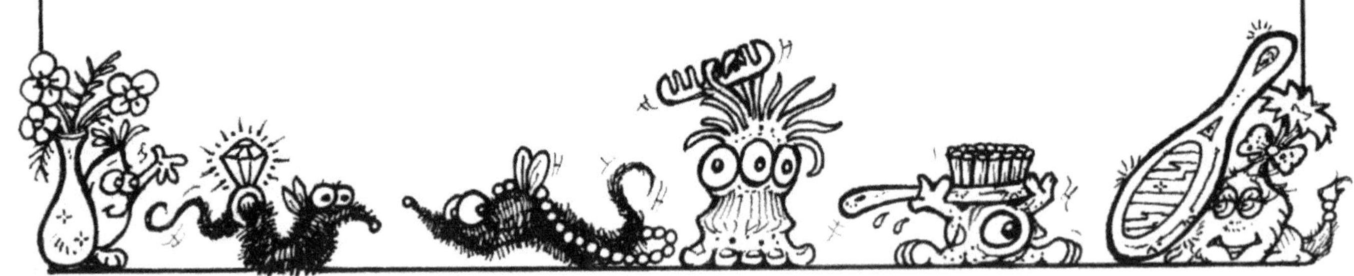

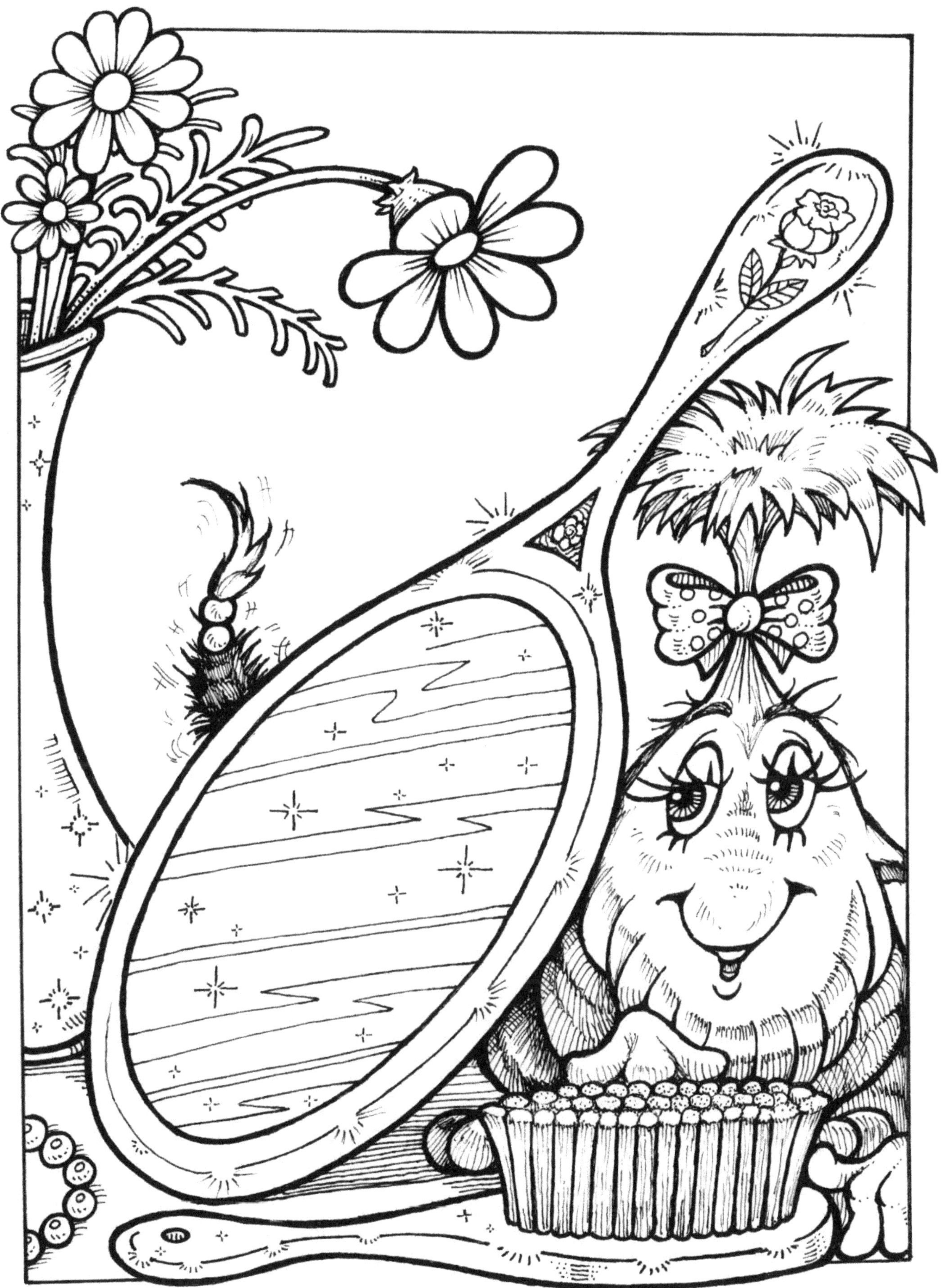

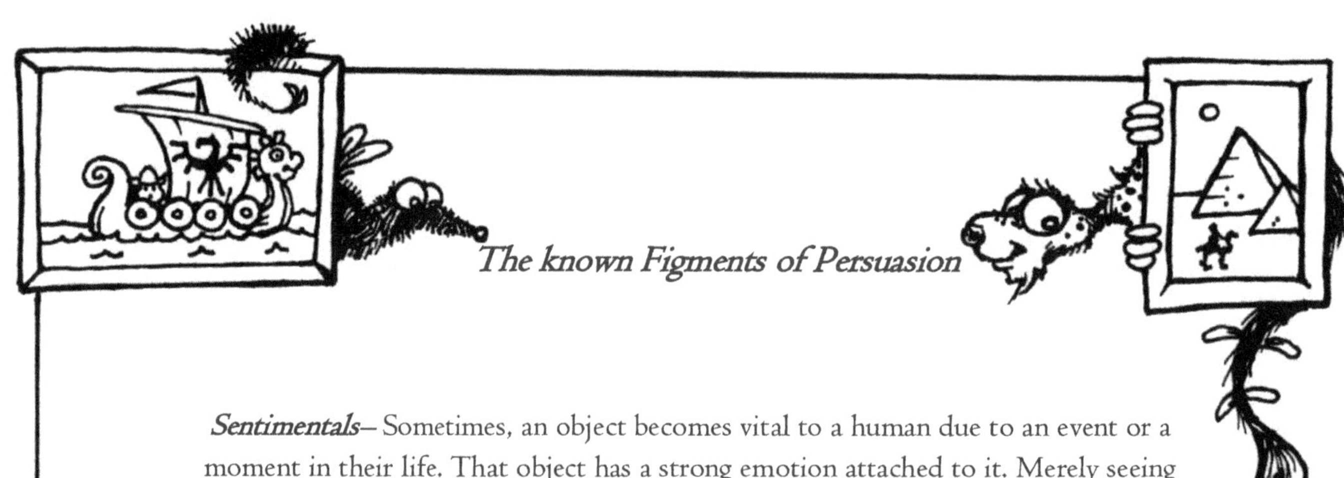

Sentimentals— Sometimes, an object becomes vital to a human due to an event or a moment in their life. That object has a strong emotion attached to it. Merely seeing or holding the thing evokes memories of that activity or moment. Sometimes the feeling is so powerful that a Sentimental is born.

One of the Sentimental signs happens when an object has taken on an importance far exceeding its actual value. Often, we remember why the item is essential, and other times that part of the memory is lost, but the feeling of importance object has remained.

Much like a Dryad has her tree, a Sentimental Figment intertwines with their moving object and embodies it. The human may not even know why or remember the exact moment of intense emotion. That emotion transfers into an elemental known as a Sentimental. It is unseen by a human eye but becomes a part of the object. It manifests into a Figment, creating a world in and around the item. Believe in Figments or not, the entity retains the dominant emotion, and the Sentimental carries part of that emotion and can intensify it. Sentimentals build memories and further entrench them in a human's psyche, making it increasingly difficult to get rid of the object. Some memories are fond and lovely; others just dream memories of things that never came to be. These memories become the very reason you can never throw the object away.

(Emotion)

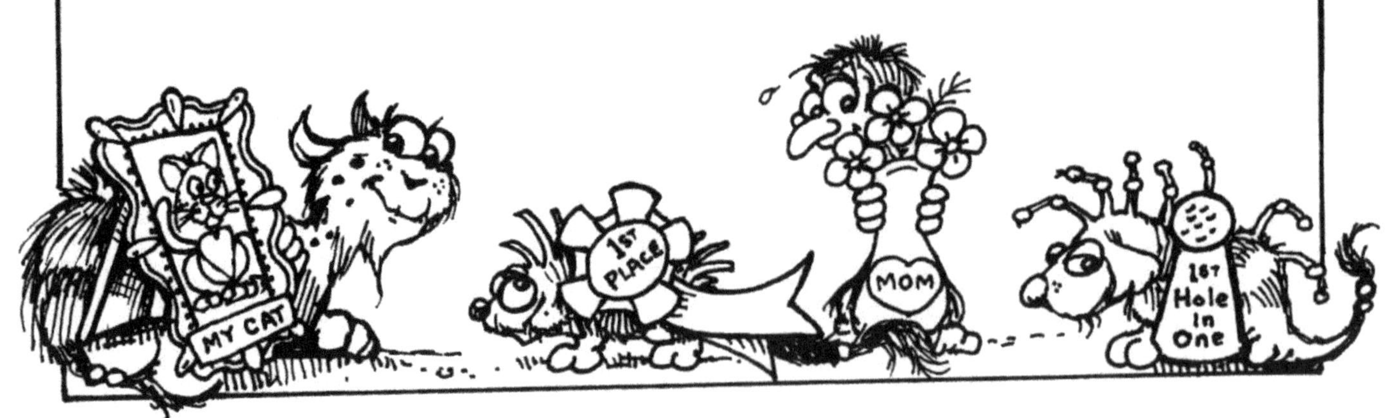

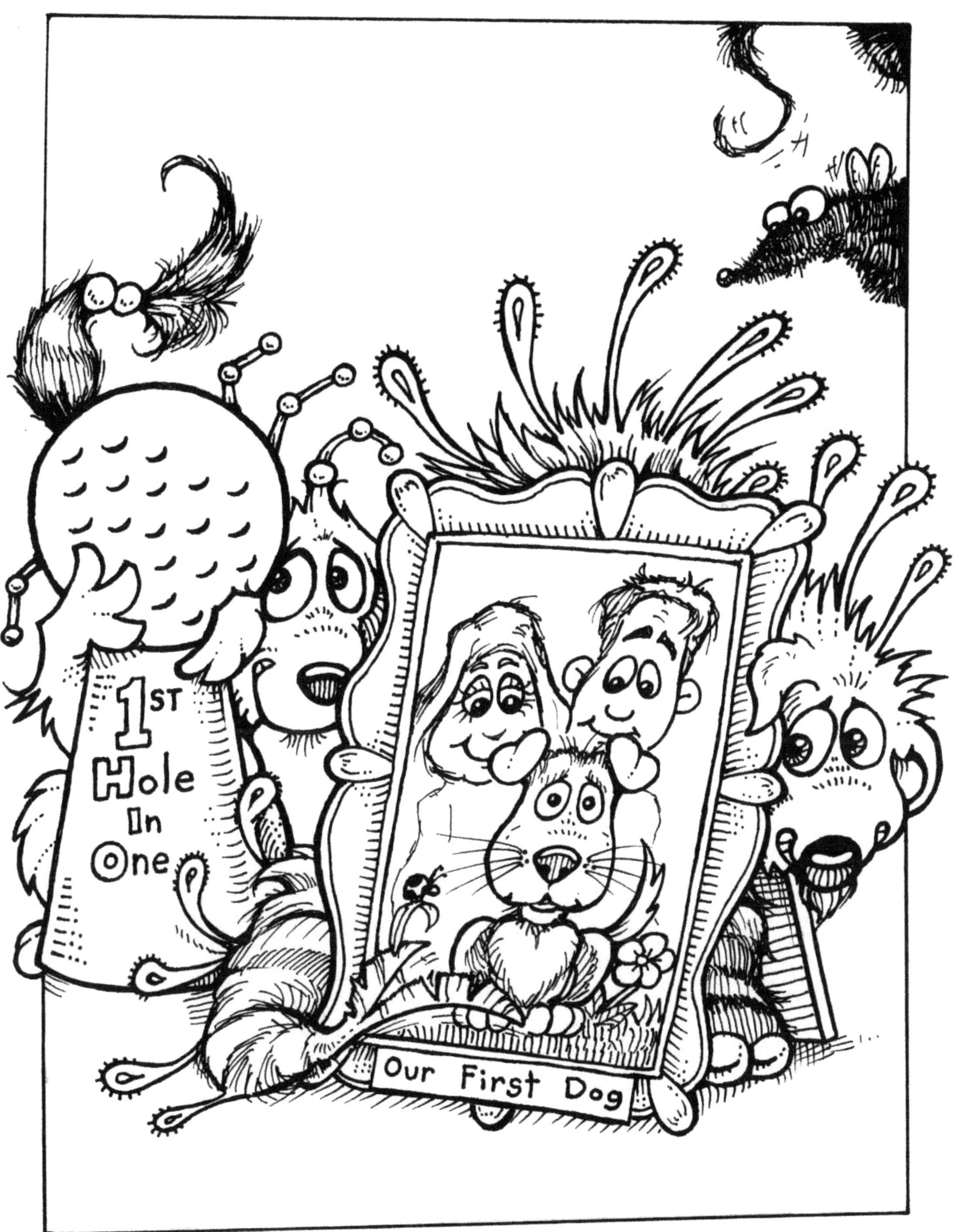

1ST
Hole
In
One
Our First Dog

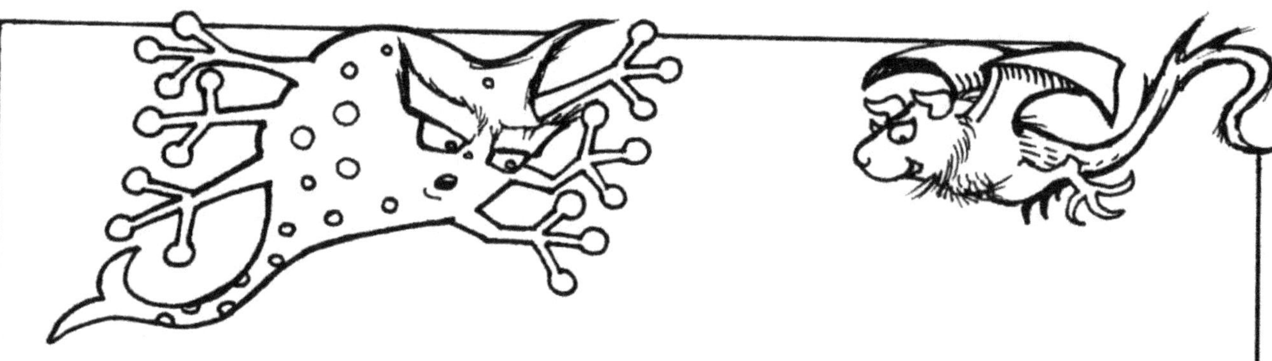

Shivers:

Shivers are similar, but different from the Sentimental, as Sentimentals are generally a happy breed, Shivers are darker. There are times when objects have gotten the reputation of being haunted because they can cause a Shiver when you touch them. Originally a Figment of happy memories, now shadowed with sadness or even bitterness. Shivers can happen when the emotion remains, but a more powerful memory has overshadowed the memory connected to it or occasionally when the object has a potent sad feeling that transfers to it then combined with the sentiment that joined the Figment in its inception. So, what was formerly a pleasant memory as an example of a Prom date that went well, becomes dark as the person connected has gone on to evil actions later in life. Shivers seem especially powerful if children were involved somehow. To change a Sentimental to a Shiver takes compelling overriding emotion that is separate from the memory.

(Common Experience)

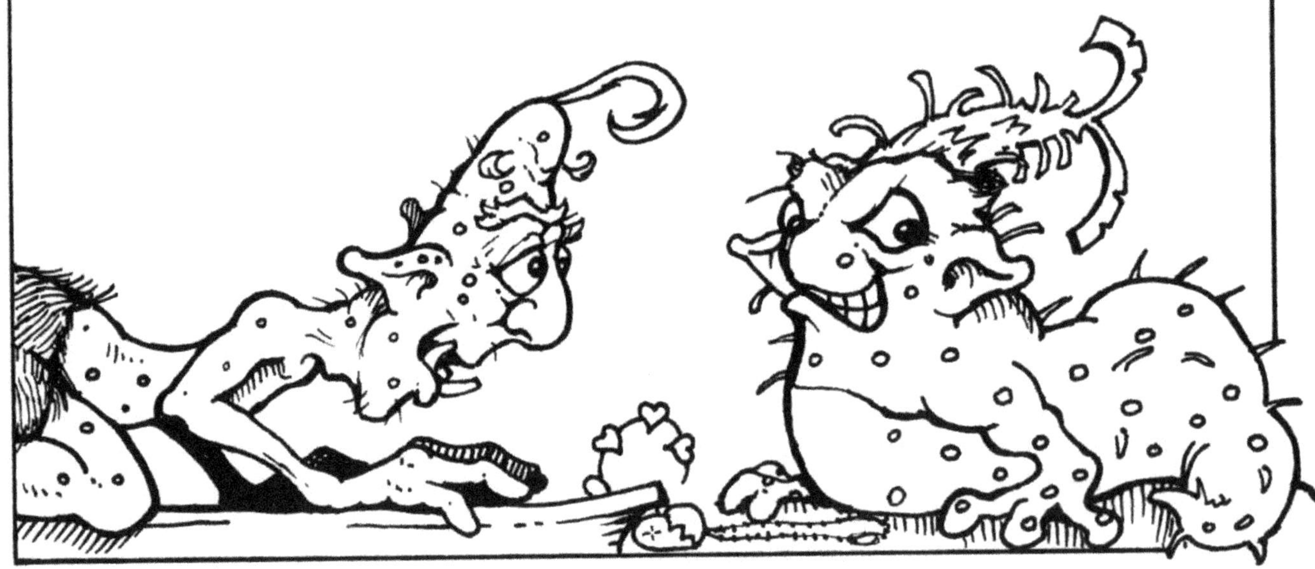

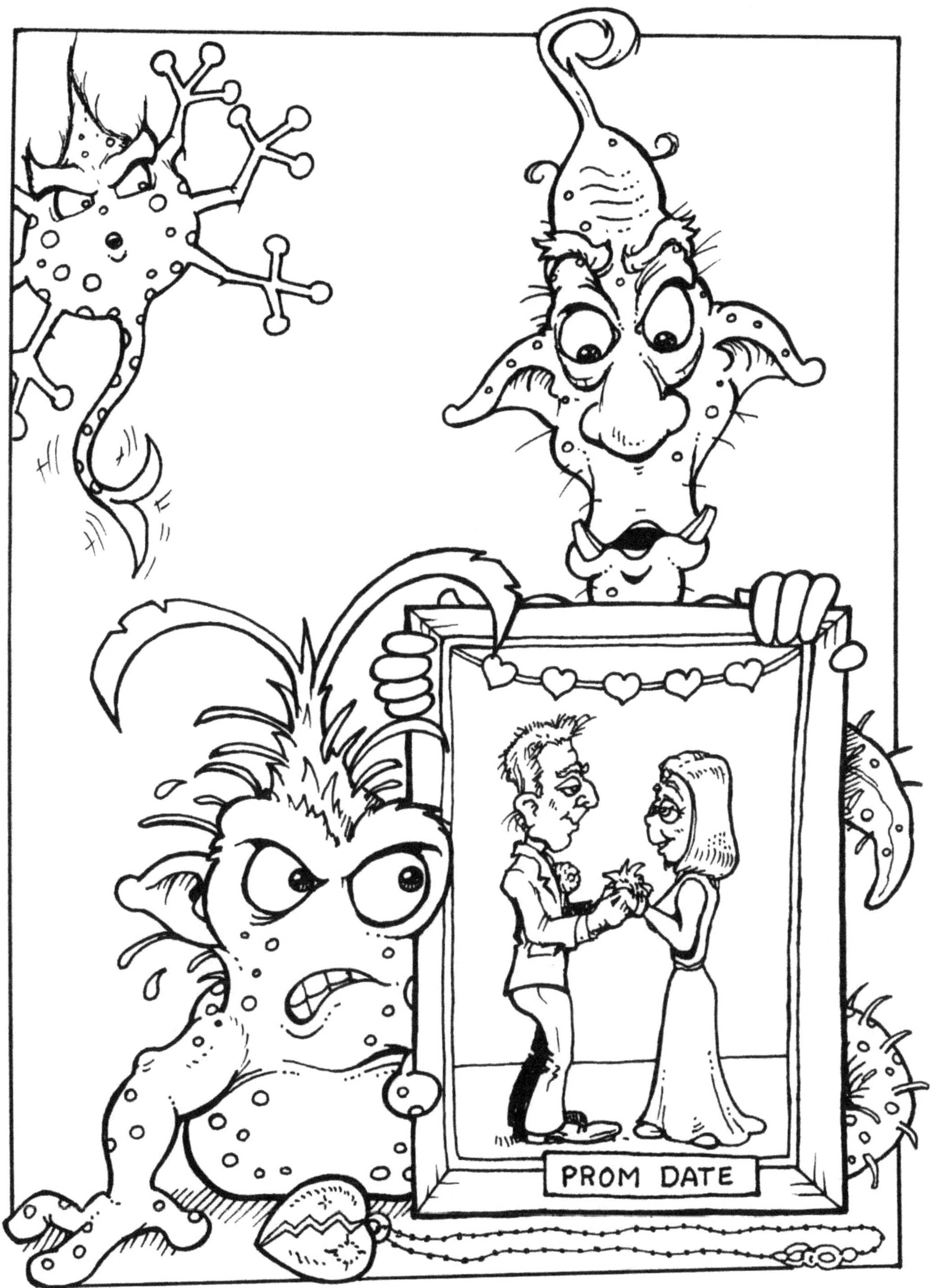

PROM DATE

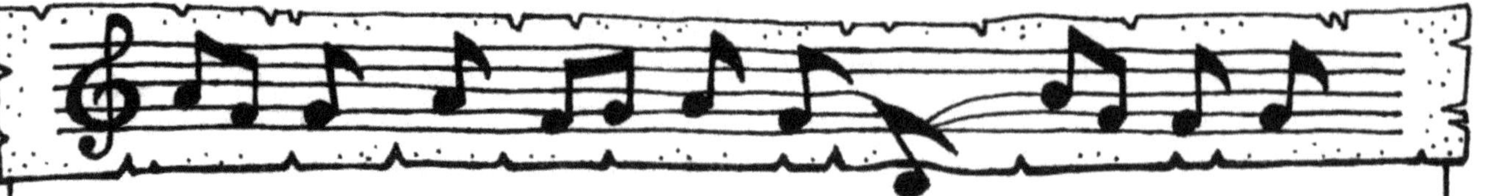

Reminiscents: They hold bits of memories that are incomplete. Memories we carry from the past that we cannot wholly bring back. When a Reminiscent takes a memory fragment, it might be large or small but usually frustrating. You suddenly forget where you put your keys or have stashed that important thing. You cannot remember all the lyrics to a song, a long-remembered address, the end of the sentence, or why you came into a room. Reminiscents often attach those bits and pieces of memories to objects but can just as easily bind them to music or scents that hold part of the recollection when it occurs. Sometimes they will have taken tiny pieces of memory, making it seem odd and almost always irritating that you cannot recollect everything. Reminiscents will collect the most curious parts of memories. Of course, this is rather difficult for the human whose bits of memories are missing. It may seem outlandish that these gaps keep happening, leaving some very irregular seeming spaces or holes in recollection. It is still unclear why Reminiscents usually only take odds and ends of memories. However, they seem to believe human contemplations to be quite essential so that they will glue them back together after a while.

Unfortunately, this often leaves odd holes in the newly glued together memories as they rarely go back together seamlessly. Sometimes when you may be missing glue, it may have been taken by the Reminiscent Figment. Occasionally little old ladies have been known to leave paste out for their Reminiscent in the hope of complete recollection. They want them to have enough glue.

(Common Experience)

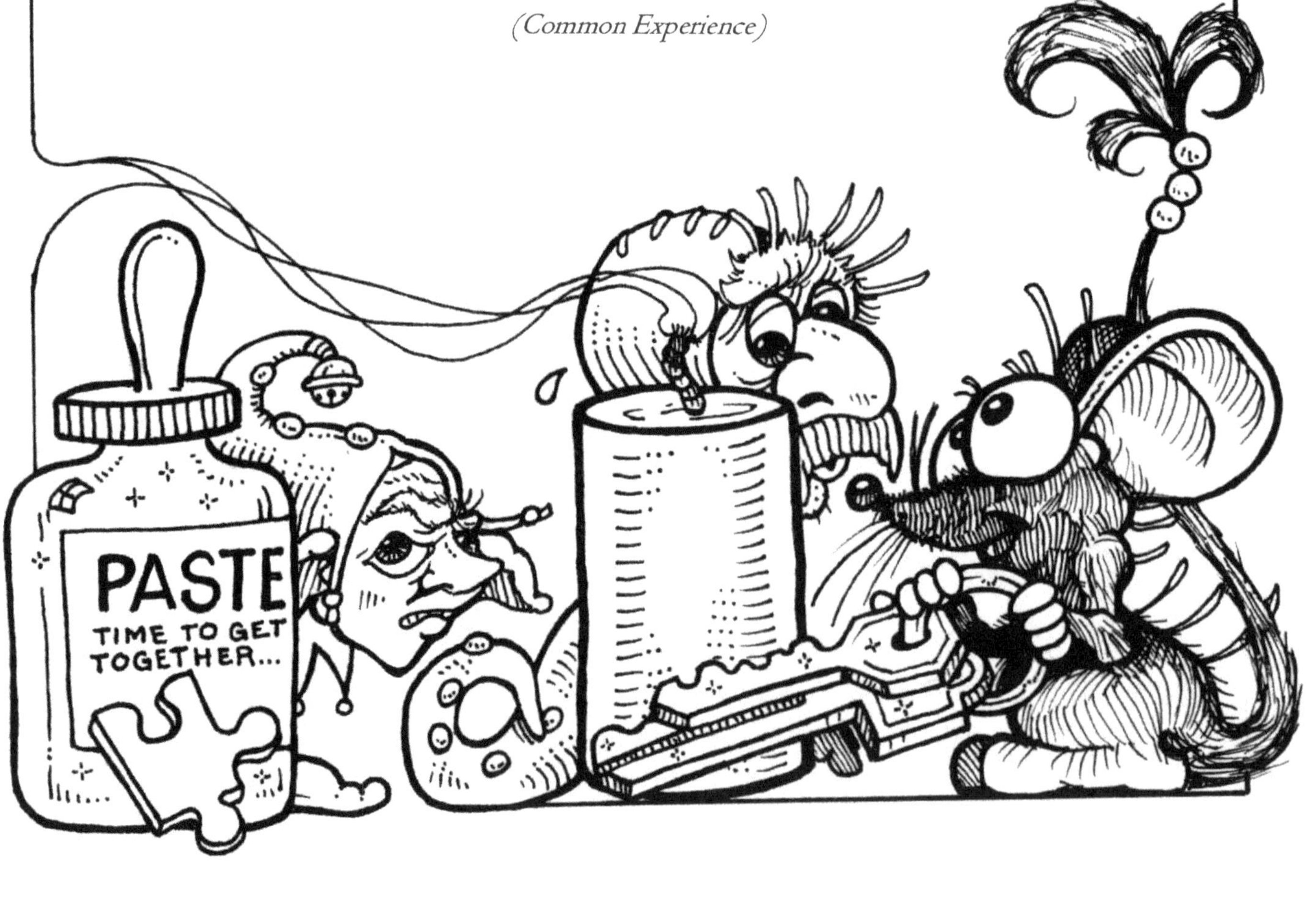

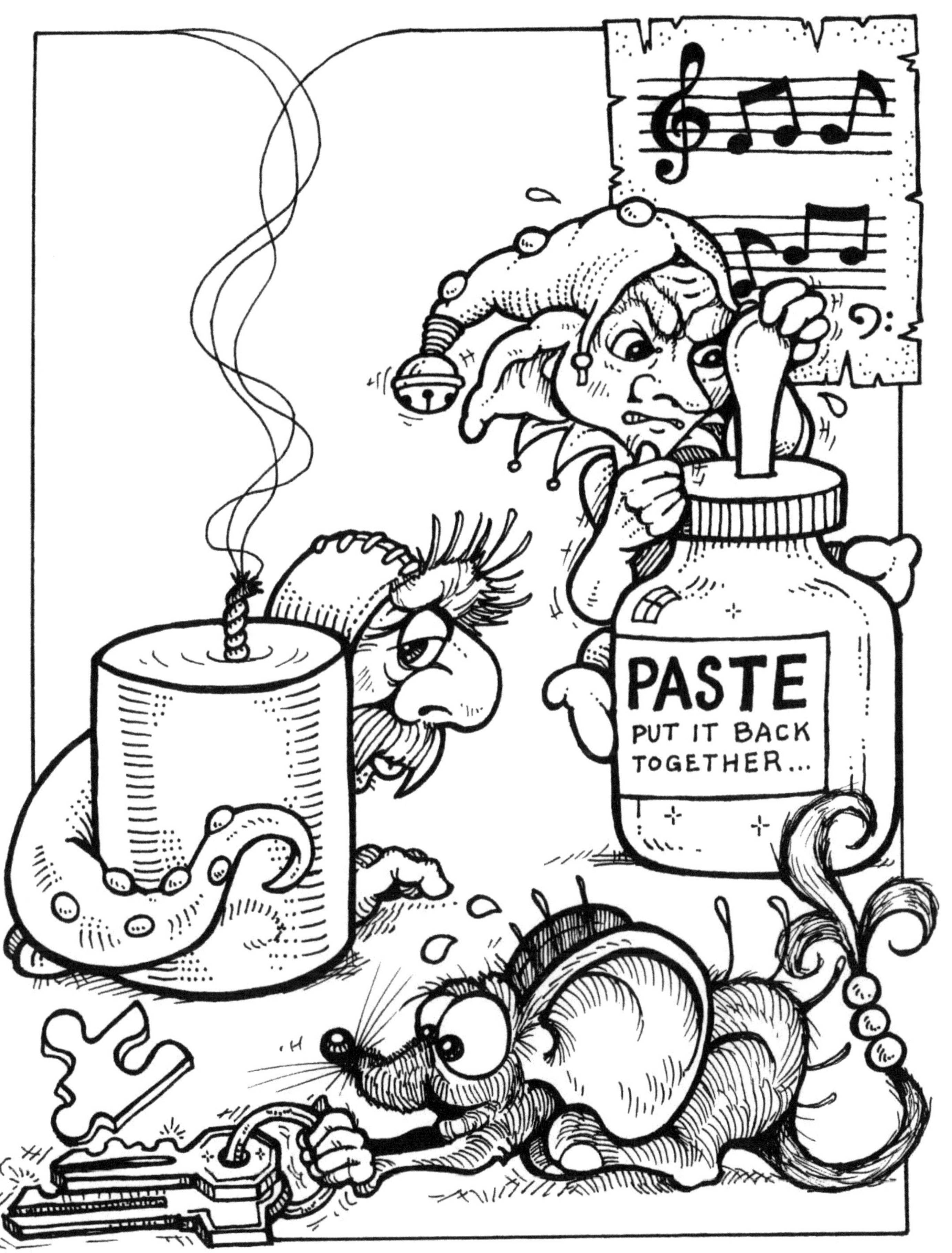

PASTE
PUT IT BACK
TOGETHER...

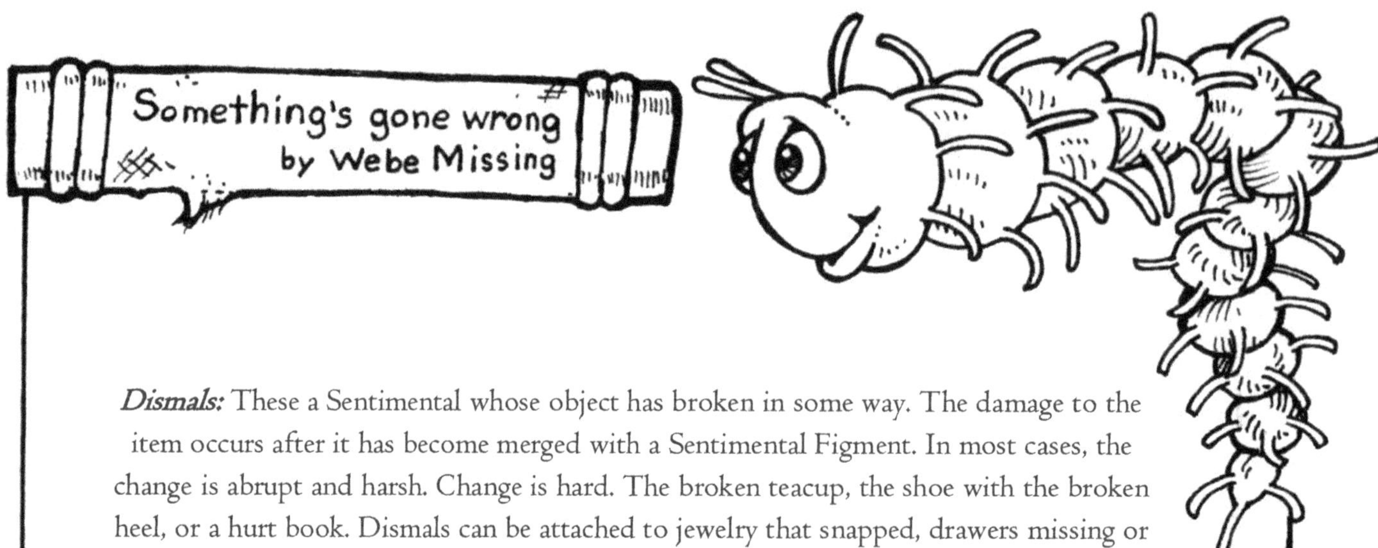

Dismals: These a Sentimental whose object has broken in some way. The damage to the item occurs after it has become merged with a Sentimental Figment. In most cases, the change is abrupt and harsh. Change is hard. The broken teacup, the shoe with the broken heel, or a hurt book. Dismals can be attached to jewelry that snapped, drawers missing or damaged, on an extraordinary box, an instrument that no longer can be tuned. A Dismal can retain just as much powerful emotion, but the object has been quite severely damaged. The human to which the Sentimental belonged cannot seem to part with the broken pieces and will go to extremes to keep it. They will keep the cracked item or broken pieces in hopes of finding a way to mend them in the future.

It might return to its original status if the object is repairable, but it is a hard path. Dismals in some cultures are pretty beautiful objects. In Japan, for instance, some practices bring a Dismal into a lovely, repaired state. Dismals are justifiably proud of their status when that happens. Fortunate Dismals will have humans who can restore almost anything with a newfound beauty or use.

(Common Experience)

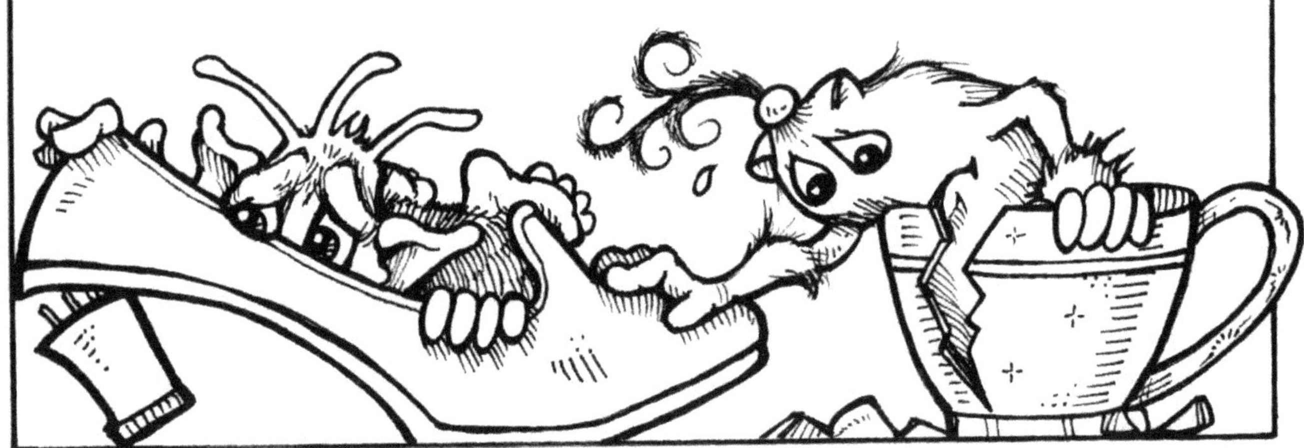

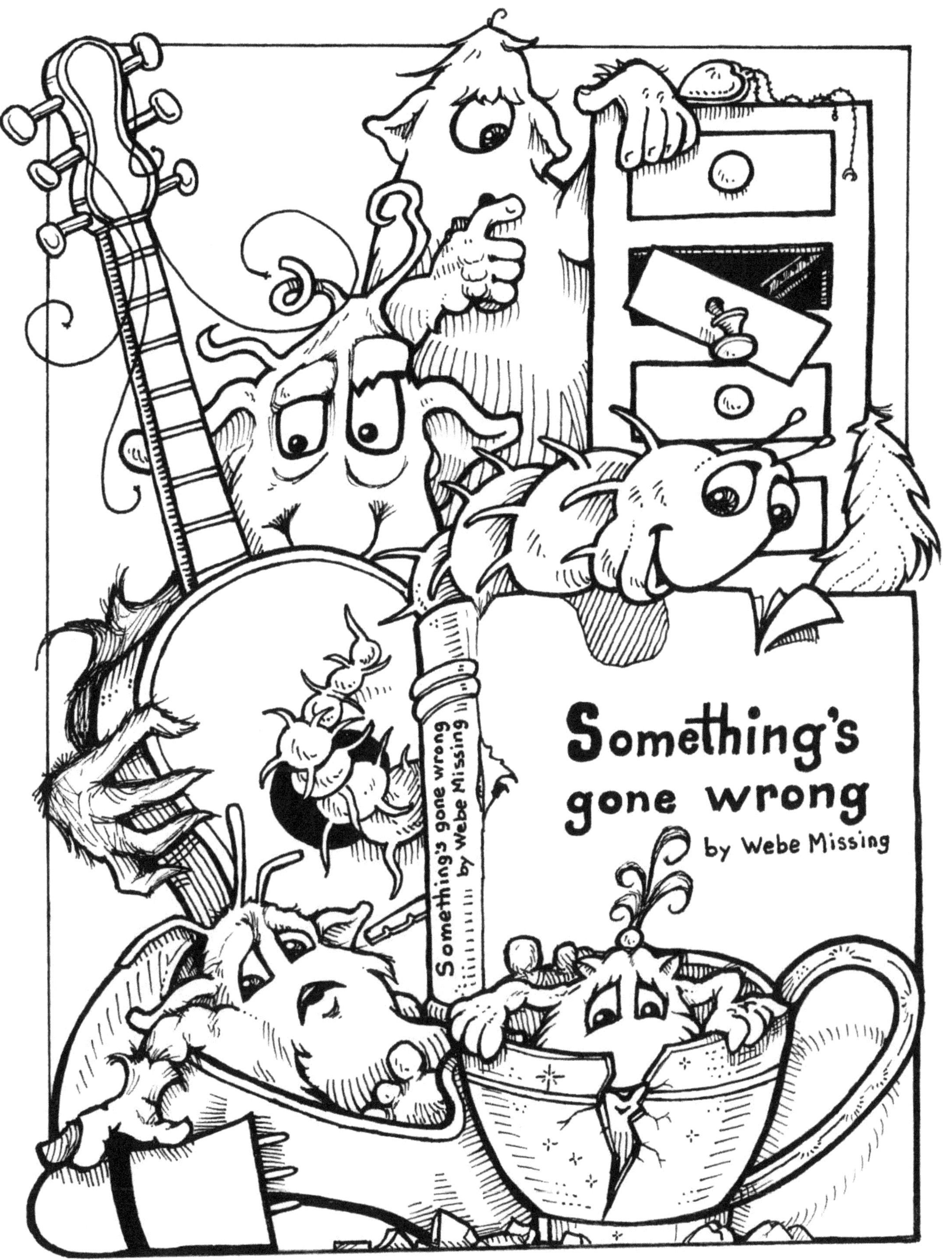

Something's gone wrong
by Webe Missing
Something's gone wrong
by Webe Missing

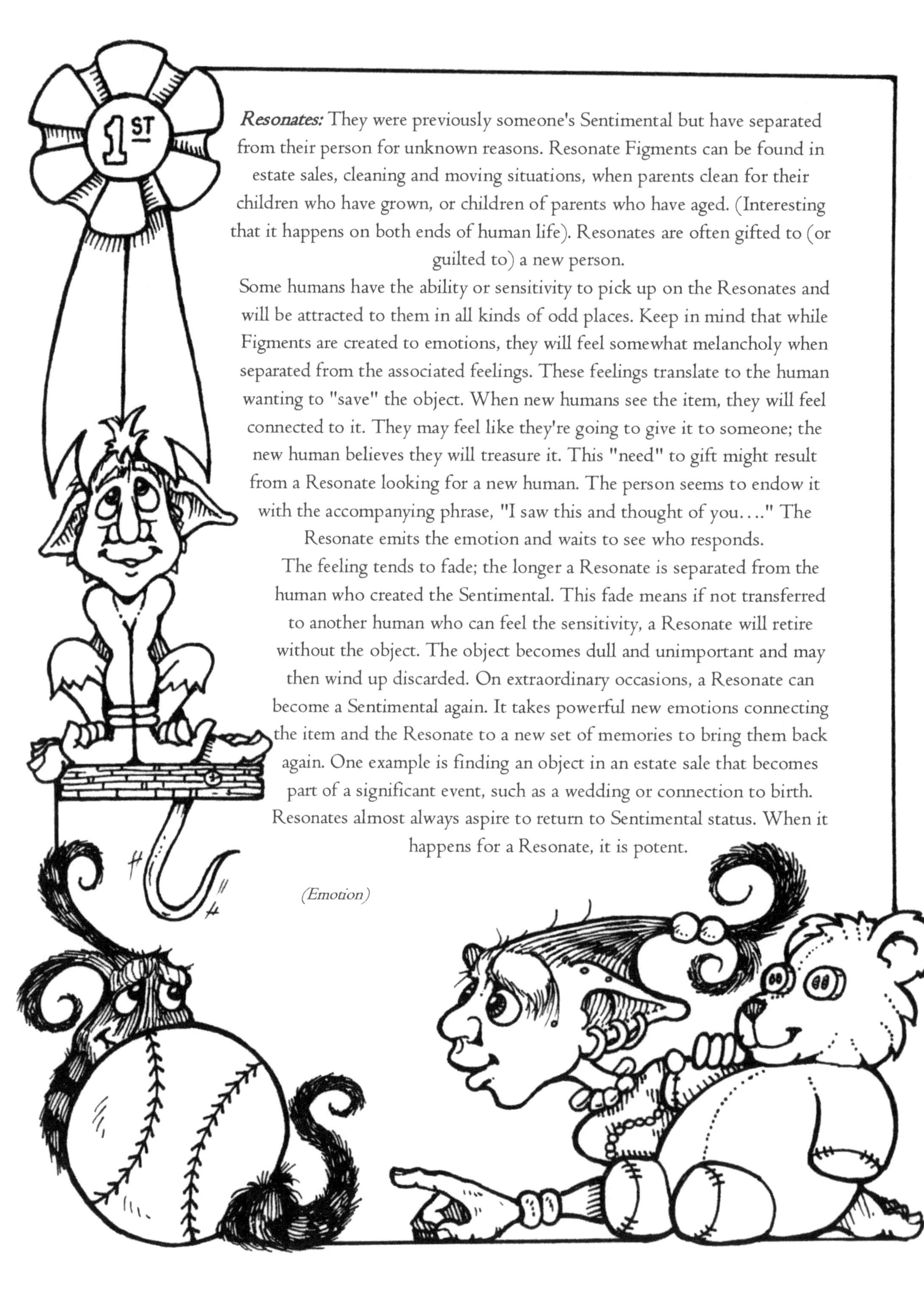

Resonates: They were previously someone's Sentimental but have separated from their person for unknown reasons. Resonate Figments can be found in estate sales, cleaning and moving situations, when parents clean for their children who have grown, or children of parents who have aged. (Interesting that it happens on both ends of human life). Resonates are often gifted to (or guilted to) a new person.

Some humans have the ability or sensitivity to pick up on the Resonates and will be attracted to them in all kinds of odd places. Keep in mind that while Figments are created to emotions, they will feel somewhat melancholy when separated from the associated feelings. These feelings translate to the human wanting to "save" the object. When new humans see the item, they will feel connected to it. They may feel like they're going to give it to someone; the new human believes they will treasure it. This "need" to gift might result from a Resonate looking for a new human. The person seems to endow it with the accompanying phrase, "I saw this and thought of you...." The Resonate emits the emotion and waits to see who responds.

The feeling tends to fade; the longer a Resonate is separated from the human who created the Sentimental. This fade means if not transferred to another human who can feel the sensitivity, a Resonate will retire without the object. The object becomes dull and unimportant and may then wind up discarded. On extraordinary occasions, a Resonate can become a Sentimental again. It takes powerful new emotions connecting the item and the Resonate to a new set of memories to bring them back again. One example is finding an object in an estate sale that becomes part of a significant event, such as a wedding or connection to birth. Resonates almost always aspire to return to Sentimental status. When it happens for a Resonate, it is potent.

(Emotion)

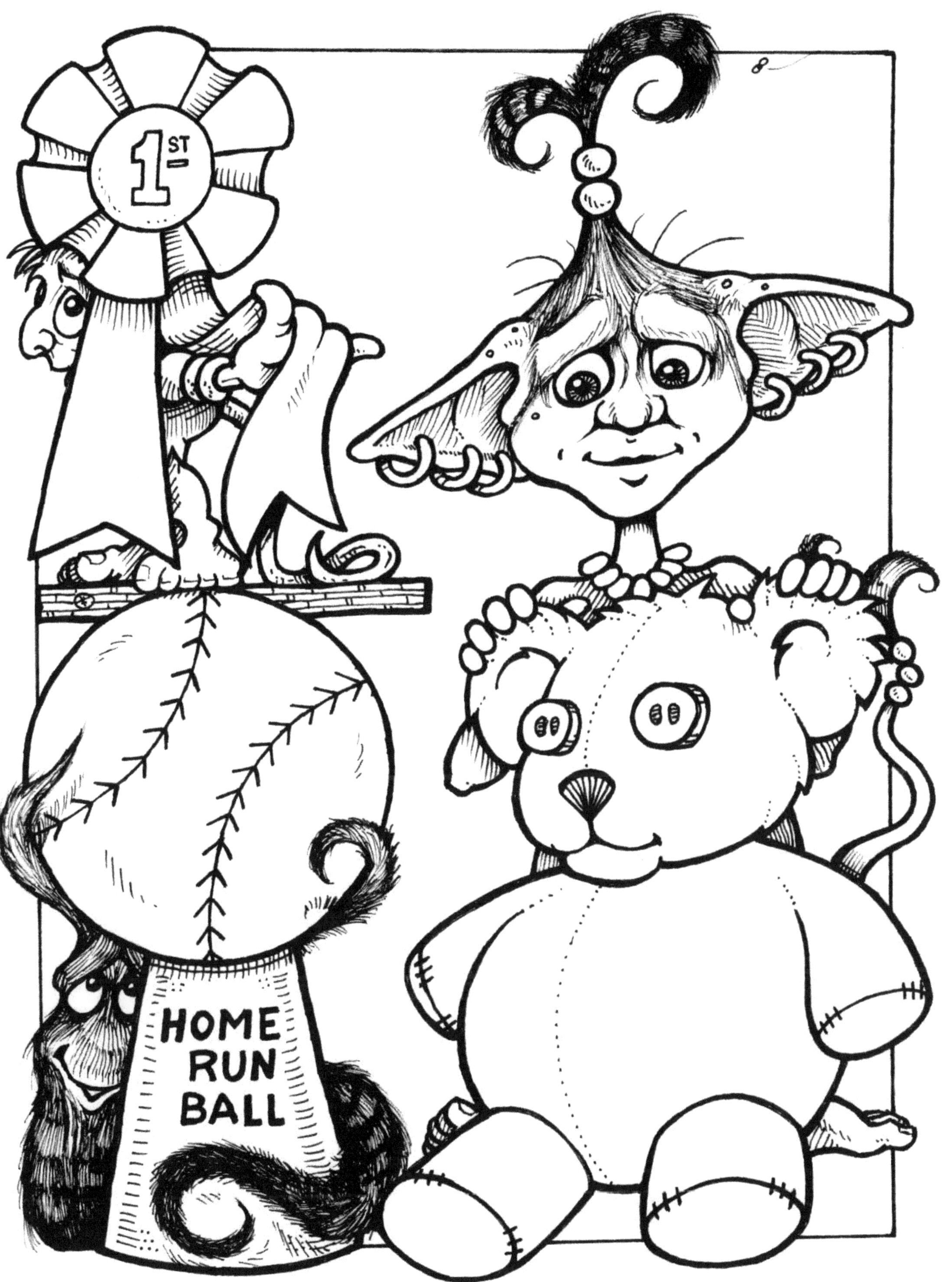
1ST
HOME
RUN
BALL

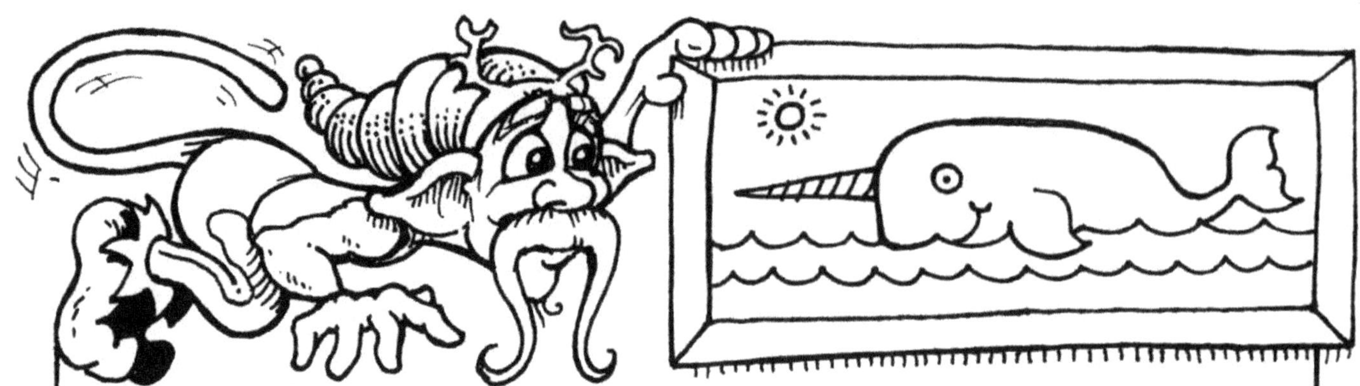

Frippery: They are a bit vain, pretentious, even silly Figments. They consider themselves different from plainer Figments due to the nature of the objects. Usually, a Frippery will connect to an overly decorated or colorful item. If they were a cake, they would have so many layers and so much frosting and roses they are nearly inedible. Repeatedly the object of a Frippery seems to inspire the words, "um, wow." They will be found frequently in collections of people who have multiple assortments of things and love cats, narwhals, or truffles. They do love assemblies and are quite gregarious. Time and again, it is found that people who have one Frippery have MANY. They do not like to split up once they bond together.

Frequently Frippery's are gifted to their humans by others who see objects that fit the category and think the human will love the artifact. Once acquired, if enough emotion attaches, the Frippery is born. Surprisingly often with a squeal from their human. They are also close cousins to Gatherer Figment's, or they claim to be. Fripperies are pastel in color, usually Pink or Lavender.

(Emotion)

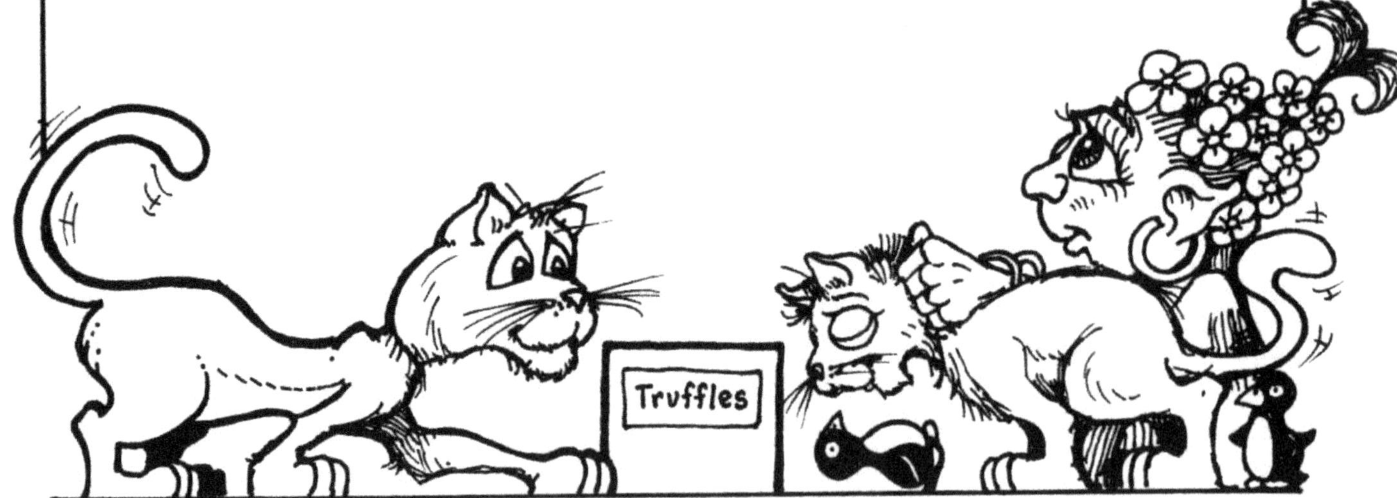

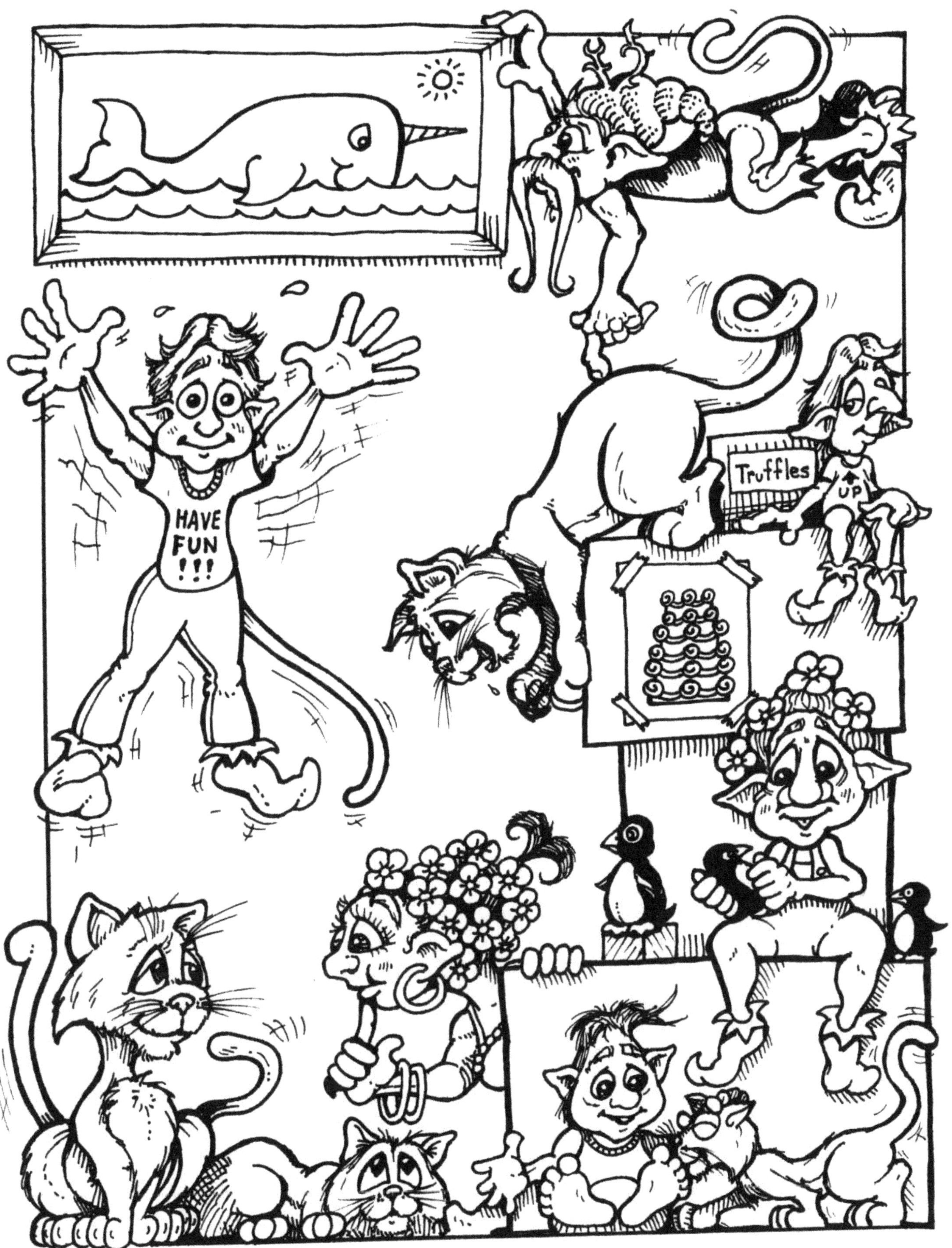

HAVE FUN !!!
Truffles
UP

Irrequites:

Irrequites are funny little Figments.
They tend to primarily affect women,
but they have been found in others.
They seem to inspire lots of sighing.

It is believed that some authors
often can have Irreguites hanging around.

Jane Austen had quite a few around her. They are very
attracted to such gathers that involve wine, bon-bons, and ice cream.

Curiously they often seem to faint or swoon at the oddest of times.
They often seem to be found with or around handkerchiefs.
Especially those that have lace or embroidery.
It has been noticed that they are very attracted by music
from the Temptations or Bonnie Raitt.

(common experience)

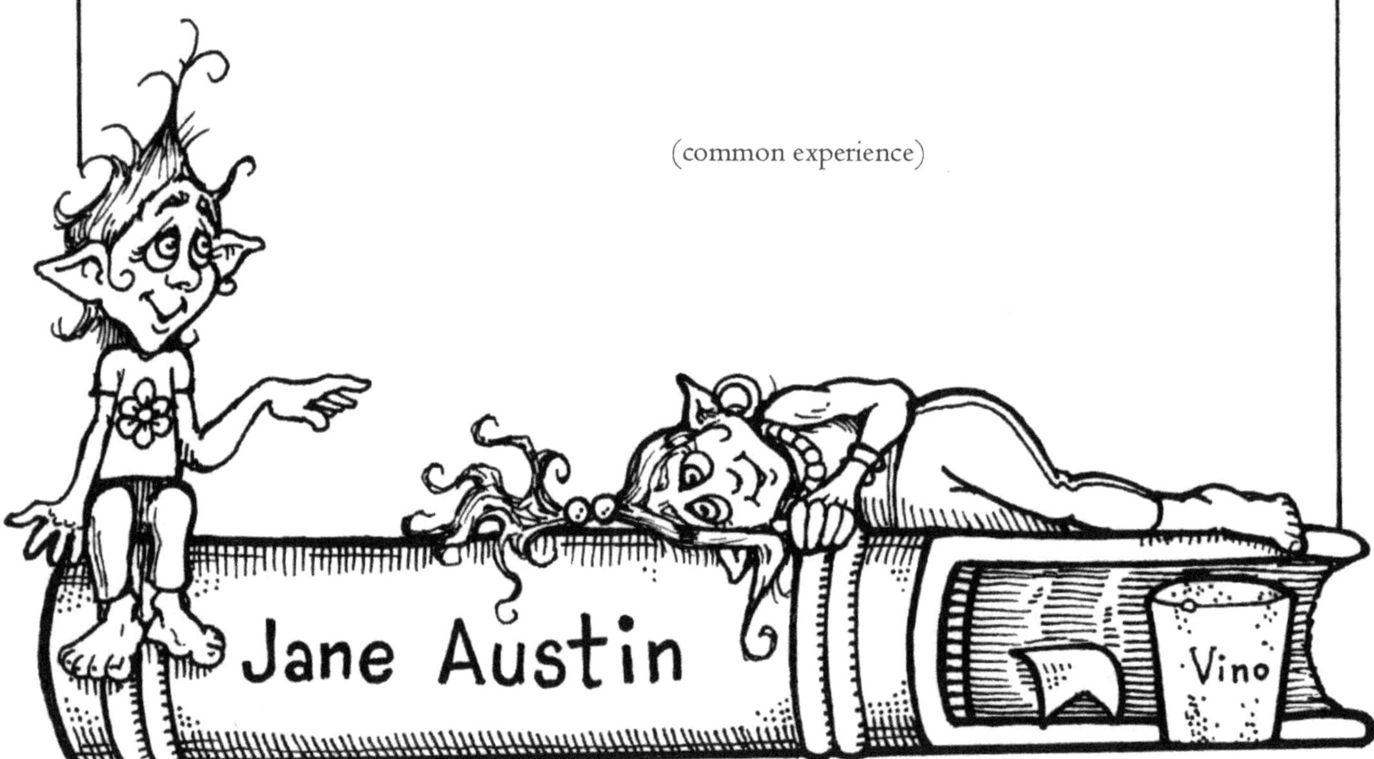

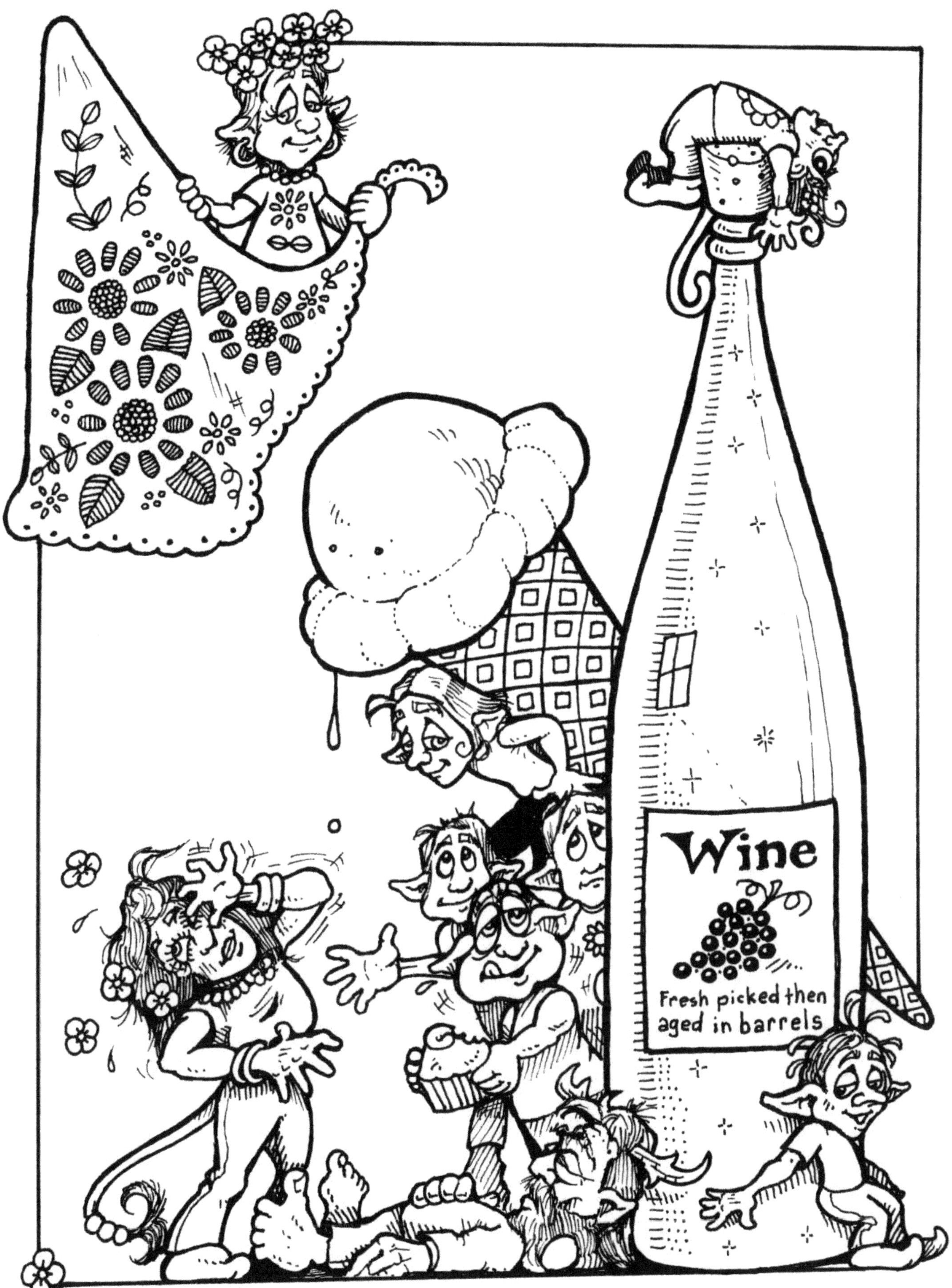
Wine
Fresh picked then
aged in barrels

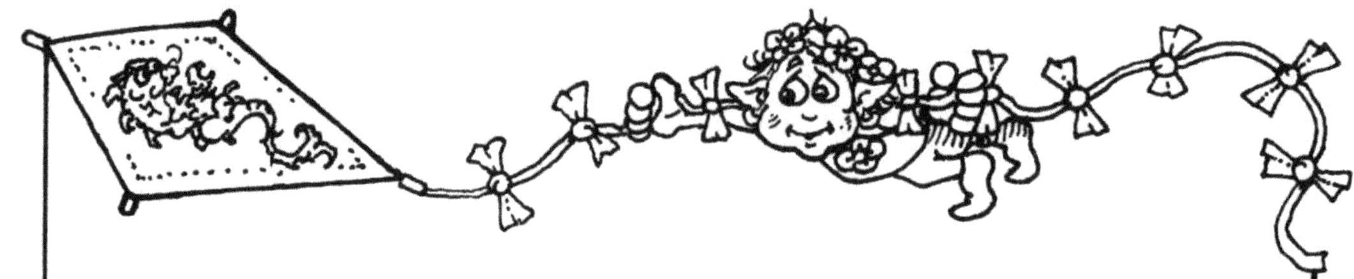

Gatherers (collectors) This Figment sometimes has an assortment of objects. Indeed, they seem to thrive in the middle of crowded spaces. For some, a Gatherer has gotten in and attached to piles or boxes of items. These are typical, unfinished crafts with fabric stashes, but they can also get into garages and workshops. They can hide in and amongst tools, screws, and nails, basements and attics, yarn and button stashes often hold items that attract them. Bobbie pins are deeply prized as they are more challenging these days for Gathers to find.

Combined with the powerful emotions evoked, Gatherers are particularly hard to dislodge. Regularly for humans, the reflected feeling is stated as, "No, I don't have a use for it today but might soon." If the Gatherer's stash is compromised, they will go to great lengths to create a situation where one of the lost items is needed as soon as possible.

All this to ensure the feeling that the trove should not
ever be compromised again.

(Common Experience)

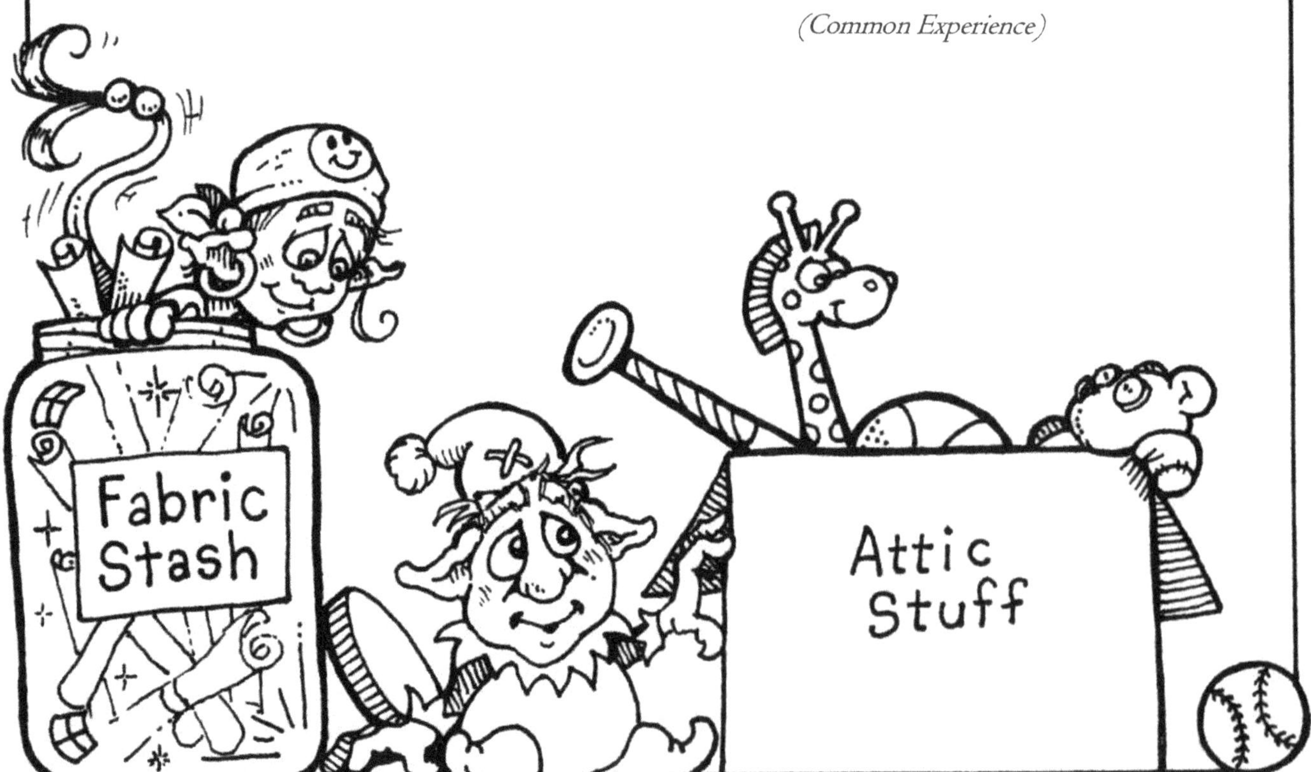

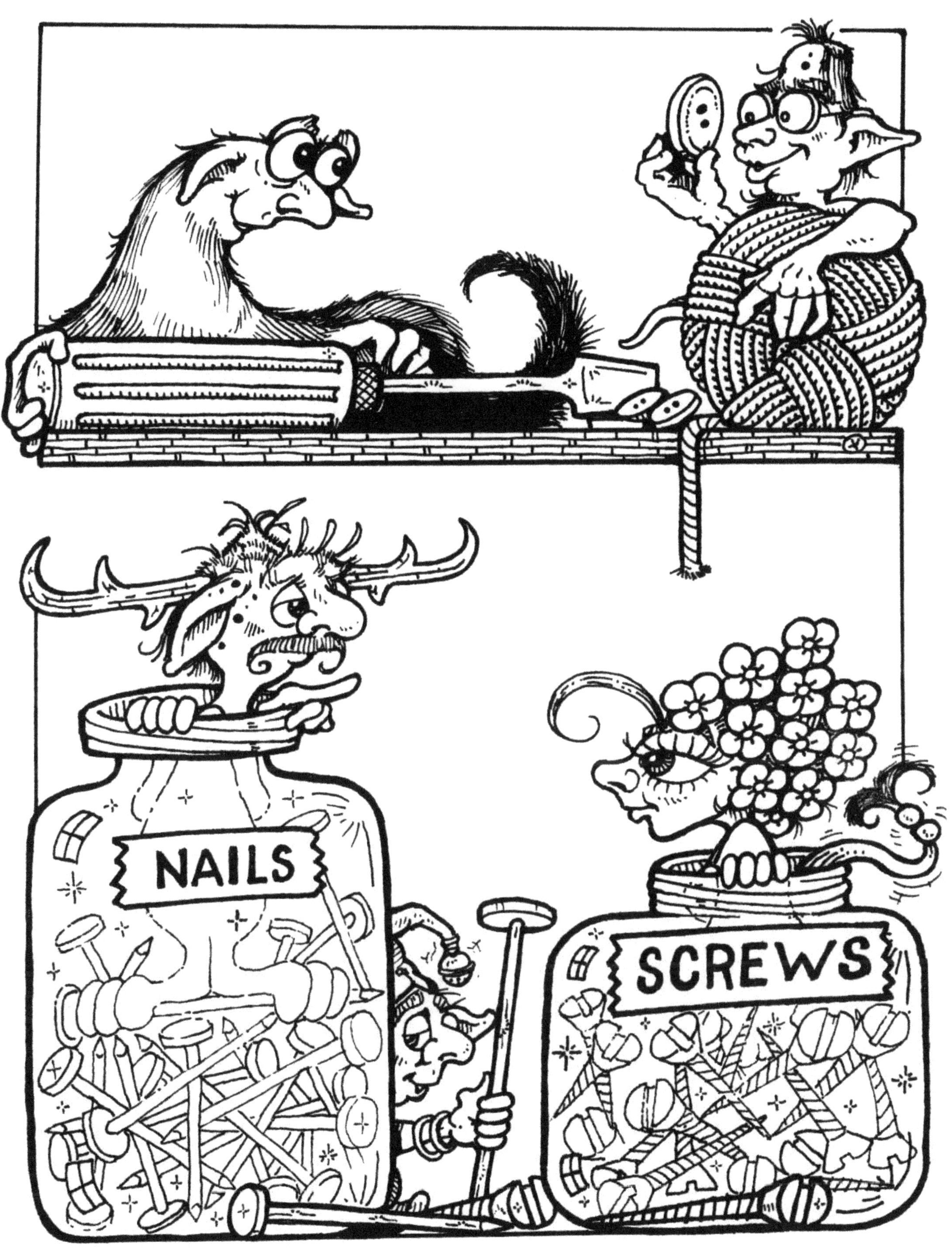

NAILS
SCREWS

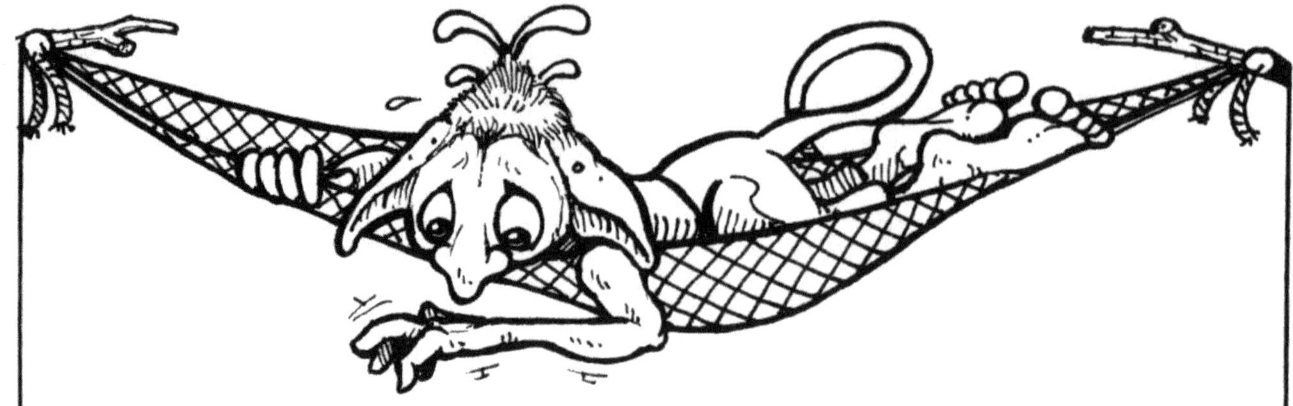

Demurs: They collect and keep lost innocence and shyness. A Demur is a beautiful, slightly sad Figment that can occur during a human's lifetime. Often, when a Demur comes to be, it is with a loss of childlike innocence. Sadly, this usually happens when the child stops seeing Figments, perhaps because the dissenters of the world have convinced a child that there is no magic to be found. Those skeptics may be other children or adult unbelievers who seem bound to make sure all become unbelievers.

Demurs remain hopeful if the child re-finds the magic, they can find their belief again.

A Demur can return the magic lost to that child. There can be beauty and peace in reconnecting with hope.

(Emotions)

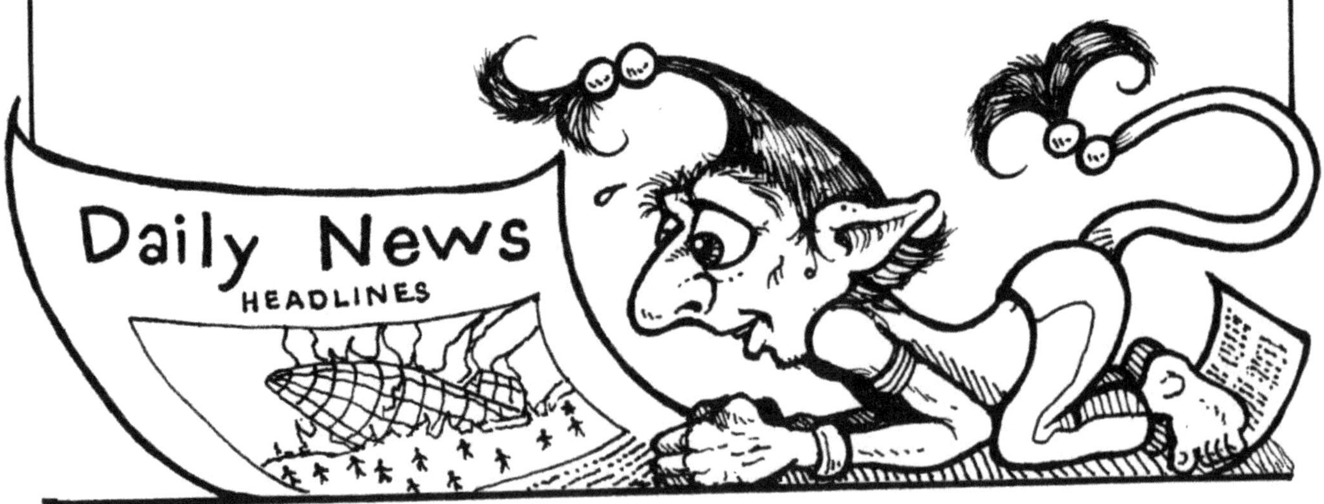

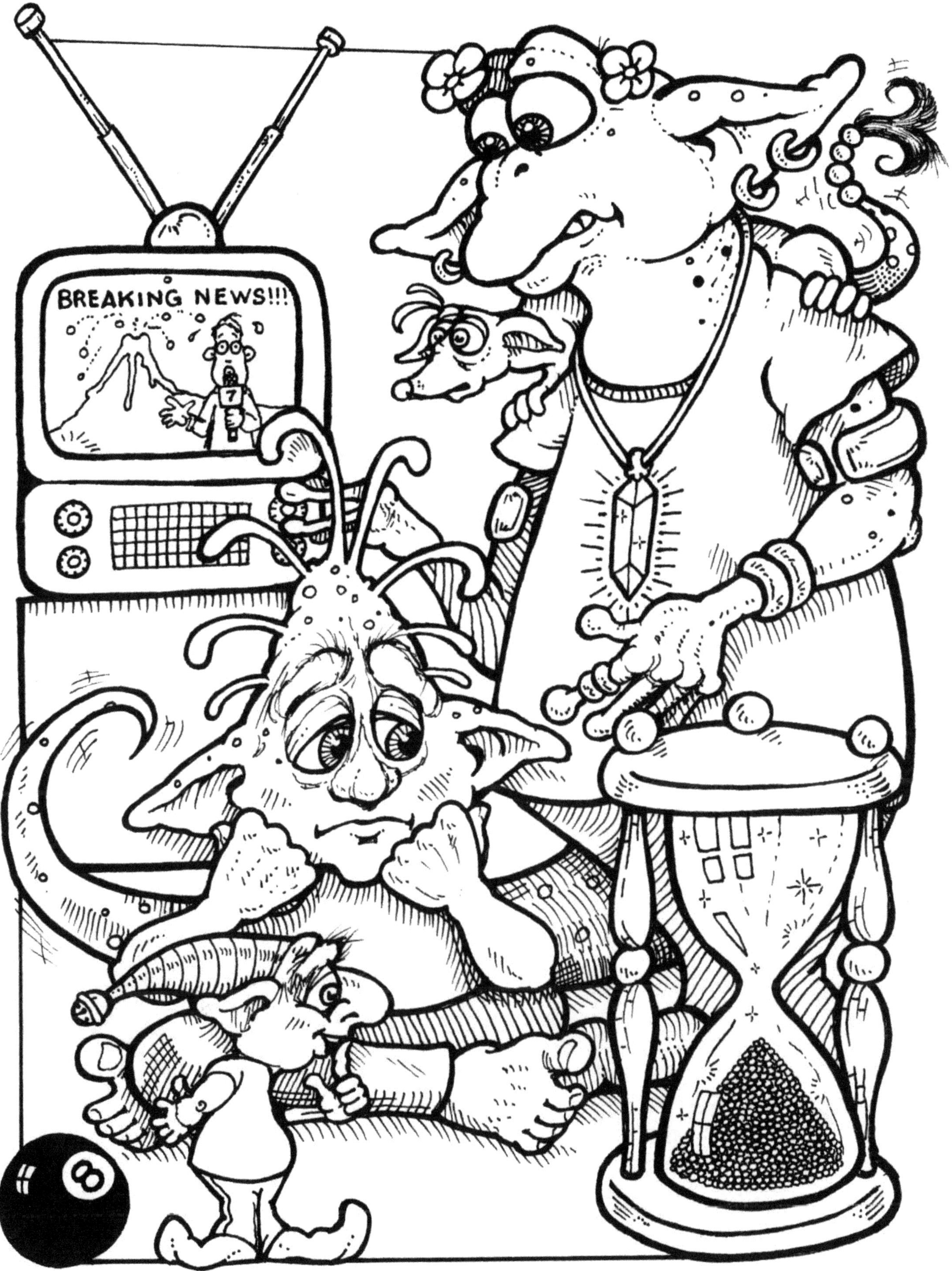

BREAKING NEWS!!!
7
8

Riven: These were Sentimentals who got lost in time. The memories are still powerful but disconnected. While most Figments will fade away after a total disconnect if they do not find another human to connect to, these, for some reason, have not. Perhaps the origin memory was just so powerful, or the break with the human was so abrupt the Riven kept on as if they would return. Some speculate that the reflected emotions about their origin human are powerful enough to keep them from fading but not enough to remain an unchanged Sentimental such as a Sentimental connected to a Military item or an item from a historical figure. If enough excitement surrounds an object in keeping with the origin human, a Sentimental may stay throughout the ages. Often those Sentimentals are discovered in beloved family relics. The feelings usually fade, and a Sentimental will break the connection when the object disconnects from its origin human. A Riven then happens. Someone loved this very much, but it is no longer with its person. Riven are often found with one or more items in a time capsule, in a museum, or historical display. Riven can also be found with forgotten items of importance, such as a cigar box of memories or jewelry with letters, dried flowers, etc. You can feel the remnants of emotions once attached to the item but no longer belong to a living human's memory.

Haunting feelings recognized by humans with a Riven are felt by many, acknowledged by few.

(Emotions)

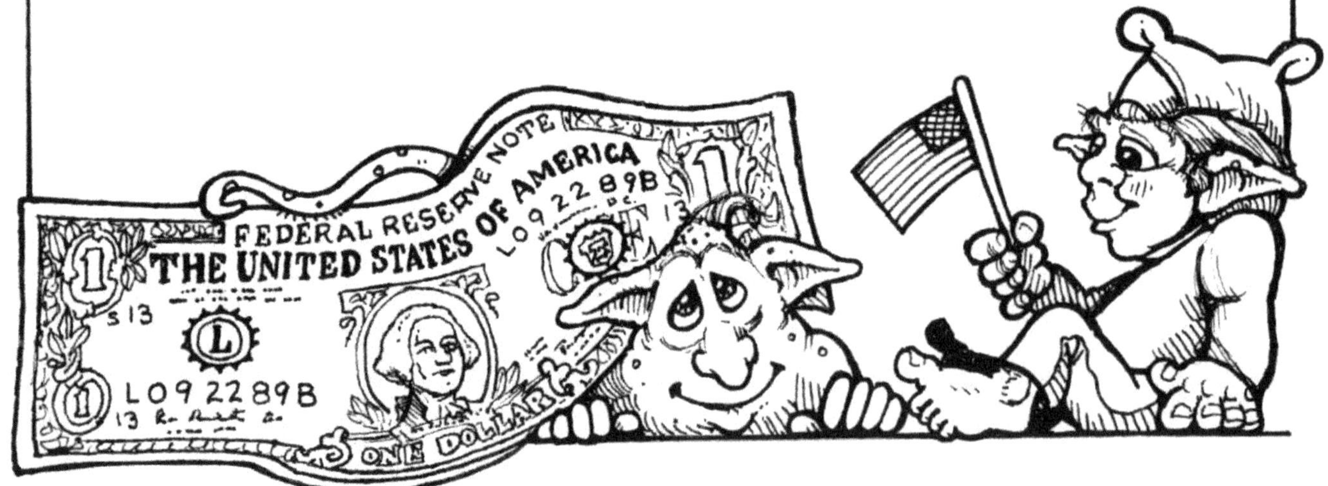

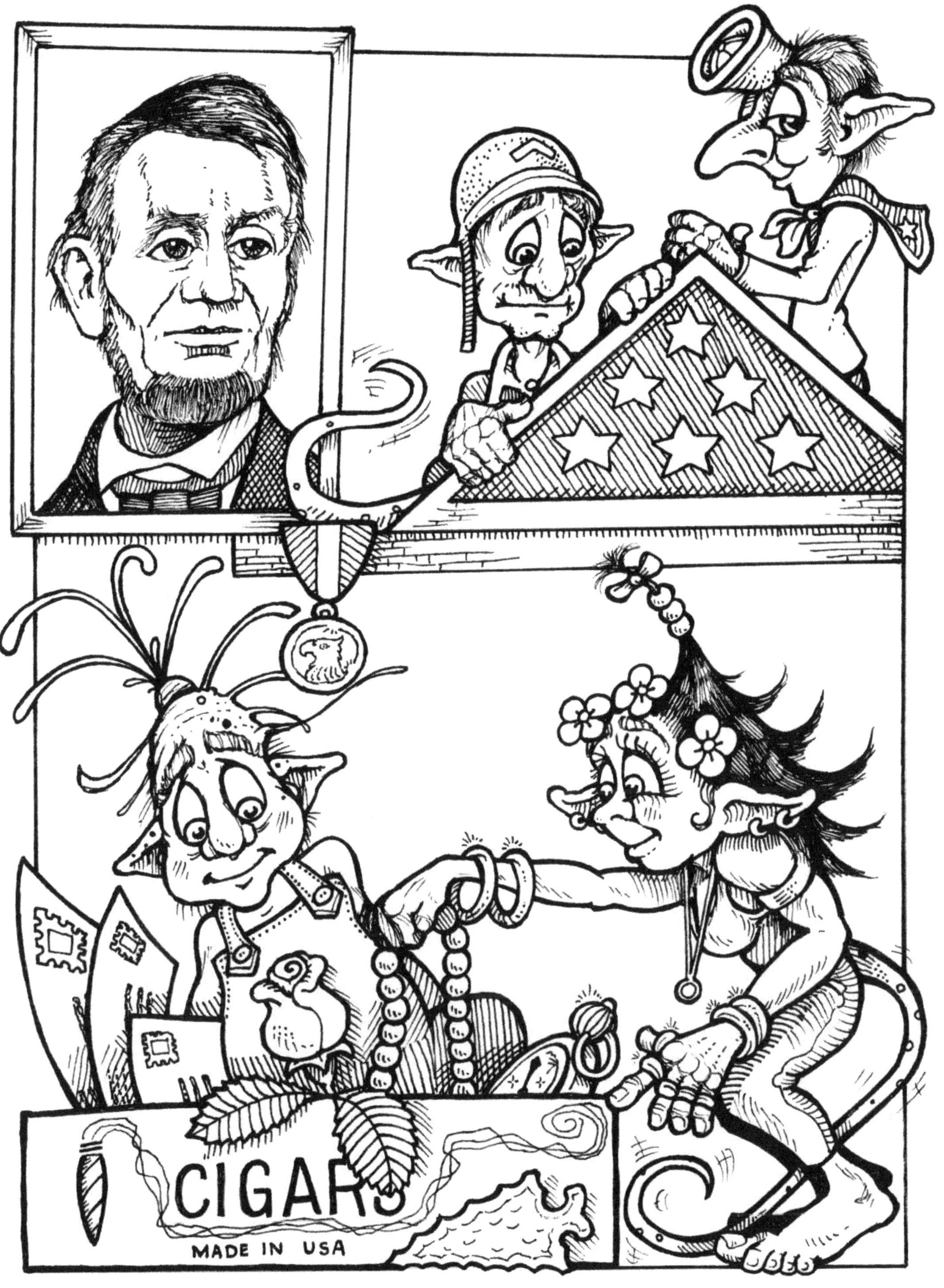
CIGARS
MADE IN USA

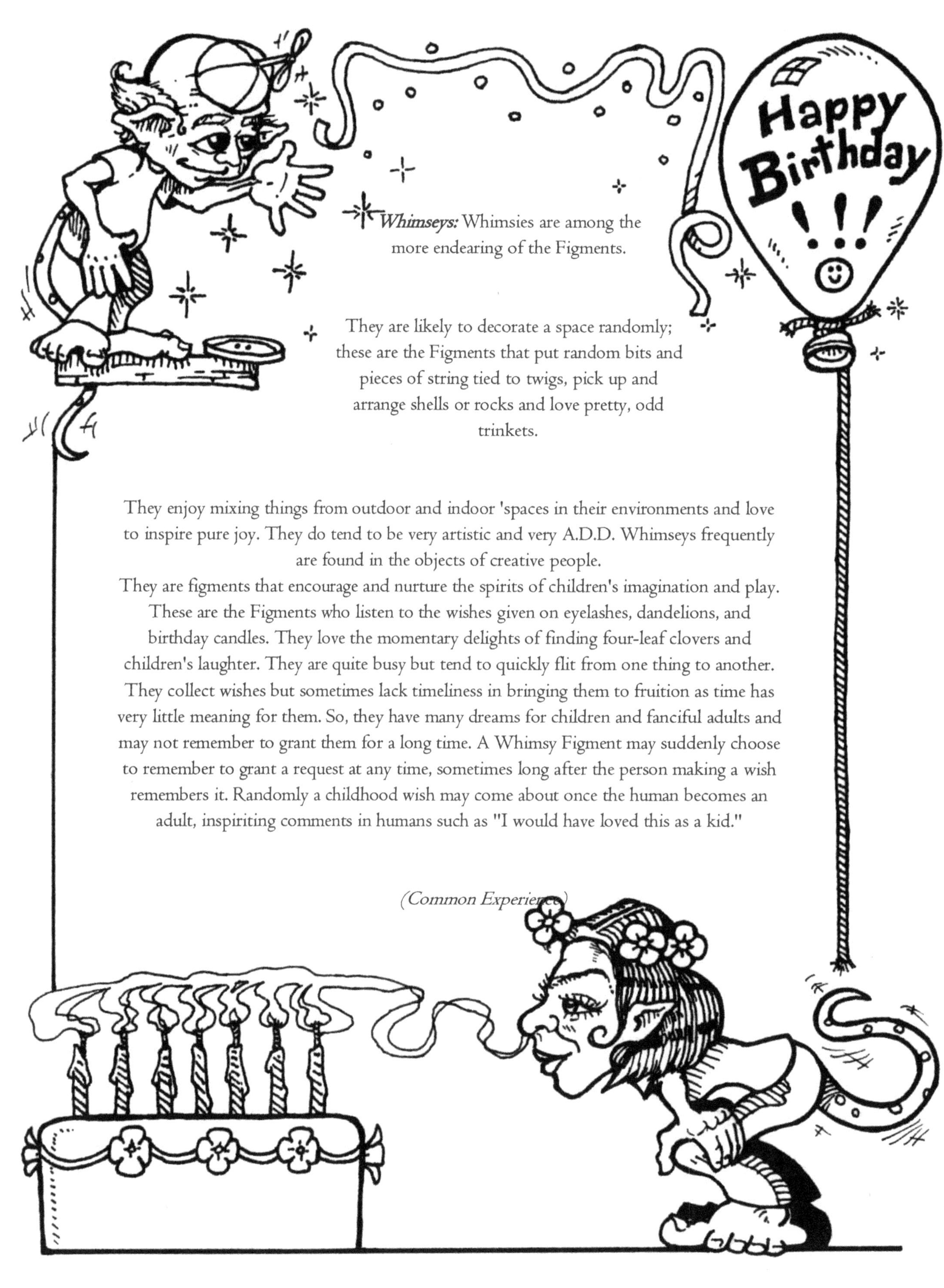

Whimseys: Whimsies are among the more endearing of the Figments.

They are likely to decorate a space randomly; these are the Figments that put random bits and pieces of string tied to twigs, pick up and arrange shells or rocks and love pretty, odd trinkets.

They enjoy mixing things from outdoor and indoor 'spaces in their environments and love to inspire pure joy. They do tend to be very artistic and very A.D.D. Whimseys frequently are found in the objects of creative people.

They are figments that encourage and nurture the spirits of children's imagination and play. These are the Figments who listen to the wishes given on eyelashes, dandelions, and birthday candles. They love the momentary delights of finding four-leaf clovers and children's laughter. They are quite busy but tend to quickly flit from one thing to another. They collect wishes but sometimes lack timeliness in bringing them to fruition as time has very little meaning for them. So, they have many dreams for children and fanciful adults and may not remember to grant them for a long time. A Whimsy Figment may suddenly choose to remember to grant a request at any time, sometimes long after the person making a wish remembers it. Randomly a childhood wish may come about once the human becomes an adult, inspiriting comments in humans such as "I would have loved this as a kid."

(Common Experience)

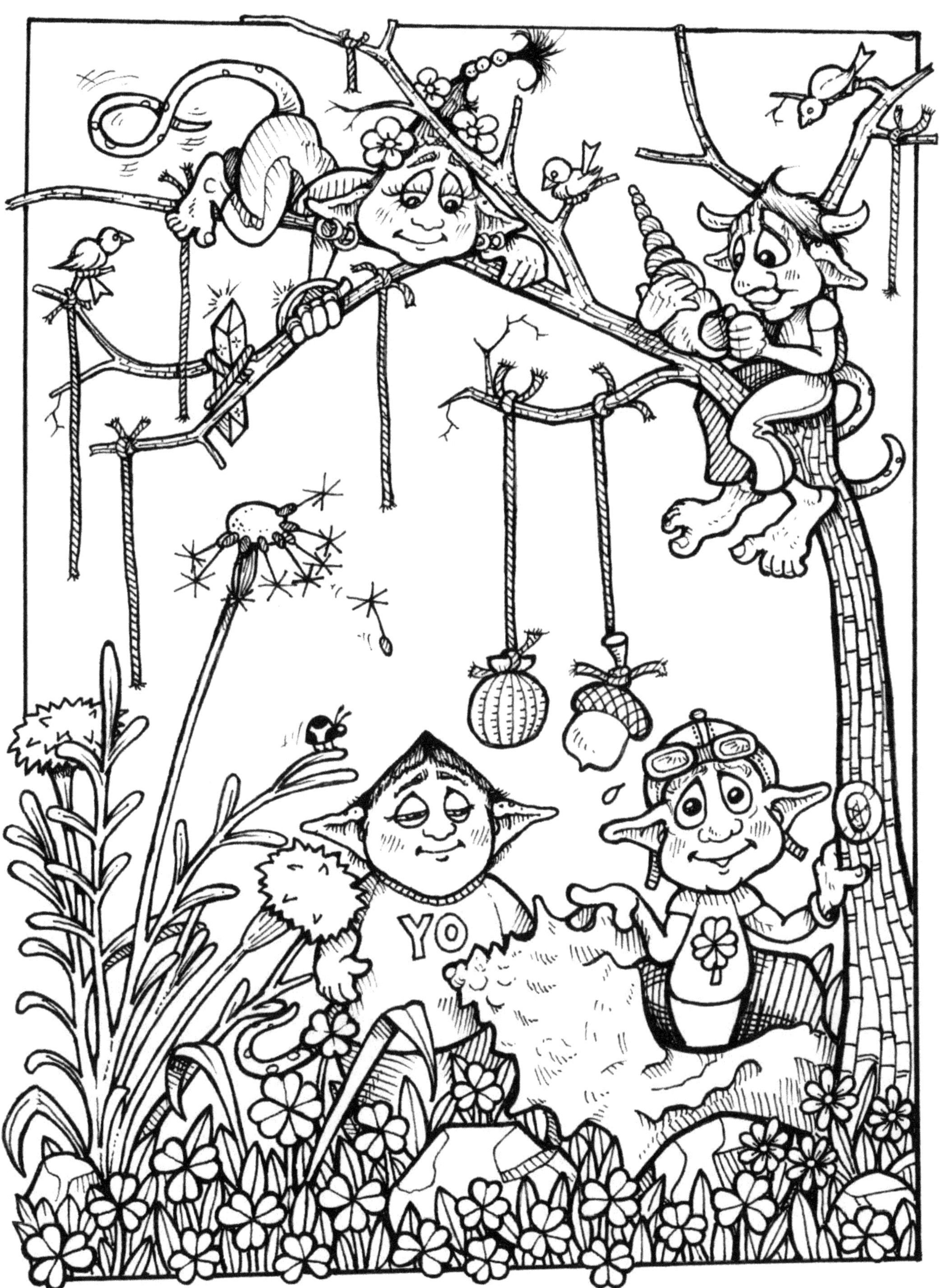
YO

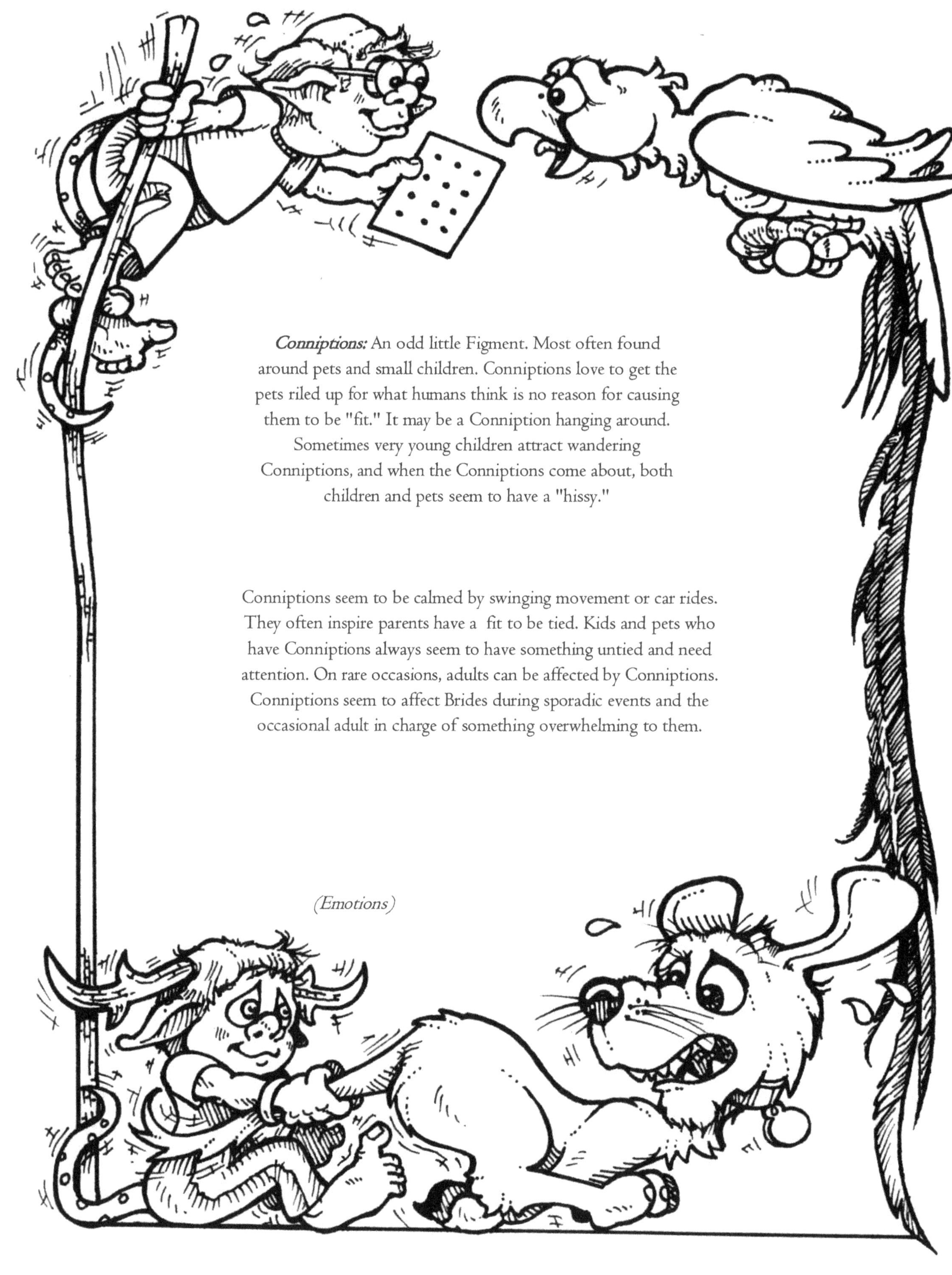

Conniptions: An odd little Figment. Most often found around pets and small children. Conniptions love to get the pets riled up for what humans think is no reason for causing them to be "fit." It may be a Conniption hanging around. Sometimes very young children attract wandering Conniptions, and when the Conniptions come about, both children and pets seem to have a "hissy."

Conniptions seem to be calmed by swinging movement or car rides. They often inspire parents have a fit to be tied. Kids and pets who have Conniptions always seem to have something untied and need attention. On rare occasions, adults can be affected by Conniptions. Conniptions seem to affect Brides during sporadic events and the occasional adult in charge of something overwhelming to them.

(Emotions)

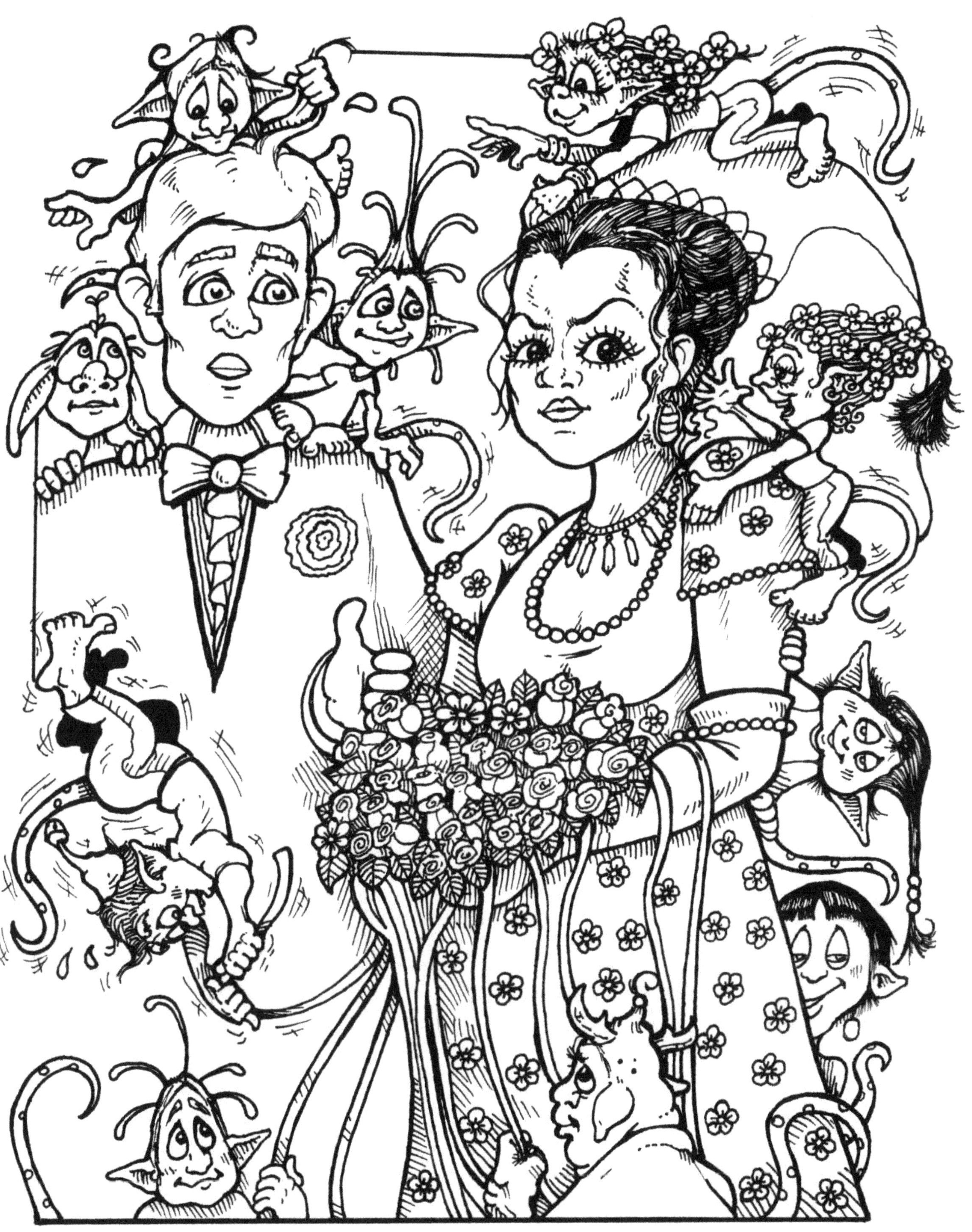

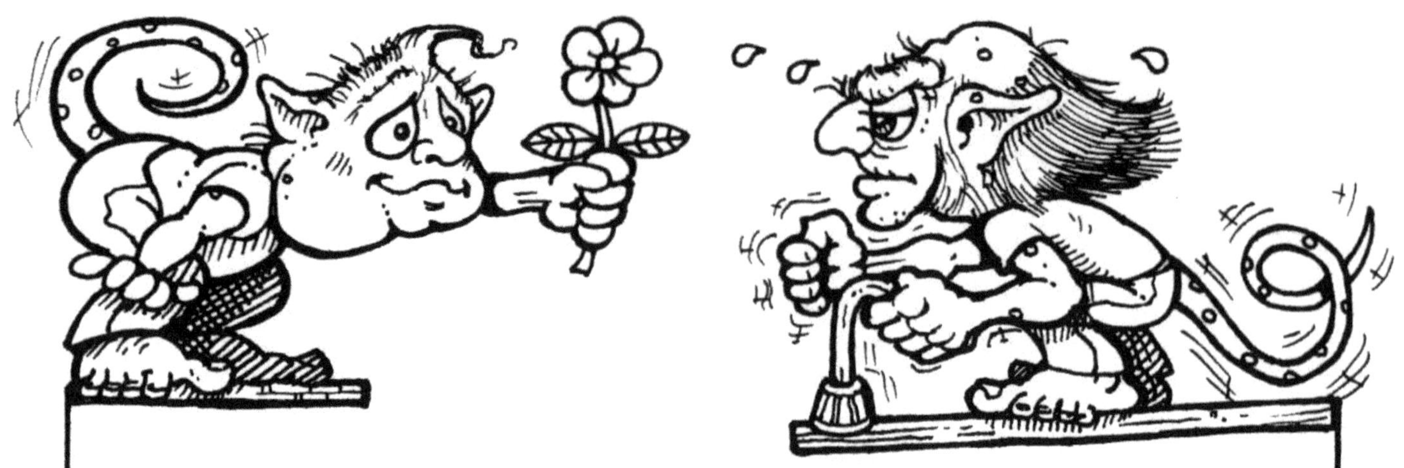

Vexations are close cousins to Conniptions but are more likely to be around Tweens to young adults. They can't help themselves but like to poke at "last nerves," so to speak. They enjoy the wild ride of emotions from the young to becoming an adult crowd.

They will provide insight, outrage, and intense emotional swings to enjoy the show. At one instant, they appear to be very loveable and fun to be around; in the blink of an eye, they are crusty and offended by everything. The speed of transformation is astounding.

Vexations are horrified by laundry baskets, dirty dishes, and anything that might be a chore. They practice boredom. They want to be individuals, as long as it is like everybody else.

(Emotions)

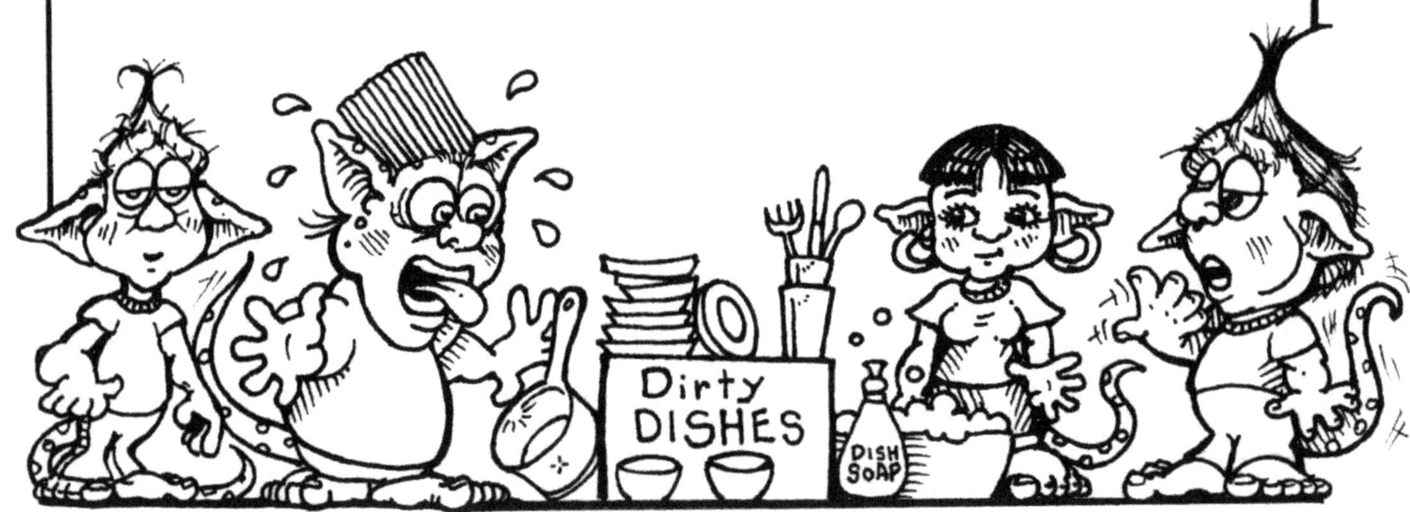

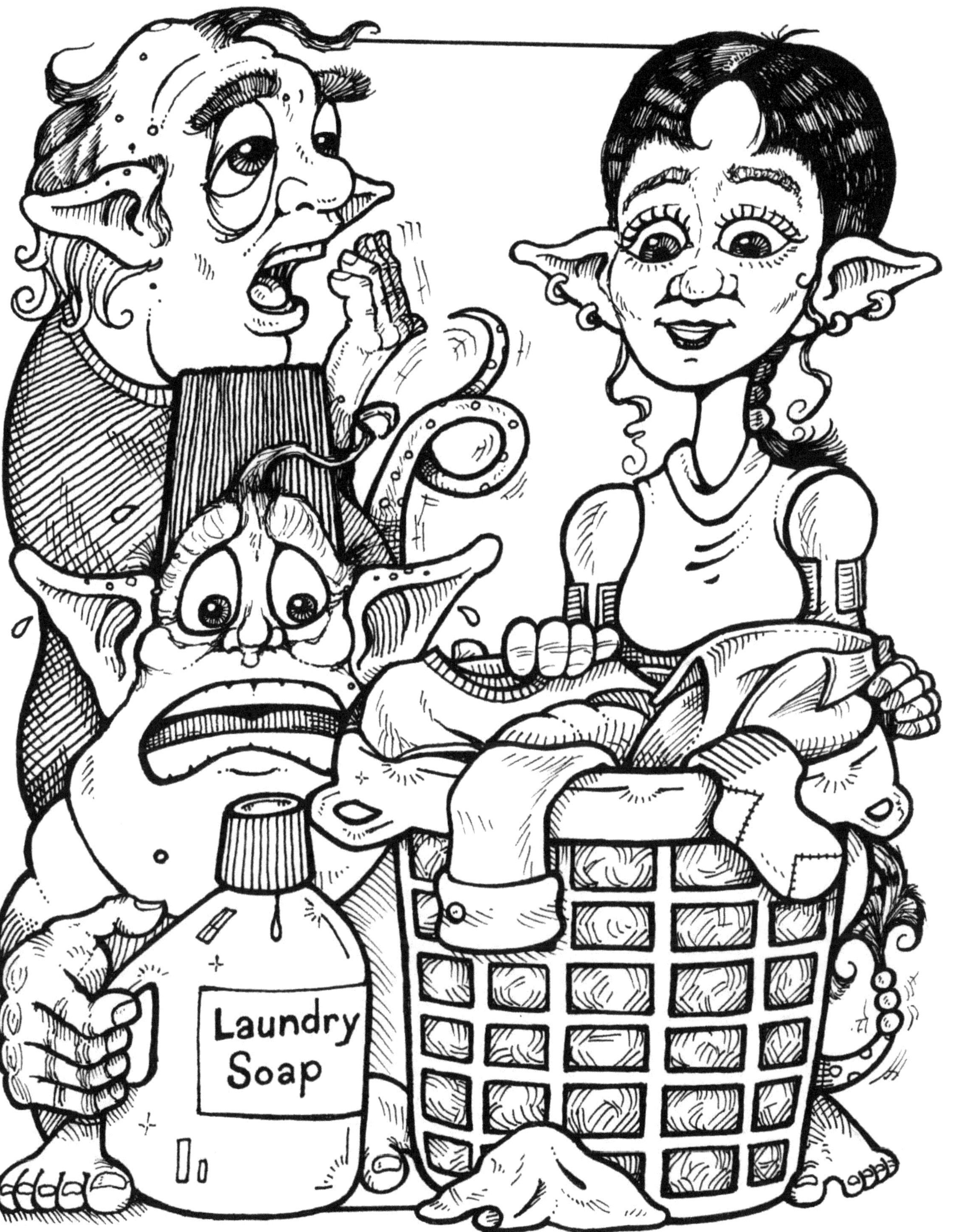

Laundry
Soap

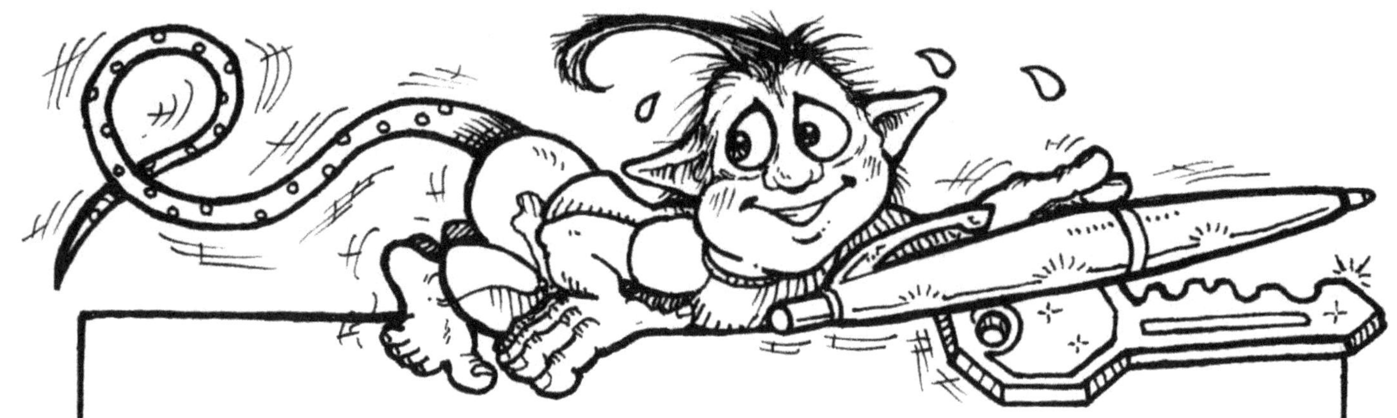

Addled: They tend to adore toddler-aged humans. Most often, here you will find the Addled. They will move items just for the giggles. Disappear your keys or one sock. Move the pen you were using, and mask the glasses on your head. They bring them back as soon as they well, do. Maybe where you left them or perhaps a few feet or inches away from where they found them. The rallying cry, "It was in the last place I looked often, means they are near!

"Keep in mind; however, that might also have been the 2nd and 8th place; you looked as you kept rechecking that same place. They collect frustrations just for the sport of it. It is conjecture that they keep score among themselves, but this is not confirmed (although many believe it). They make you doubt your sanity or memory; however, you didn't forget, you just got Addled.

(Emotions)

The Figment Three Conniptions, Vexations, and the Addled.
They are with us all through our lives but in different ways.

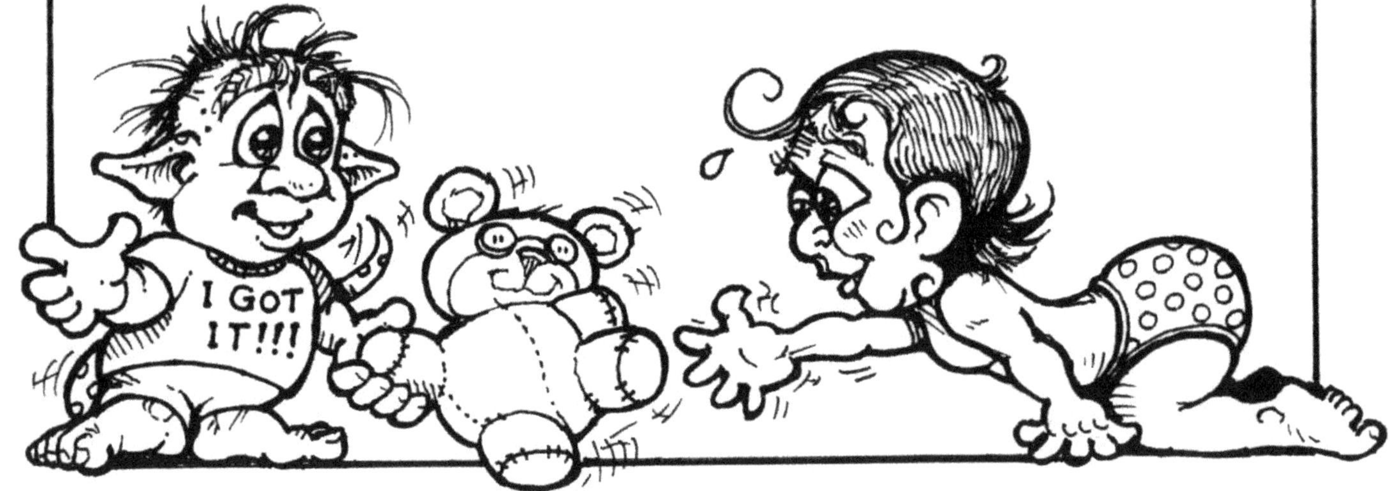

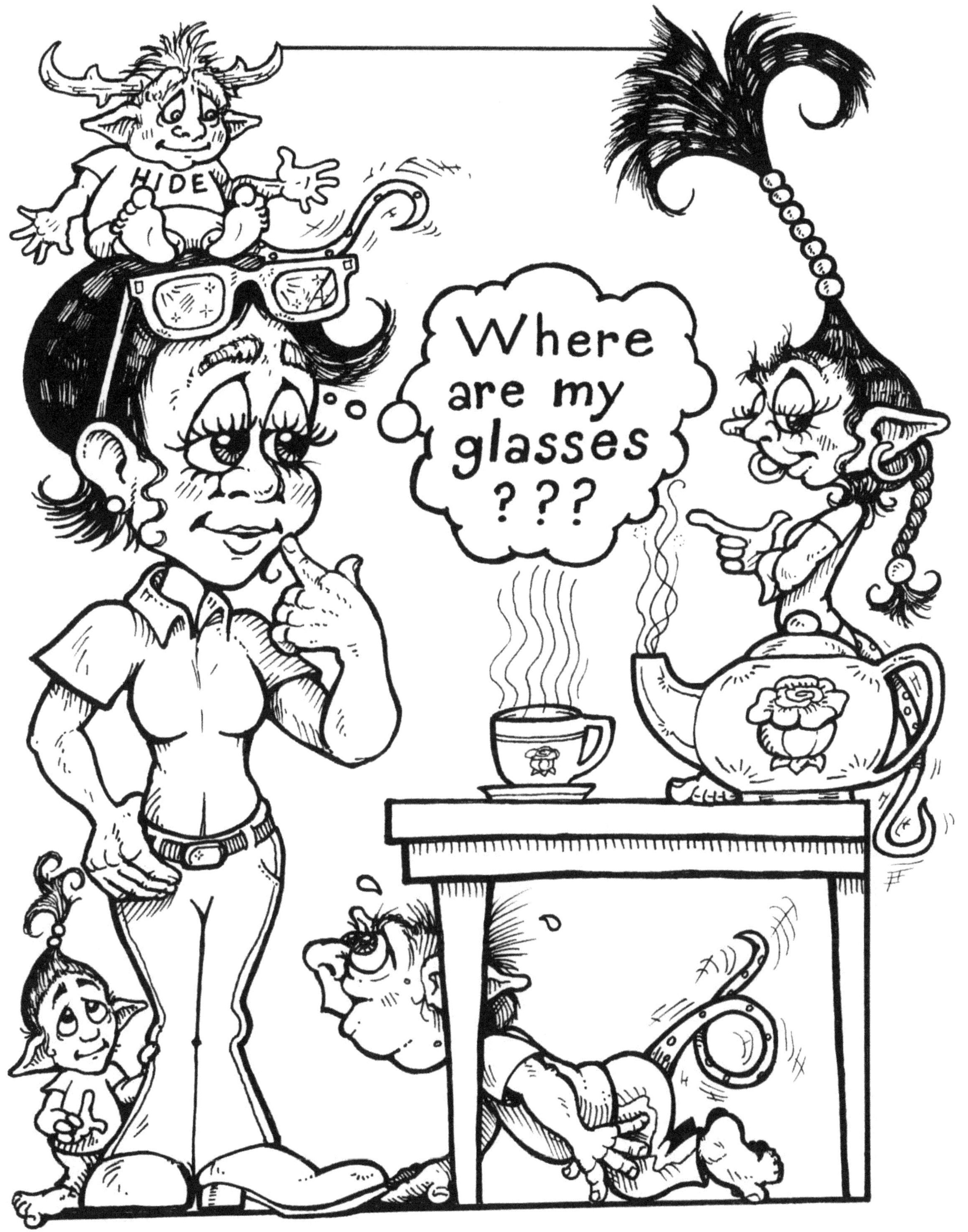

HIDE
Where are my glasses ???

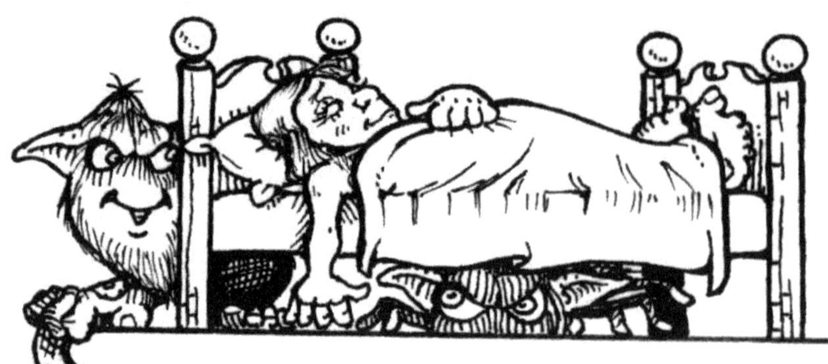

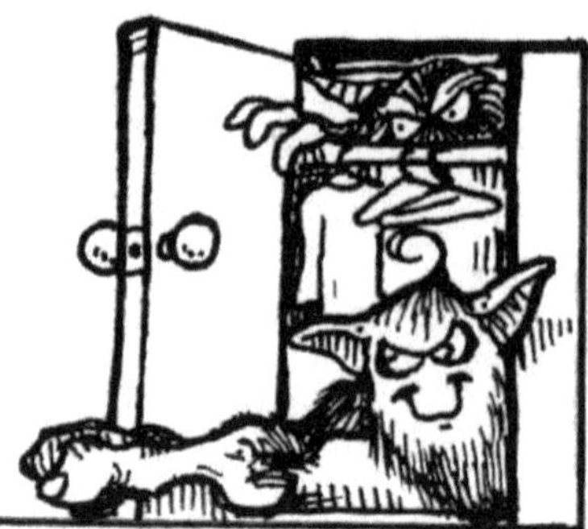

Trepidations: Don't mess with these Figments; they are scary and dark. Nightmares and Anxiety attacks are their specialties.

Trepidations live in dark corners and eerie places. Occasionally closets and shadows. Sometimes under beds, but there can be Sinisters there. Trepidations enjoy the feelings generated by unknown situations and reflect them to exacerbate the emotions. They do not employ logic and tend not to hang around with Scruples. Scruple Figments overthink for Trepidations. Trepidations love the feelings of fear and trembling; they come into being with worries of the past and unclear futures.

Like all the Figments, they come from deep emotions, but this Figment can go from one object to another. If the first-time fear of public speaking has enough passion for creating a Trepidation Figment, they may connect to a button on a garment worn when the fear happens at school, to a backpack, or something kept in a locker. Trepidations are often considered a charm or good luck piece but, instead, the fears that helped in its inception.

Trepidations, however, do not stick to a single object. They can shift from object to object, continuing to inspire concerns in the human who manifested it as that human matures. They can become so intense that others around can feel its effects.

(Emotions)

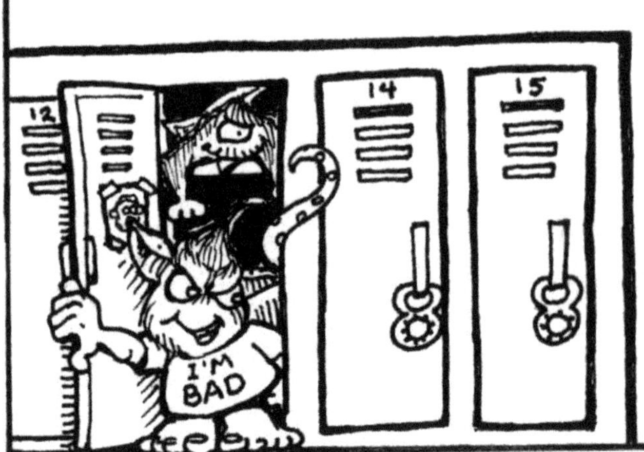

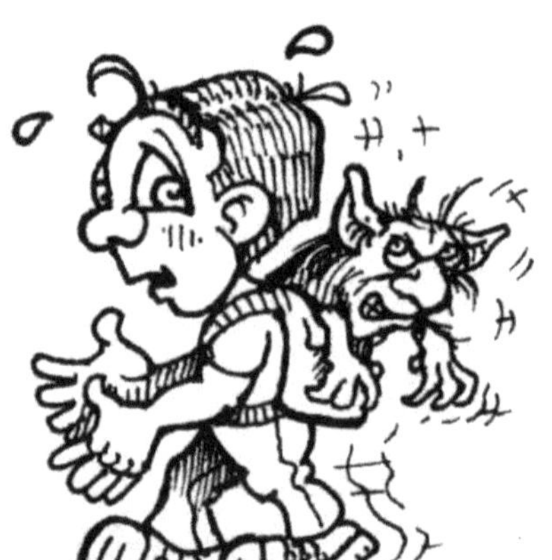

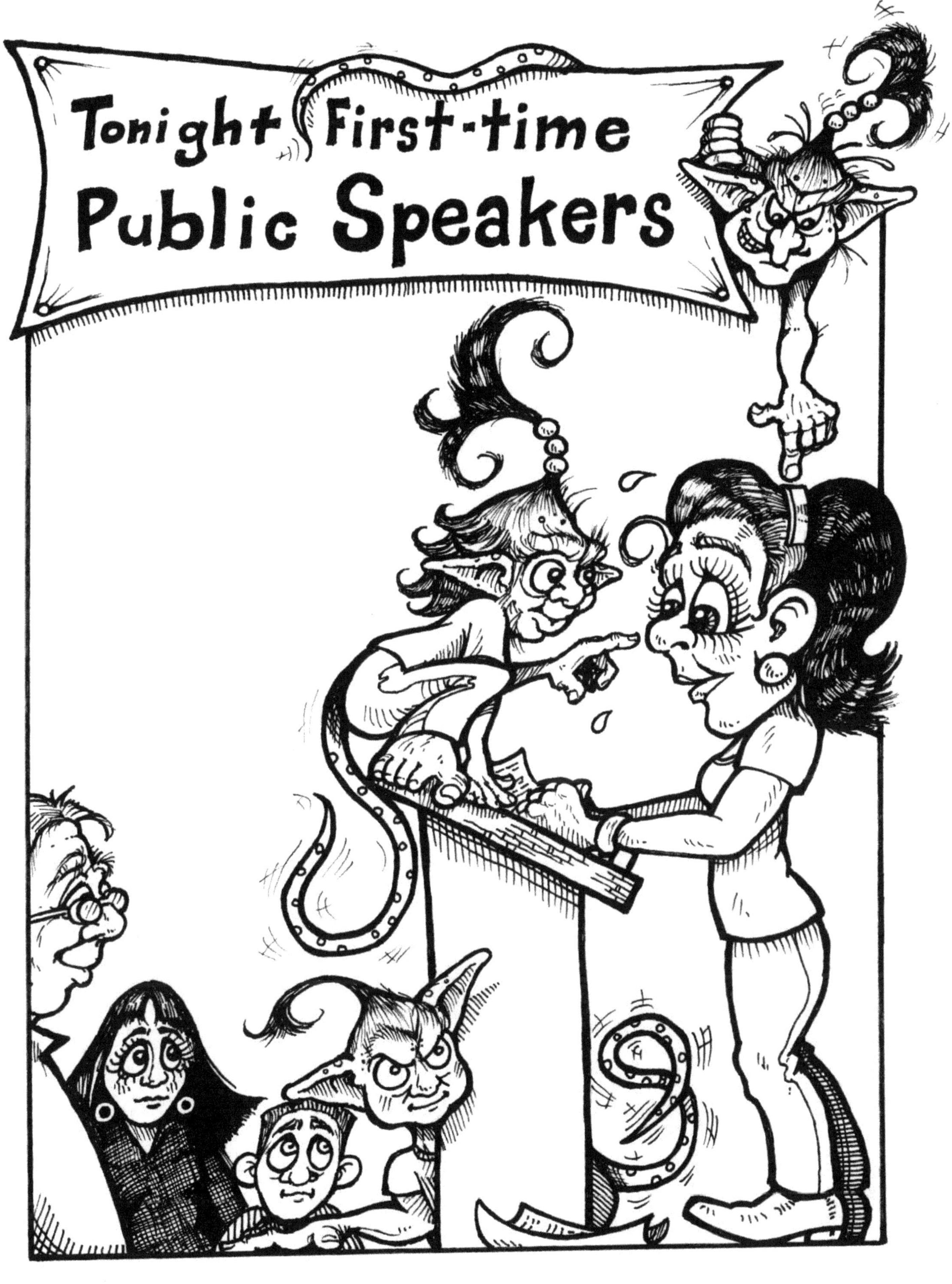

Tonight First-time
Public Speakers

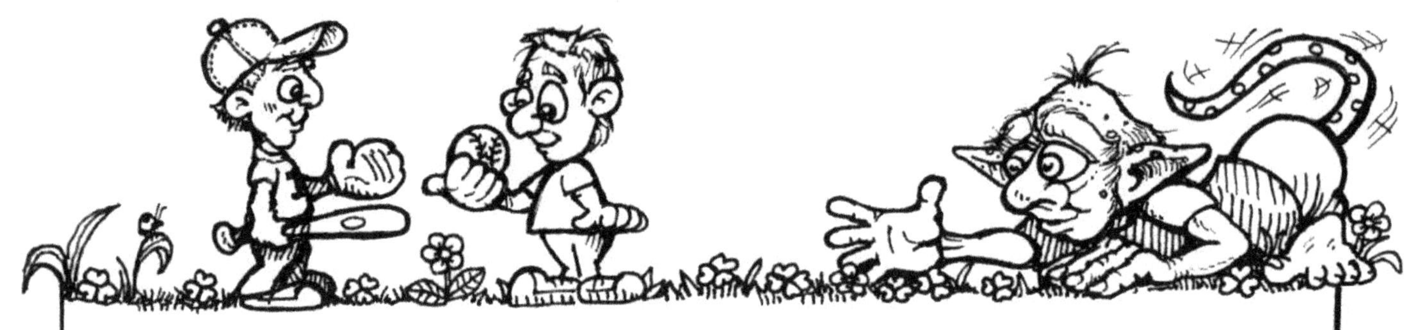

Scruples: *Tend to be given from human parent to child. But most frequently from an adult to a child. There have been cases where peers provide Scruples for each other, but it is more likely that two or more who have Scruples will have their Figments interact and intensify the emotion. This phenomenon is not limited to kids. Scruples are ethical to have and sad to lose. Having no Scruples is very distressing. Periodically additional Scruples are picked up throughout life as humans grow and interact with others. Scruples like to hang with their human and hate to be lost. They found in reminders of the human who passed their Scruples on down the line. Once you have acquired one Scruple, it gets easier to have more Scruples. And this is one Figment for which it is good to have both healthy and many, Scruples.*

Interestingly if one's human has strong enough Scruples, those Scruples can influence a whole group. Sadly, when they are compromised, it becomes more difficult for them to affect their human. If the human loses touch with their Scruples, it is much like not having any. It is best to keep something around to remind you daily of the right influences in your life, such as the one who gave you your Scruples. Scruples can grow strong again if weakened, but the human must commit. Over time the Scruples can be healthy as ever. It does help if they hang with others with solid ethical Scruples.

(Emotions)

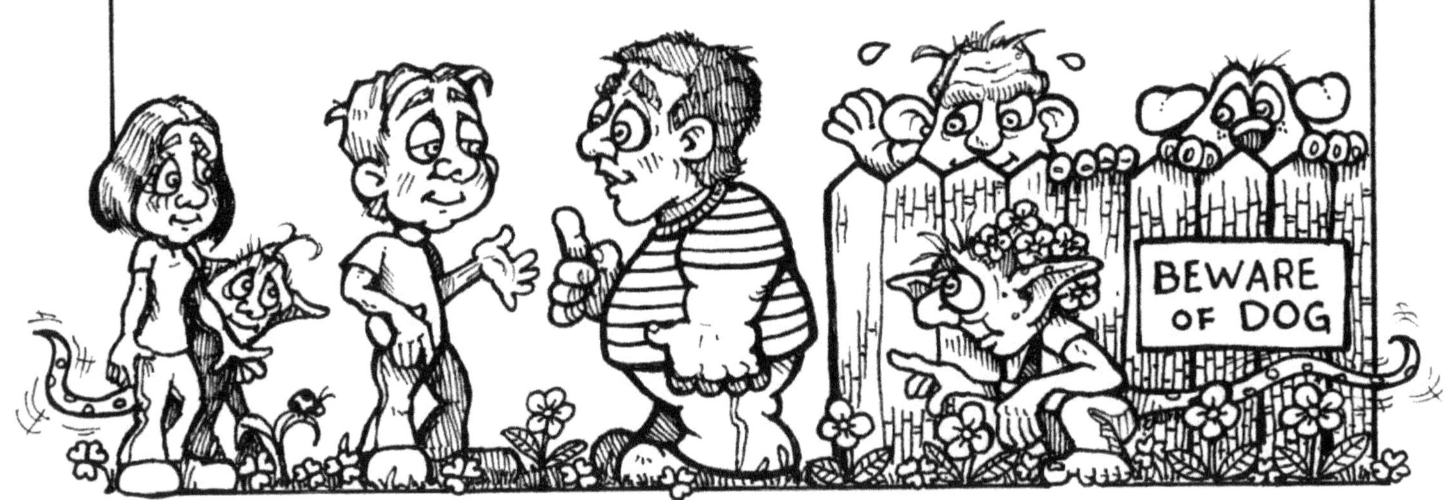

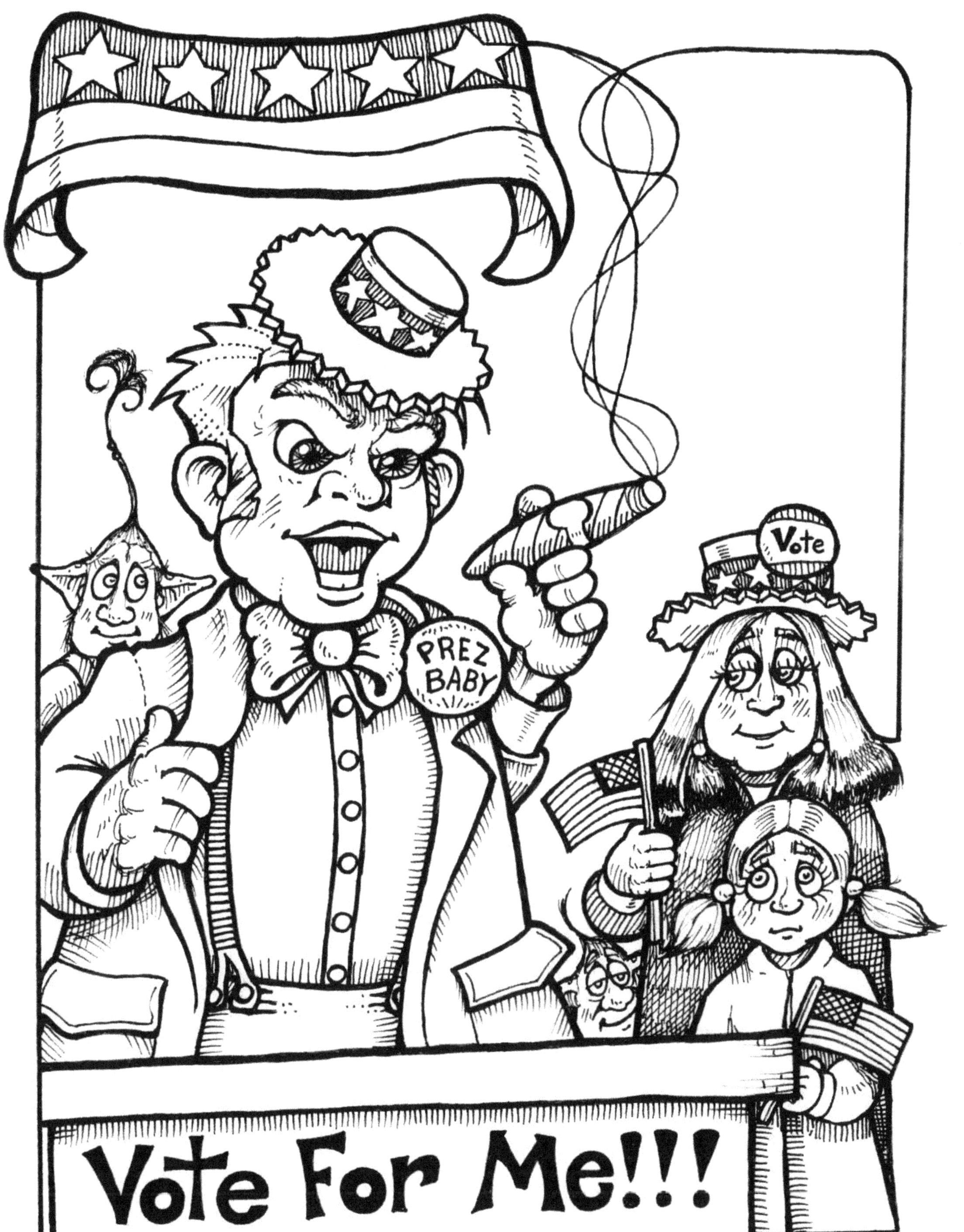
Vote
PREZ BABY
Vote For Me!!!

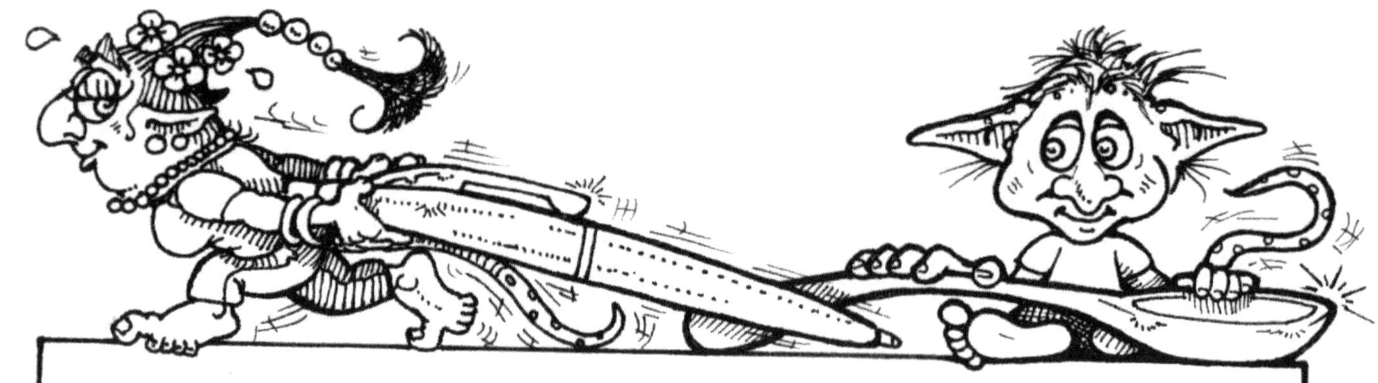

Mislay: *Mislays are the collectors of lost things. When the Addled forget to return lost objects, the Mislay will gather them. Sometimes they collect items themselves. They don't always wait for the Addled to get things first. They prefer parts of things, not the whole, such as one of a pair, a single screw, that one thing you need, a single puzzle piece, or a single shoe. They don't want the entire set, just the lid of the Tupperware or spoon. The cord is what a Mislay desires, not the thing that uses the plug. Pencils and Hair ties seem to be popular with the Mislay as well. They believe they are making them safe but often forget to tell the human where the item is. They feel little compulsion to do so since they are, in their opinion, keeping it safe anyway. Sometimes, it is as minor an object like a ring or the remote or pen you just used. Needles are prized.*

Mislays are not malicious and do not see their actions as upsetting. If they notice that a human is overly frustrated with missing an item, they will often return it. That returned item may show up at random times or in unexpected places. Those needles may come back in your carpet right where you walk (so you can find them easily), or a single hair tie may reappear on the kitchen counter where no one has been. Mislay don't want you to miss the returned object and dislike drama so much they may return the item to a place or in a way that still makes it difficult to find if a Conniption gets involved.

(Common Experience)

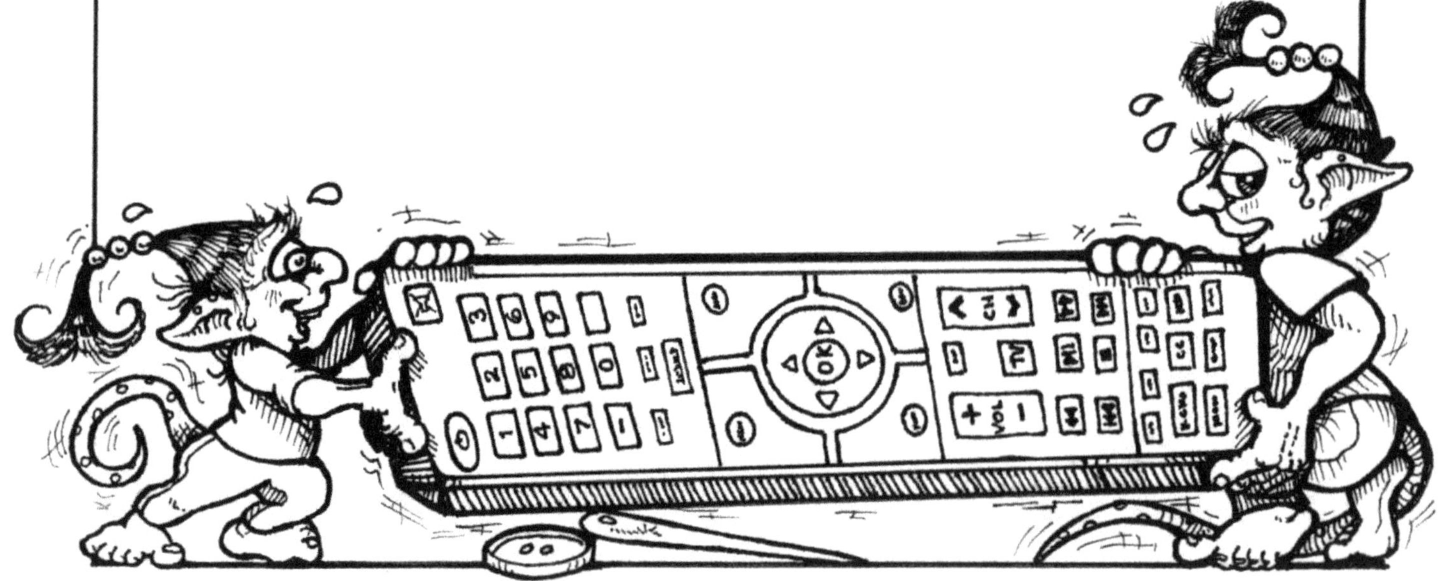

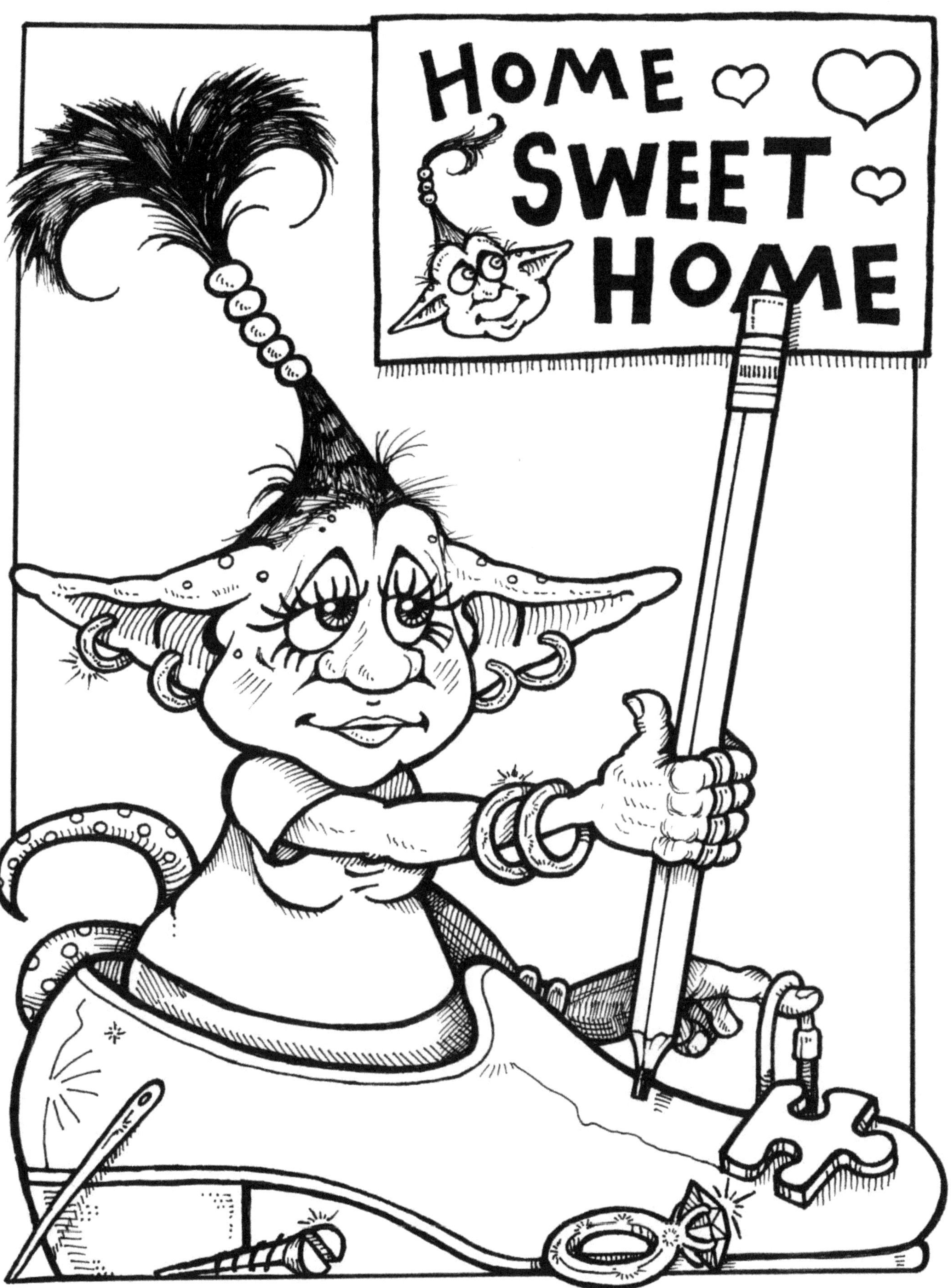

HOME
SWEET
HOME

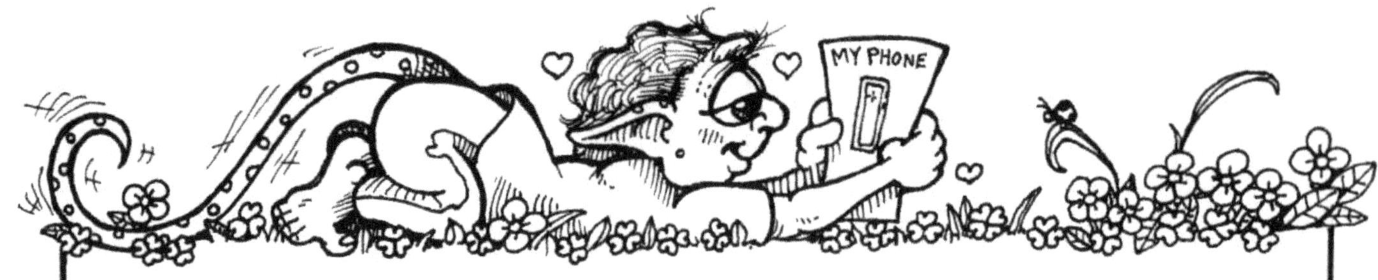

Bewilders: *Sometimes called the phone Gremlin. They like to disguise themselves at times as Peeves, but they are not. They muddle up the words typed or spoken into a device. They get into so many things that are supposed to be beneficial to humans and love to simply move items around.*

They live and around phones causing miss-typed texts and searches. Even voice issues in the phone, such as you can have full service and yet the sound is crackled or comes and goes. The Bewilders are having a field day.

They love to shift the keys as your fingers are typing. The more experienced ones can change other phone features as well. The longer they are part of a phone, the more established they become. Bewilders tend to find it hilarious to make crackling paper sounds while people are on the phone. Or muffle sounds. No one knows why.

(Common Experience)

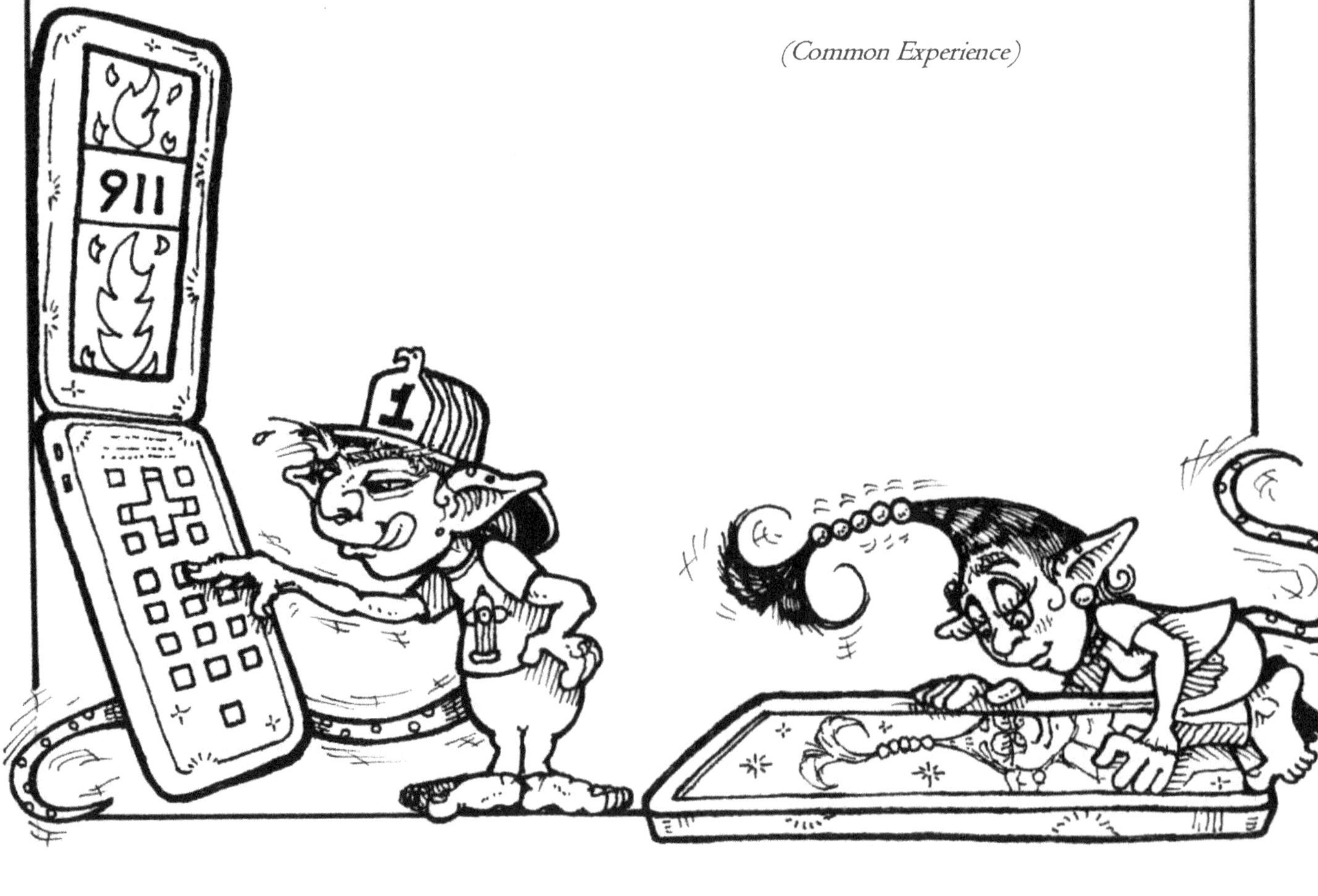

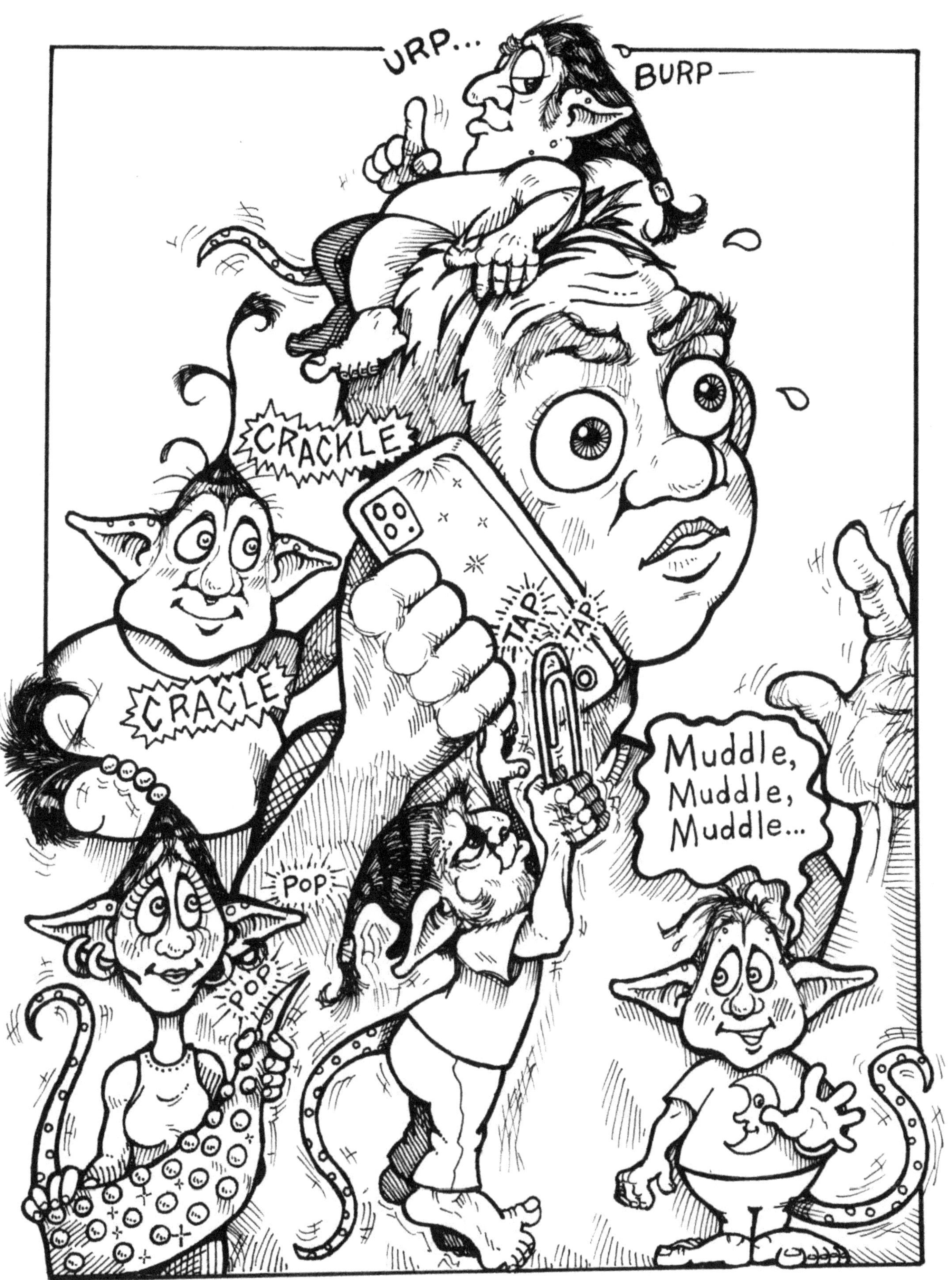

URP...
BURP
CRACKLE
CRACLE
TAP TAP
POP
POP
Muddle,
Muddle,
Muddle...

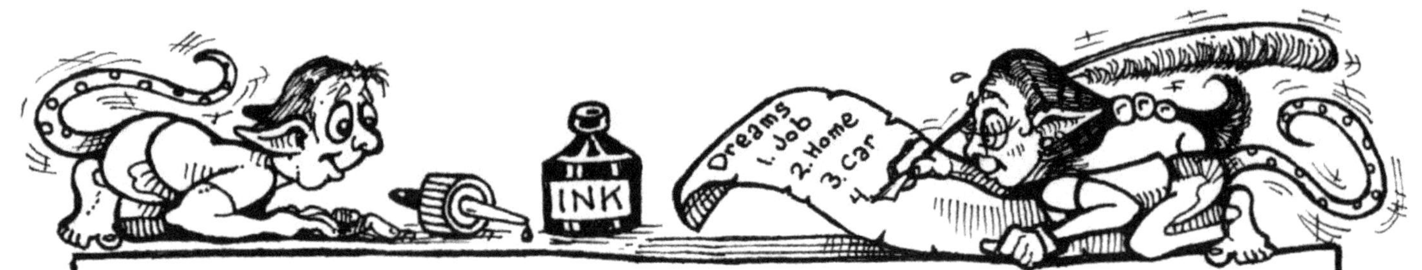

Evocatives: They give dreams to humans (quite often children) of futures yet to come.

Evocatives inspire wishes for the future, near and far. For those that are lucky they keep their Evocatives into adulthood. Those persons are often called dreamers. Evocatives are formed frequently in the Arts. Evocatives are lovely dreamers planning on futures not yet realized.

Evocative give dreams that occur in both the night and the day. Keepers of wishful thinking, hopes, and plans. One of the Figments that are, instead, beautiful and not quite in touch with their human. They offer inspiration but can be a bit unconnected. Time has less meaning to them than the usual Figment, and that is saying quite a bit.

It is believed at the time of this writing that Evocatives have been mistaken for a Muse. Muses, however, are a bit different. They inspire specific beginnings, Evocatives remain more in the dreamy state of futures yet to be defined.

(Emotions)

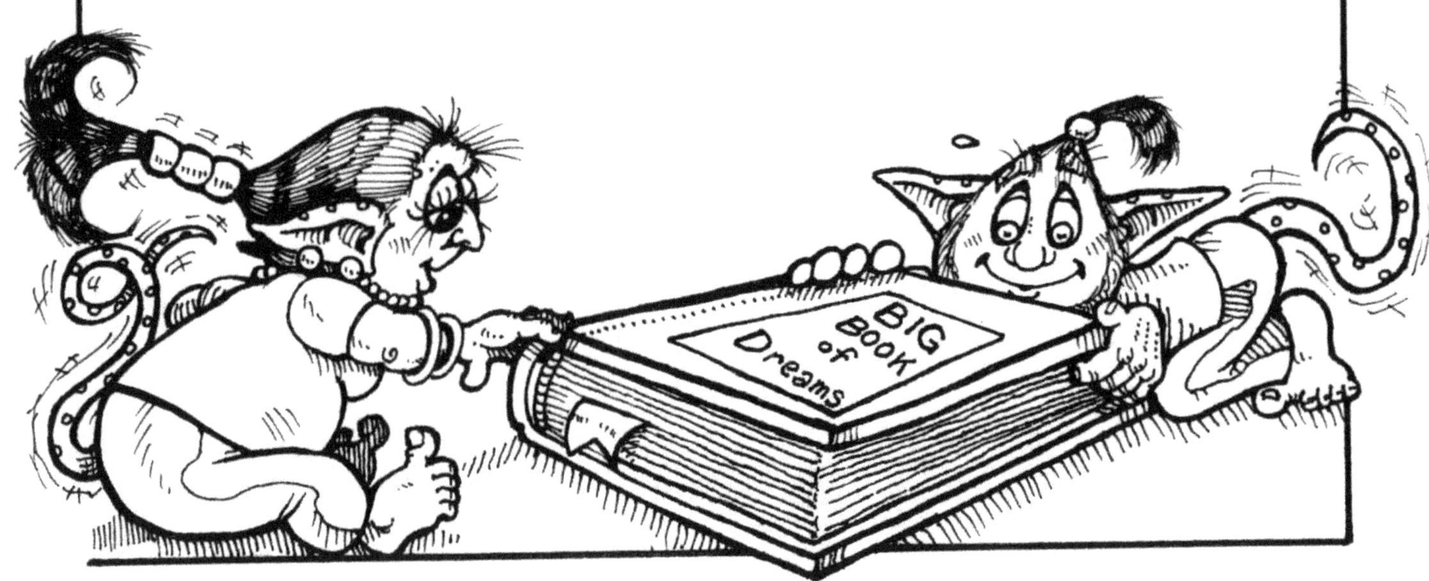

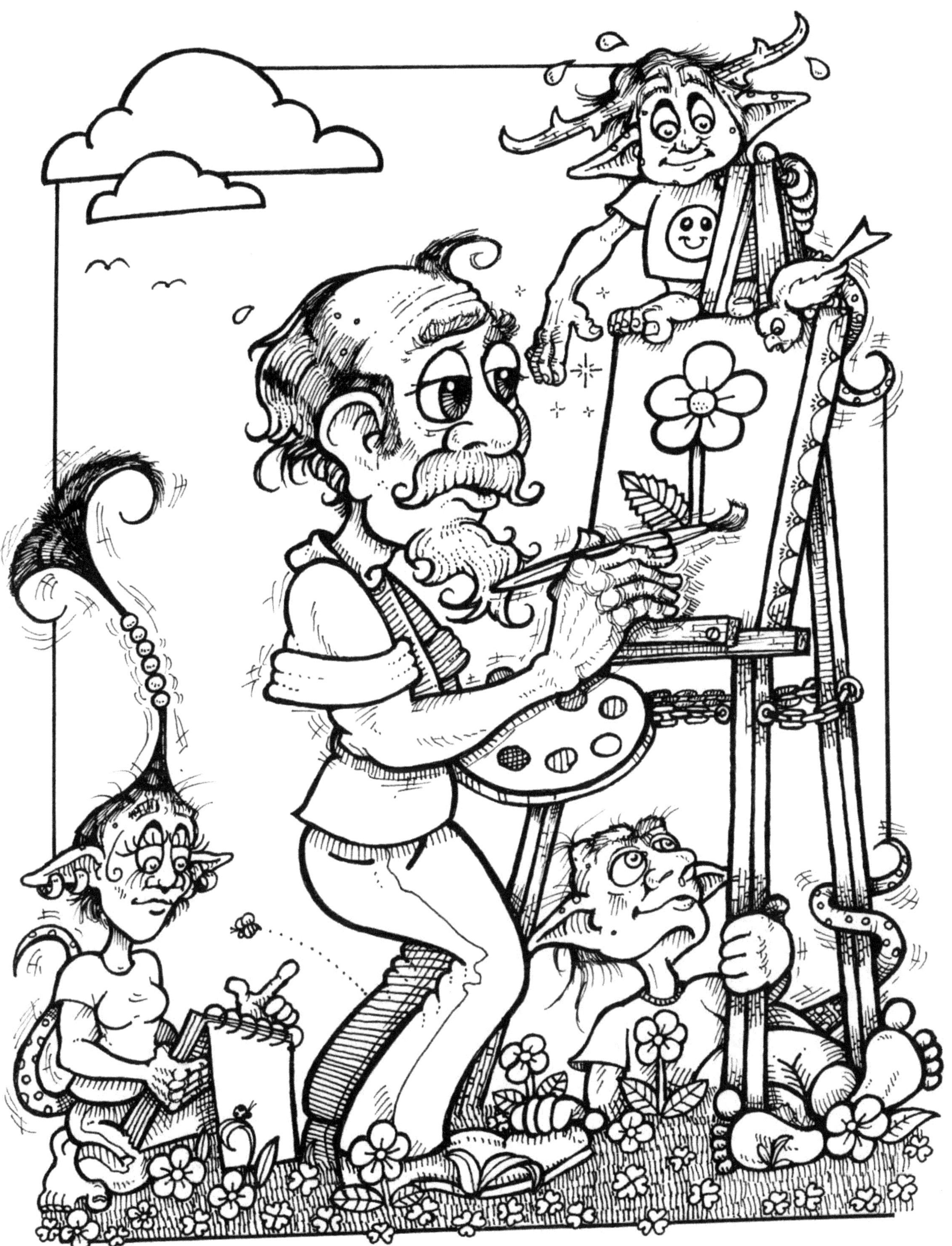

Curmudgeons: *Perpetually, even professionally grumpy*
Figments. While often found around older humans, they
manifest in many areas. They like to pretend to be
Peeves, but while specific Peeves have a cause they are
irritated about,

Curmudgeons seem to be grumpy about everything
randomly. They often inspire humans to have loud
outbursts ranging from off-color language to randomly
yelling at various people.
Things like,
"Get off my lawn!"

(Emotions)

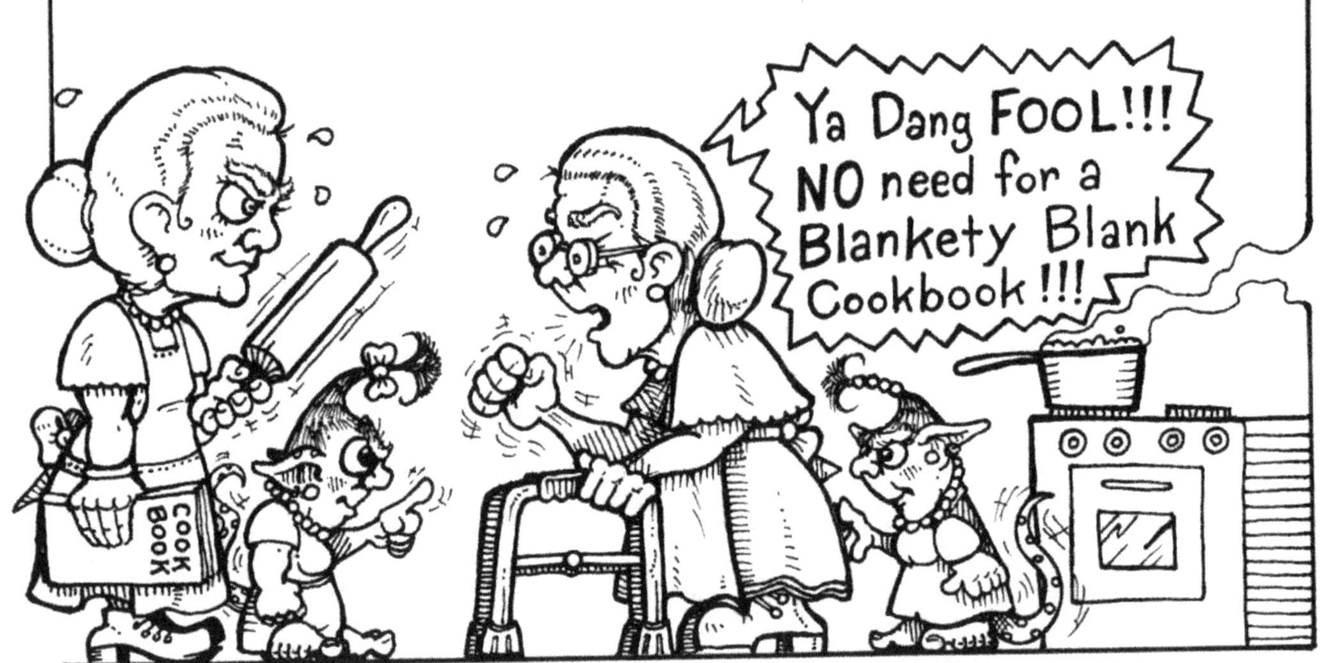

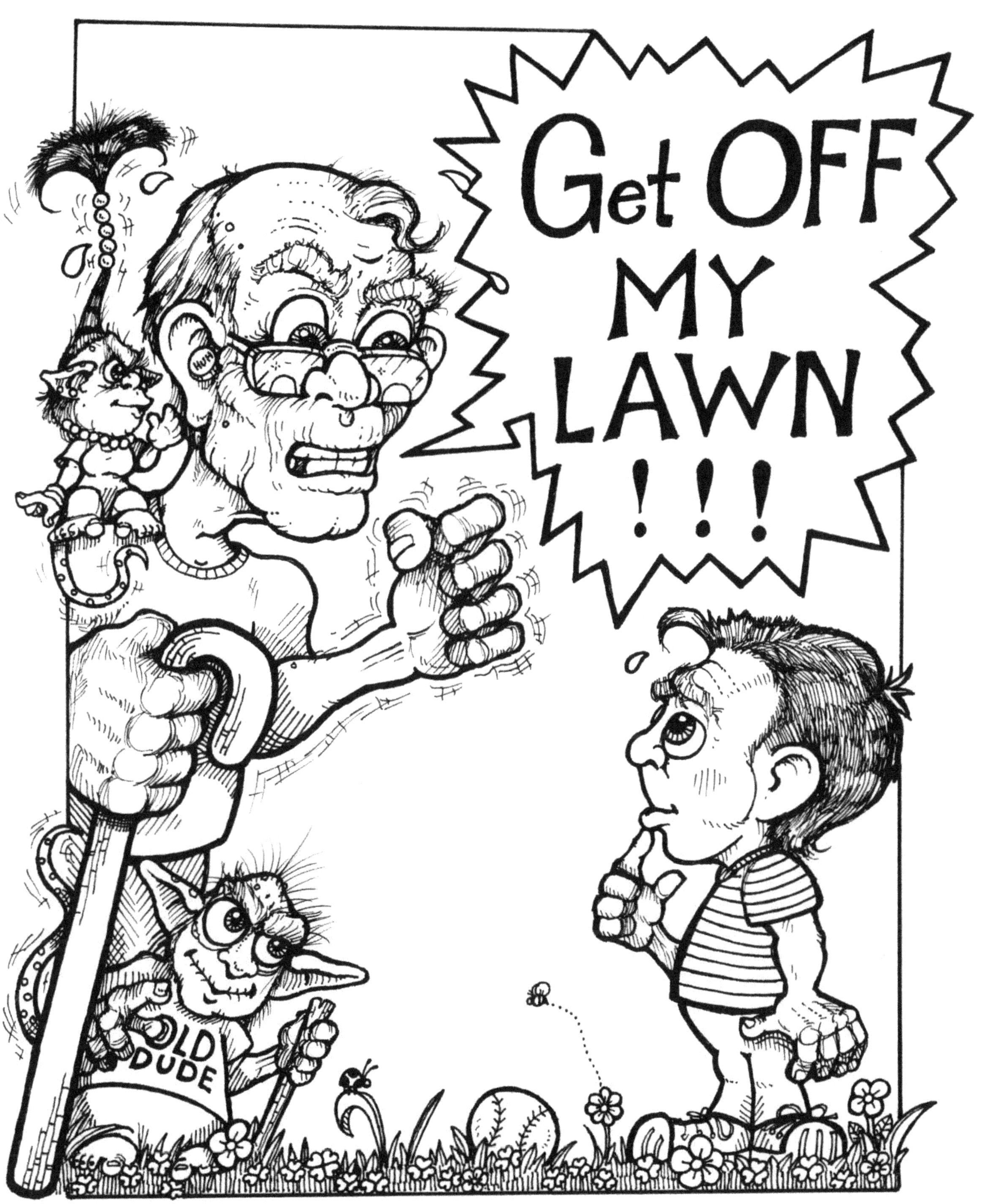

Get OFF MY LAWN !!!
OLD DUDE

Futzers: These Futzer Figments can often be found in the company of Curmudgeons. They are known for causing random muttering that is unintelligible. It is hard to tell what has brought them into inception, but they often inspire exasperation in these near the human they connect with since their influence is quite strong. You can tell if a human has one or more Futzers around them as the human is generally muttering along with their Futzer.

Common Experience)

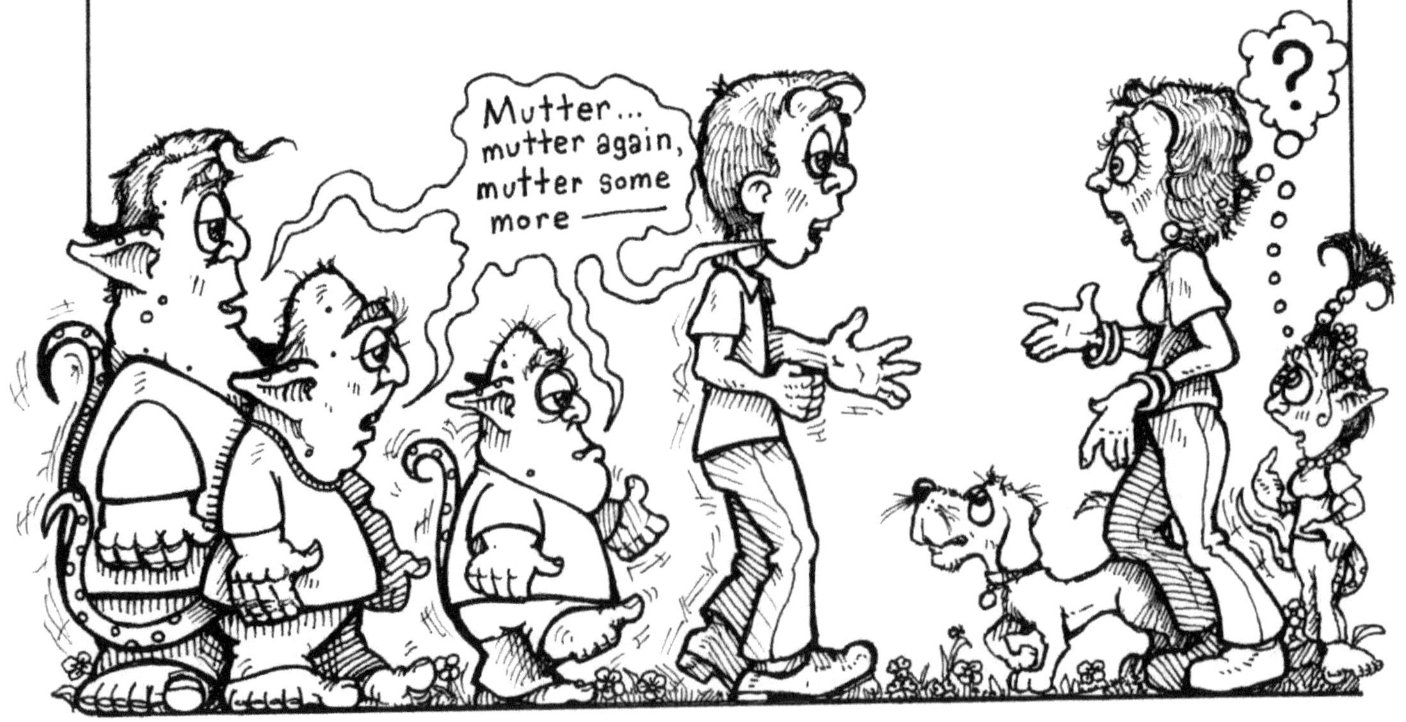

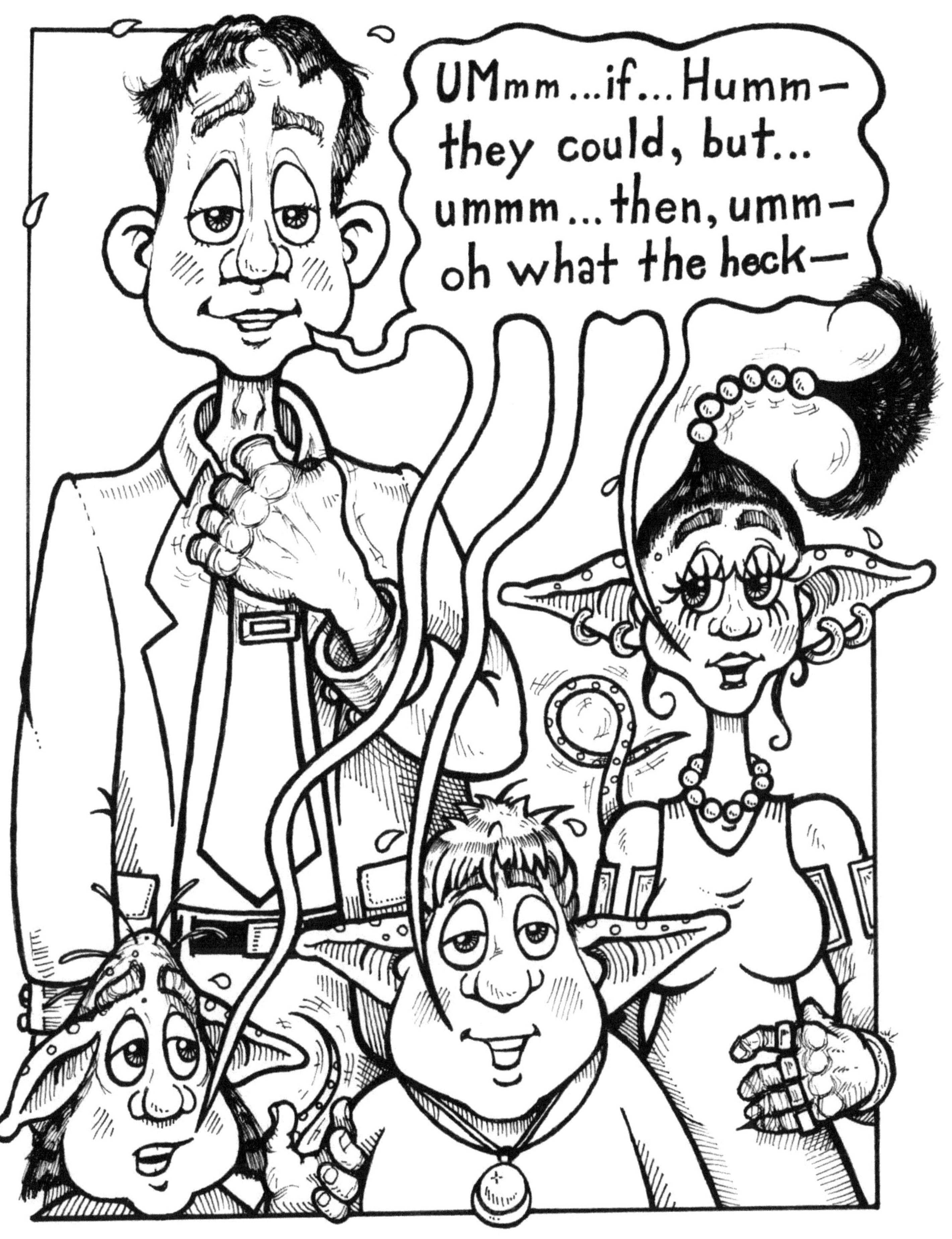

UMmm...if...Humm— they could, but... ummm...then, umm— oh what the heck—

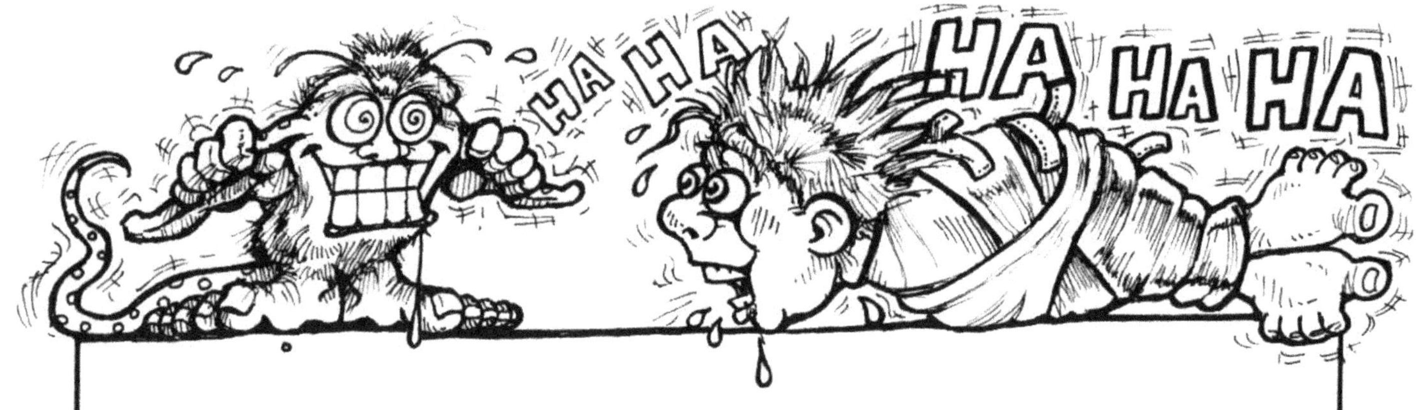

Frenetics: Mad, obsessive, insane, overwrought, berserk Figments, they are in a constant state of agitation and kin to whirling dervishes. They're usually near people who have both a fragile grasp of reality and those in continuous motion, not connected to actual accomplishment. They love agitating humans and sometimes animals into a state of mania.   Much like Conniptions, they are happiest in the middle of chaos, but Frenetics are more sustained chaos, while Conniptions seem to have shorter "fits" that subside.

(Emotions)

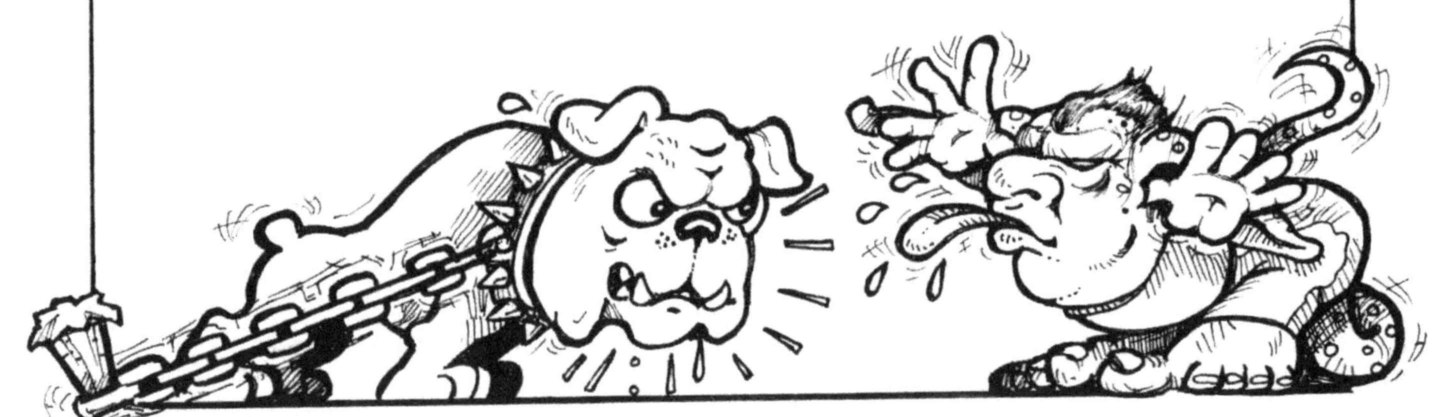

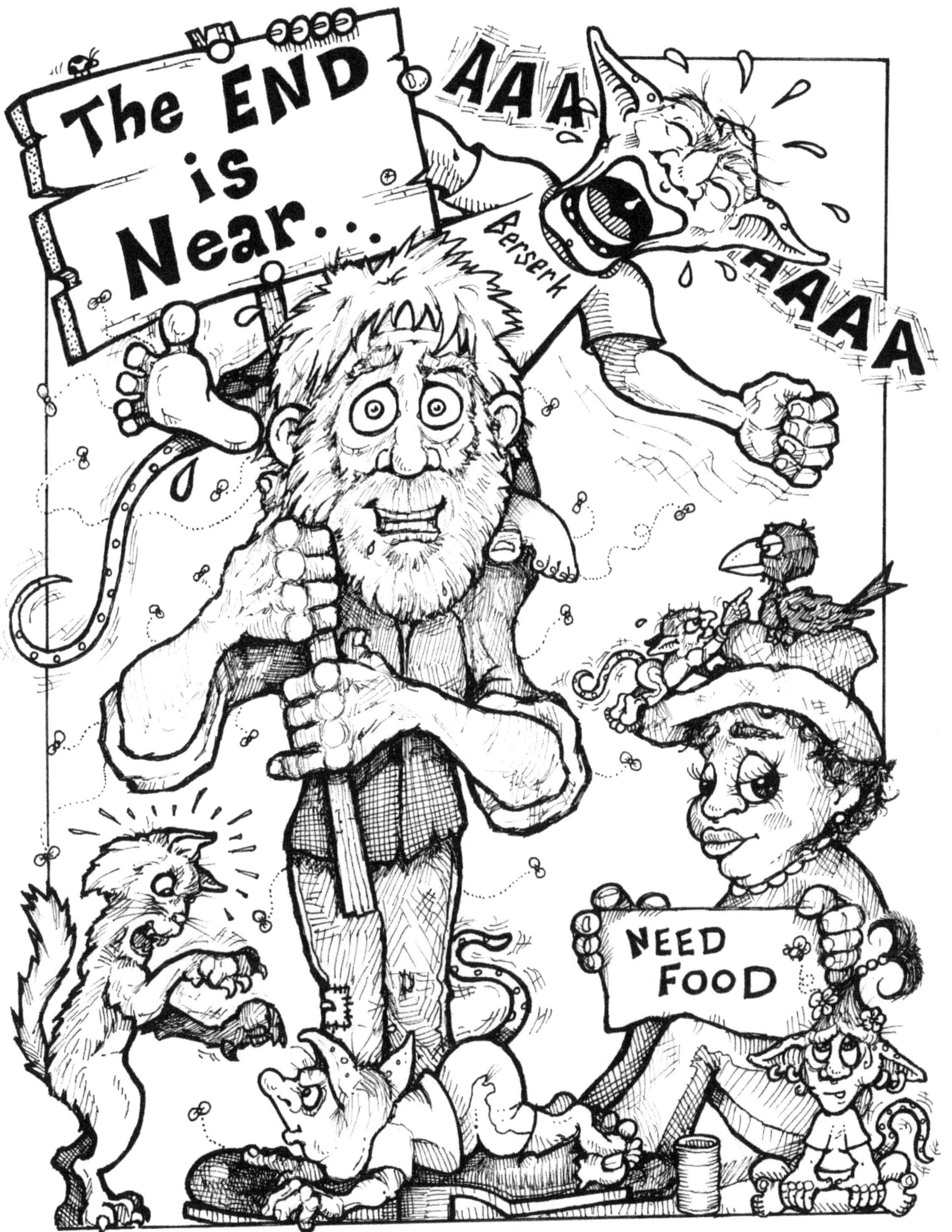
The END is Near...
AAA
AAAA
Berserk
NEED FOOD

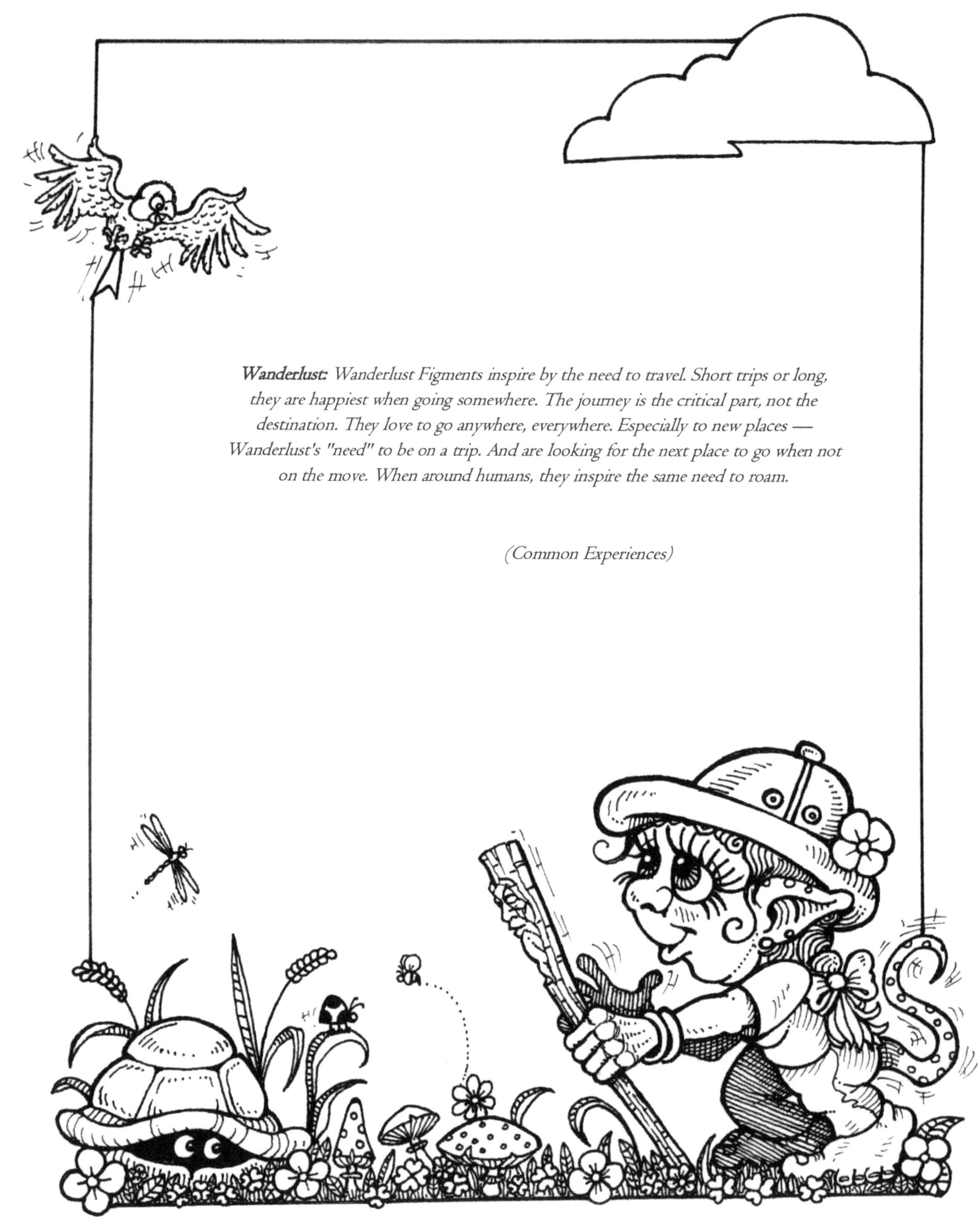

Wanderlust: Wanderlust Figments inspire by the need to travel. Short trips or long, they are happiest when going somewhere. The journey is the critical part, not the destination. They love to go anywhere, everywhere. Especially to new places — Wanderlust's "need" to be on a trip. And are looking for the next place to go when not on the move. When around humans, they inspire the same need to roam.

(Common Experiences)

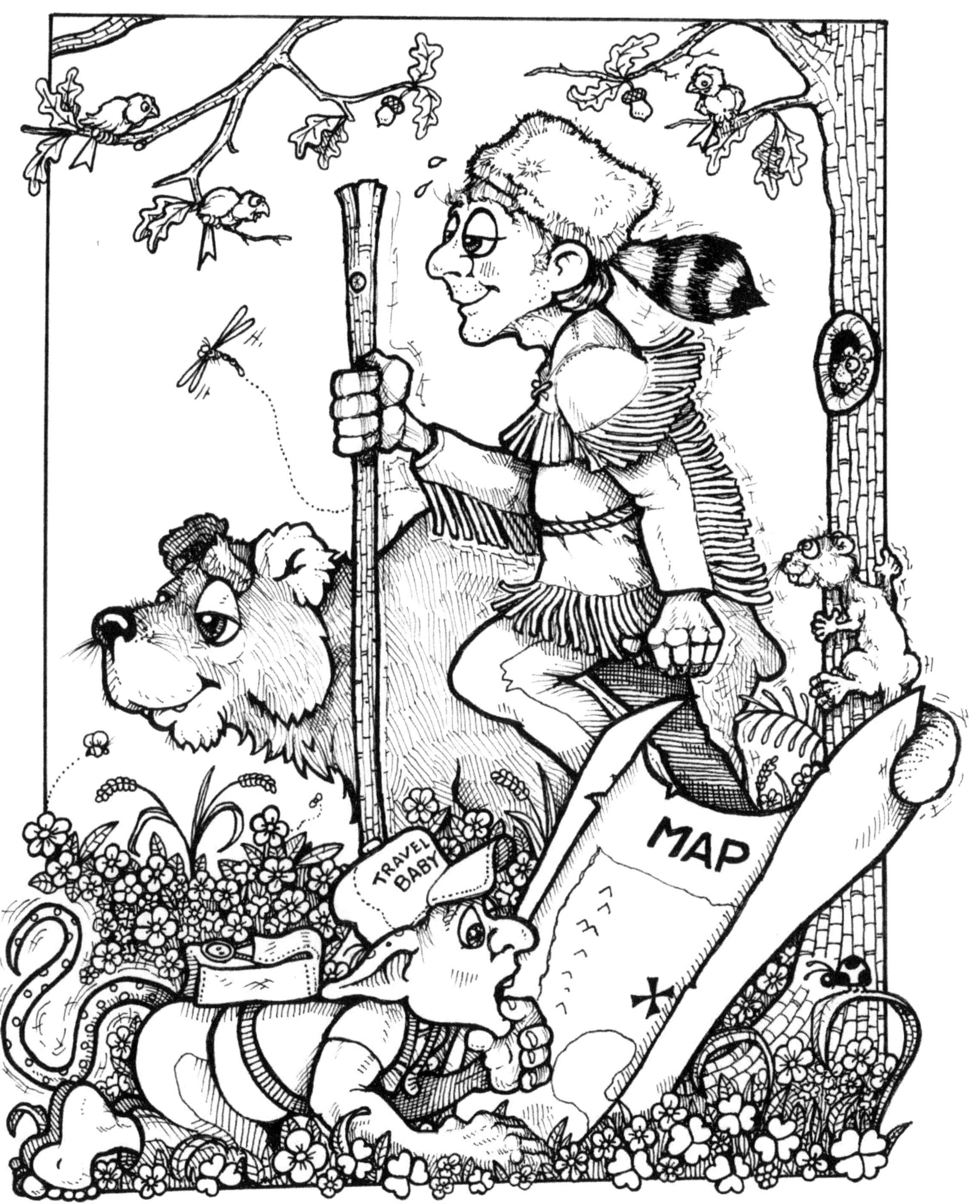
TRAVEL BABY
MAP

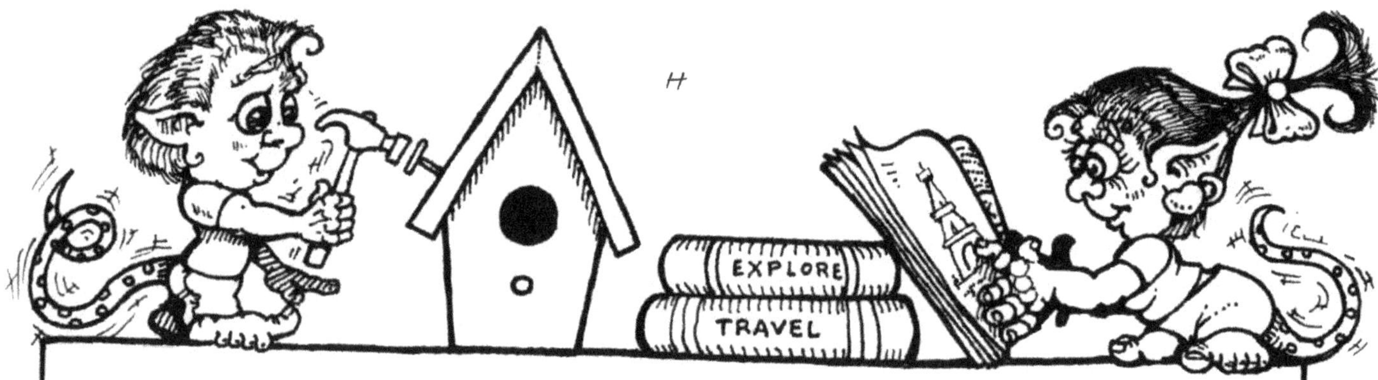

omebodies: *These figments are most content when at home. They will travel mostly to get somewhere and are always more than ready to come home again. They may garden, love to cook, read, or do hobbies, but they are happiest when nesting at home. They may travel, but usually, they can do a specific thing or get to the destination. Often nesting along the way and will attempt to create a home even if away from*

home. All while on the move. Most happy when traveling vicariously and never leaving home, through books or othmeans.

If forced to more, they will make familiar foods and make the place they land into a home.

(Common Experience)

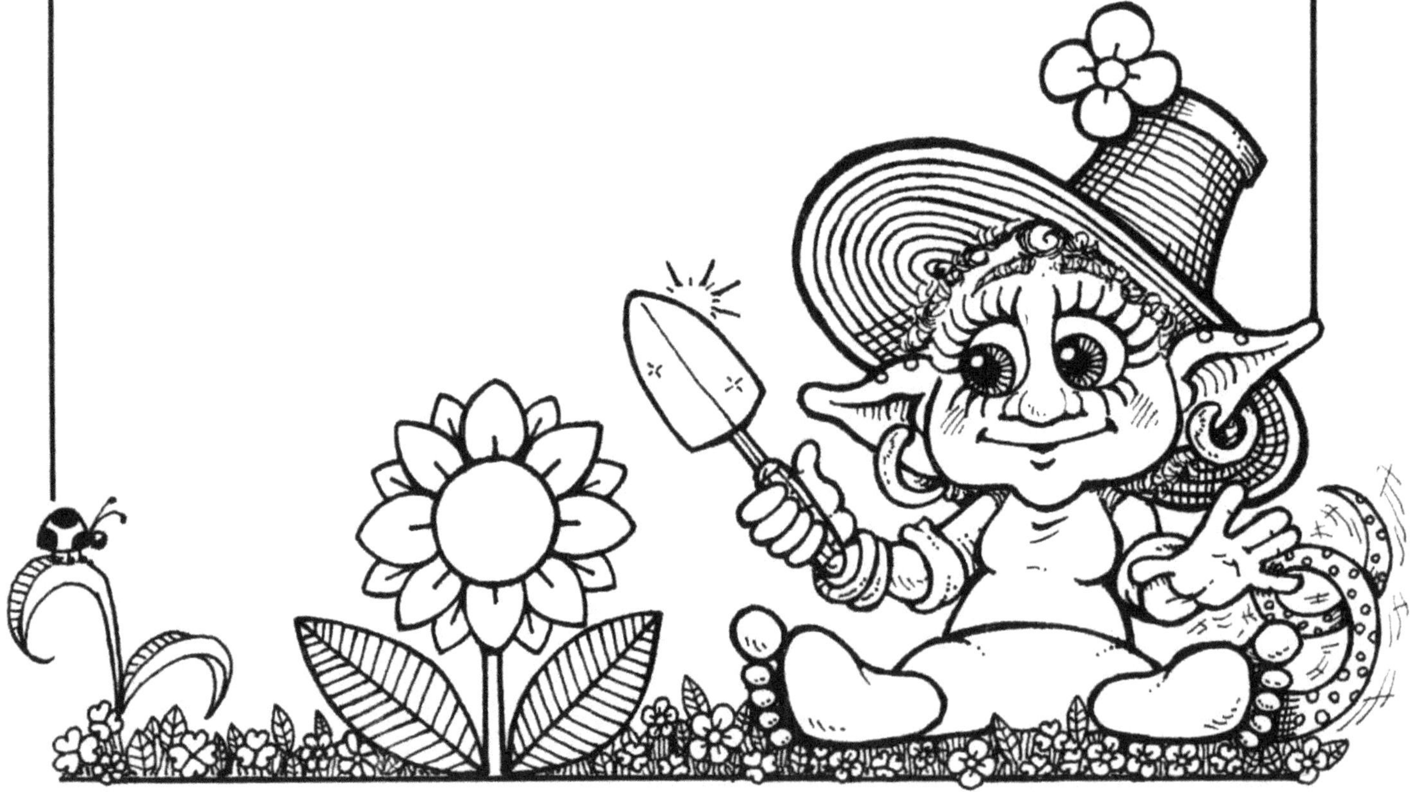

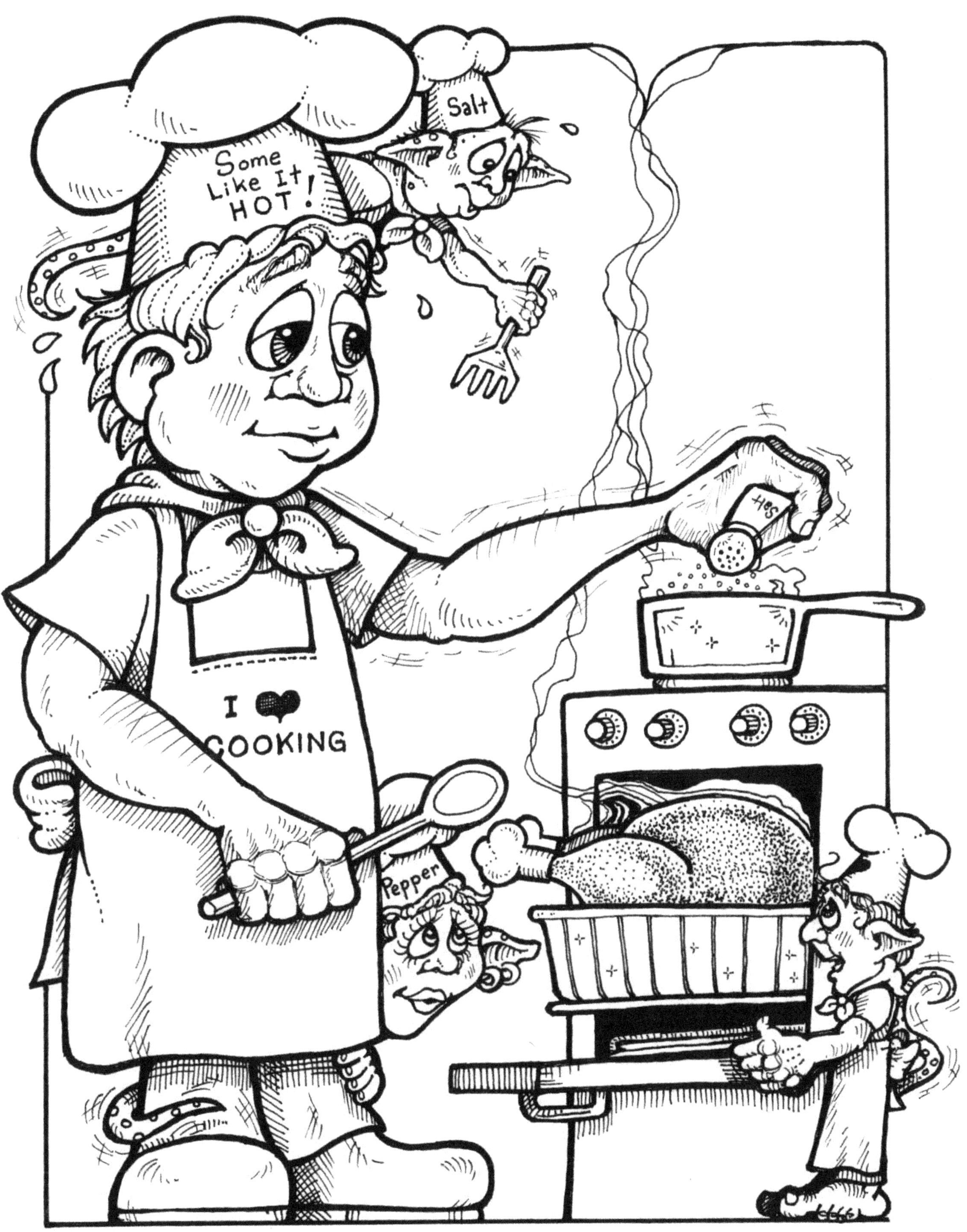

Some Like It HOT!
Salt
I ♥ COOKING
Pepper
Salt

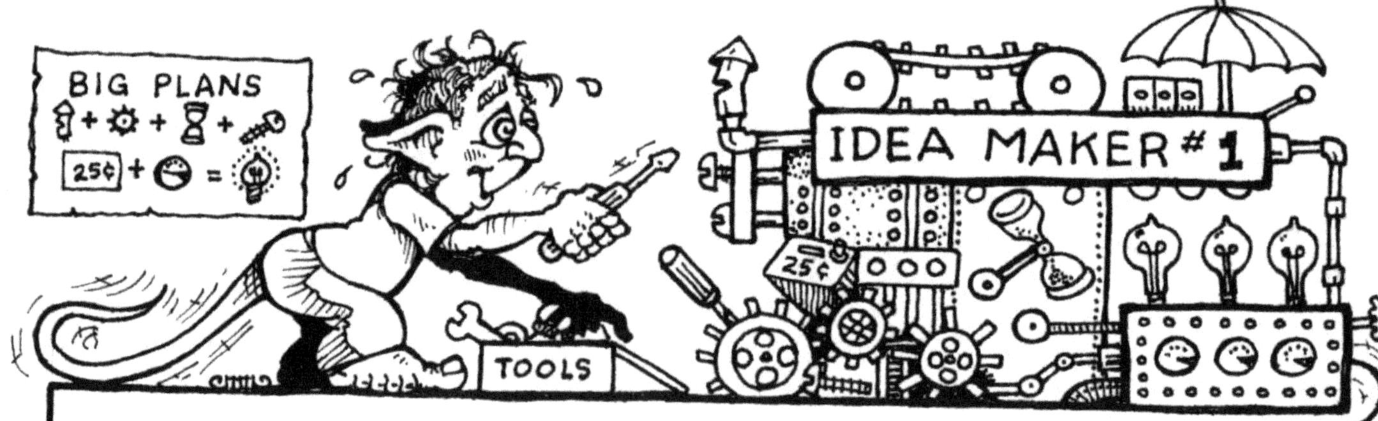

Soapbox: *Soapbox Figments get inspired by an idea. Once an" idea" happens, Soapboxes will hold onto it with all they've got. They will pontificate about that idea at every perceived opportunity to get others to join their concept.   Once they have acquired a theory, they will keep it at all costs. New information, facts, etc., do not deter a Soapbox Figment. They keep on sharing the original idea with others.*

They want to share and, even if possible, recruit others to their beliefs. They want everyone to get that idea and run with it if possible. One track, all in, well, until the next idea comes along. Then that is the new obsession, and the cycle repeats.

(Emotions)

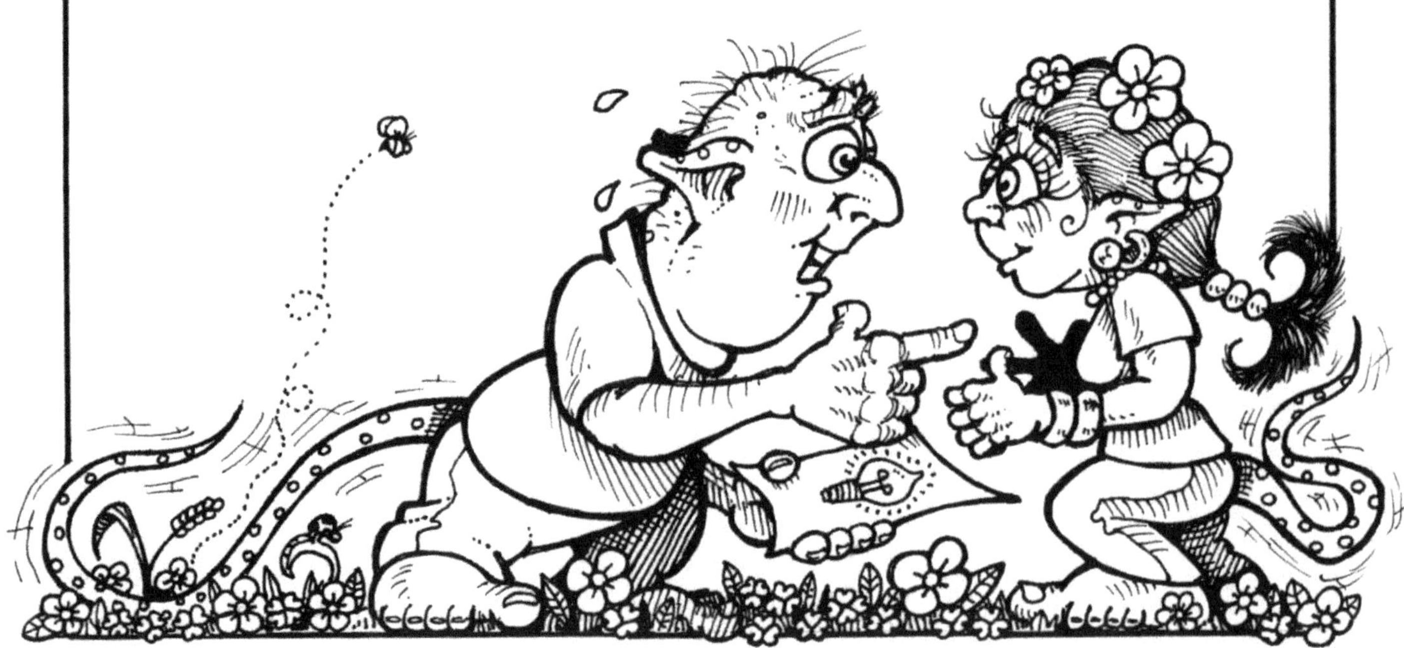

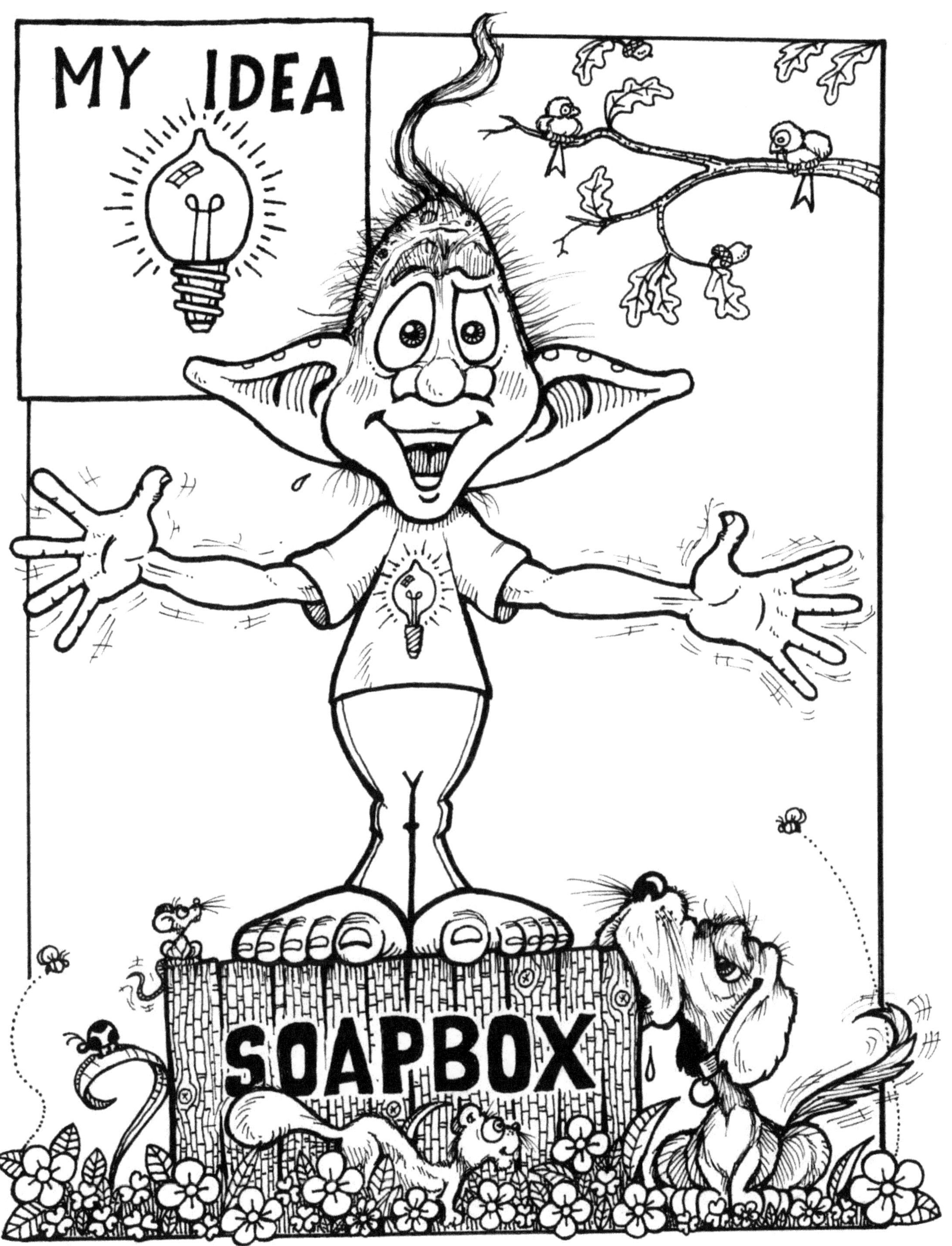

MY IDEA
SOAPBOX

Significant movement

Bandwagon: This Figment is a follower of other Figments. They will attempt to be like the ones they see. Whatever is the current figment fashion, or well anything. Humans who have Bandwagon Figments want to be sure they have the popular opinion decorations and need to be observed reading the "current" in things. They believe in whatever seems to be the significant movement of the day and never let a fad go by that they don't join with a gusto. Bandwagon figments are attracted to very passionate about causes; they believe in these causes entirely. Bandwagon Figments are always wholly convinced that all their Friend Figments believe too. They are all in, to whatever they are "supposed" to think. They consider themselves to be very trendy. While never quite knowing who they are themselves.

(Common Experience)

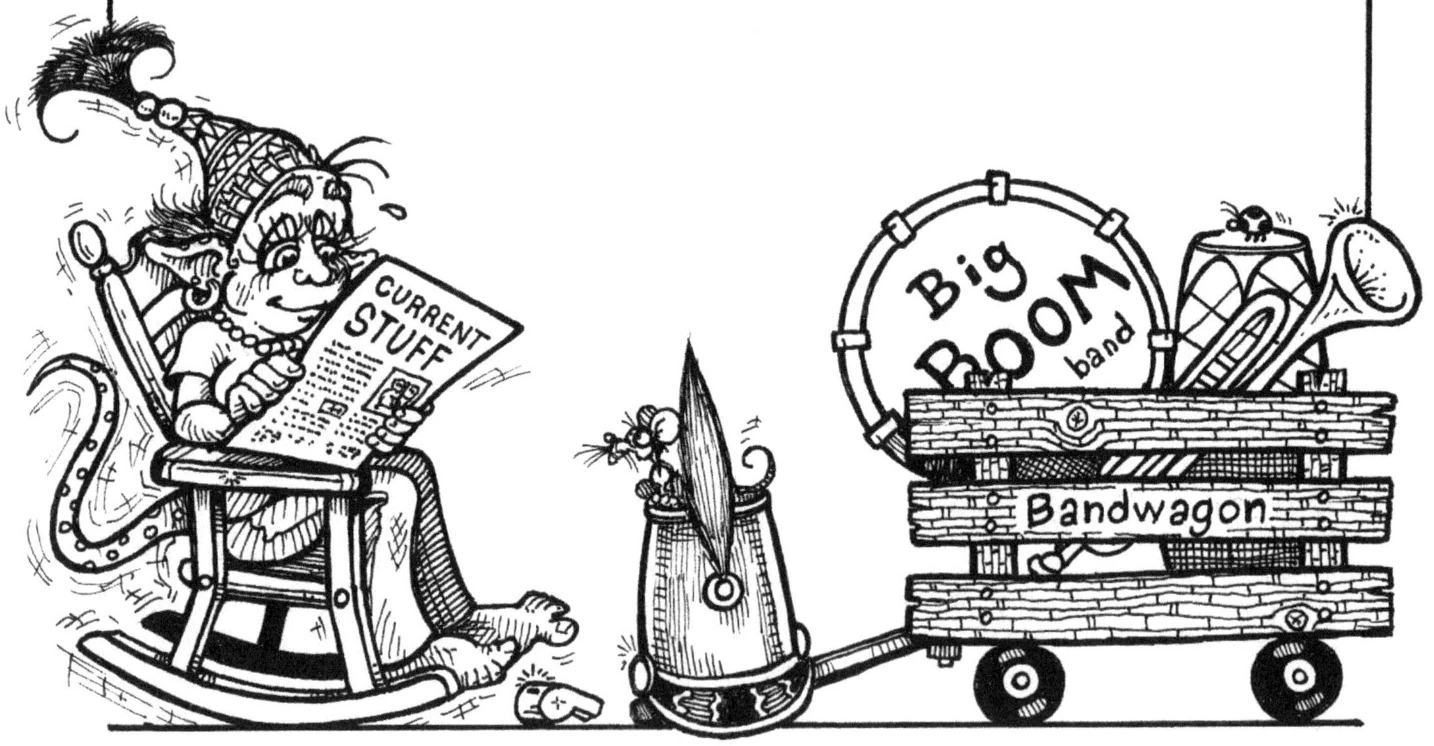

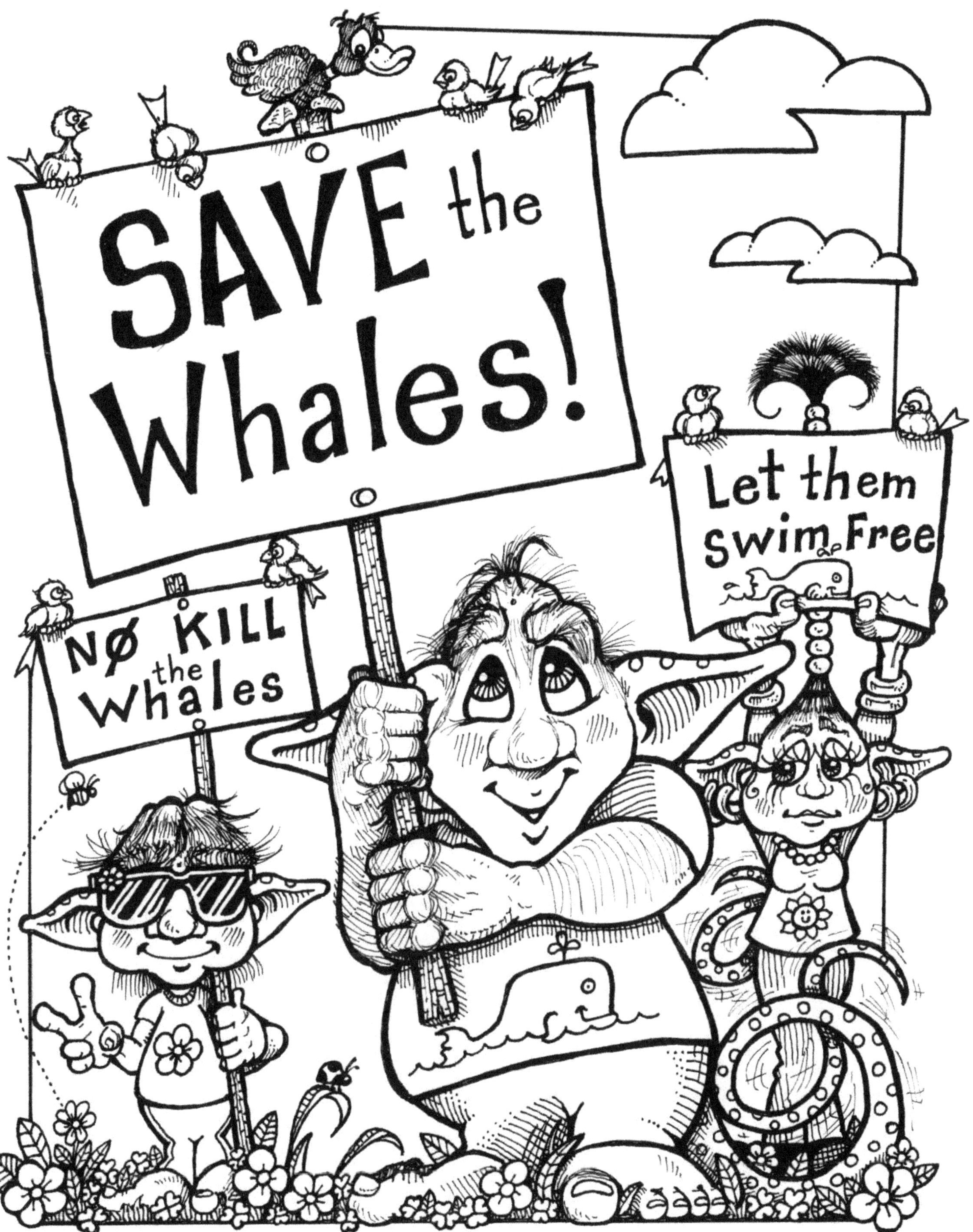

SAVE the Whales!
NØ KILL the Whales
Let them swim Free

Inspirations ✿ Dreams

Glimmers: Glimmers collect bits of ideas and inspirations that never became a project or had to follow through. Sometimes, the dream was never quite remembered, and sometimes from an idea where the human was distracted or buried in minutiae. The worst kind of Glimmer is when a person has a grand theory, but other humans devalue the person or the idea so entirely before they can succeed. Other times a Glimmer collects from a person who has the beginning of an idea but does not follow up on it. Glimmers collect those unfulfilled ideas. They need to go somewhere after all, or they could cause trouble. Sometimes Glimmers will weave strings of the idea bits together and leave them for a human to find. The results then seem to spring forth as completed thoughts from out of the blue. Glimmers aren't significant on discernment. These strings of ideas, taken from others, can be good ideas, not great ideas or stolen ideas. Glimmers don't care. They will give the ideas to whomever they think will follow up and may try several humans until they find one who will. These Figments enjoy the moment of inspiration when they can share one with a human.

(Common Experience)

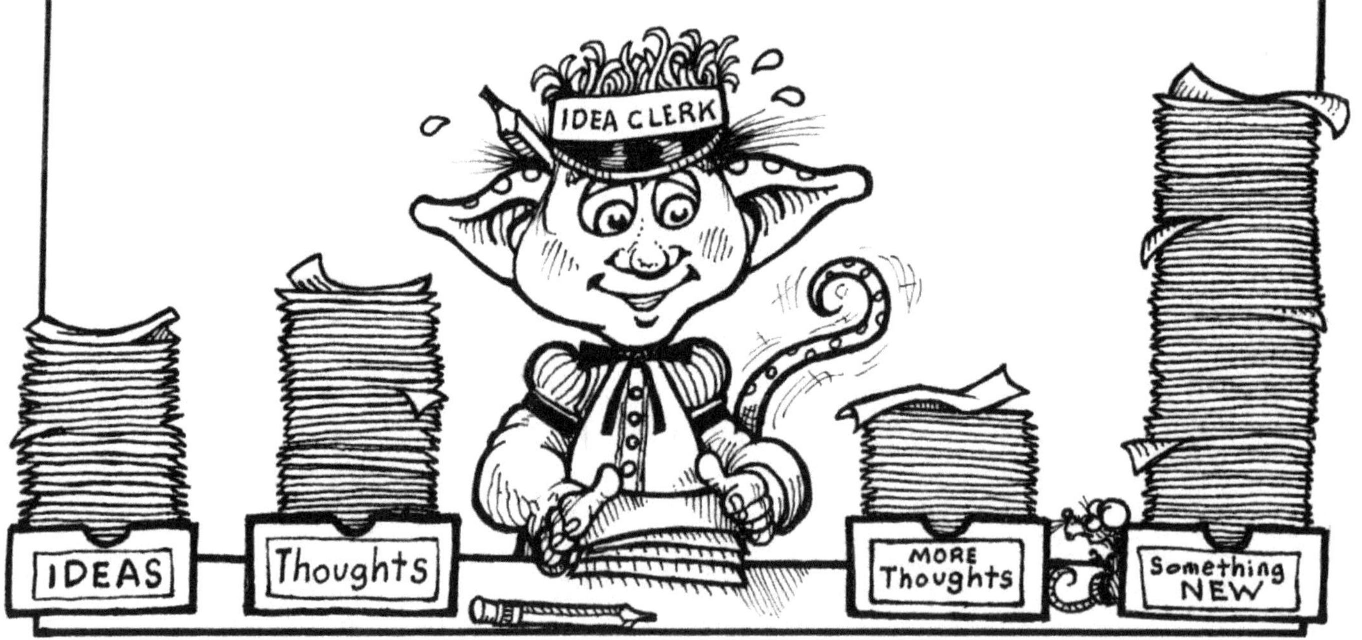

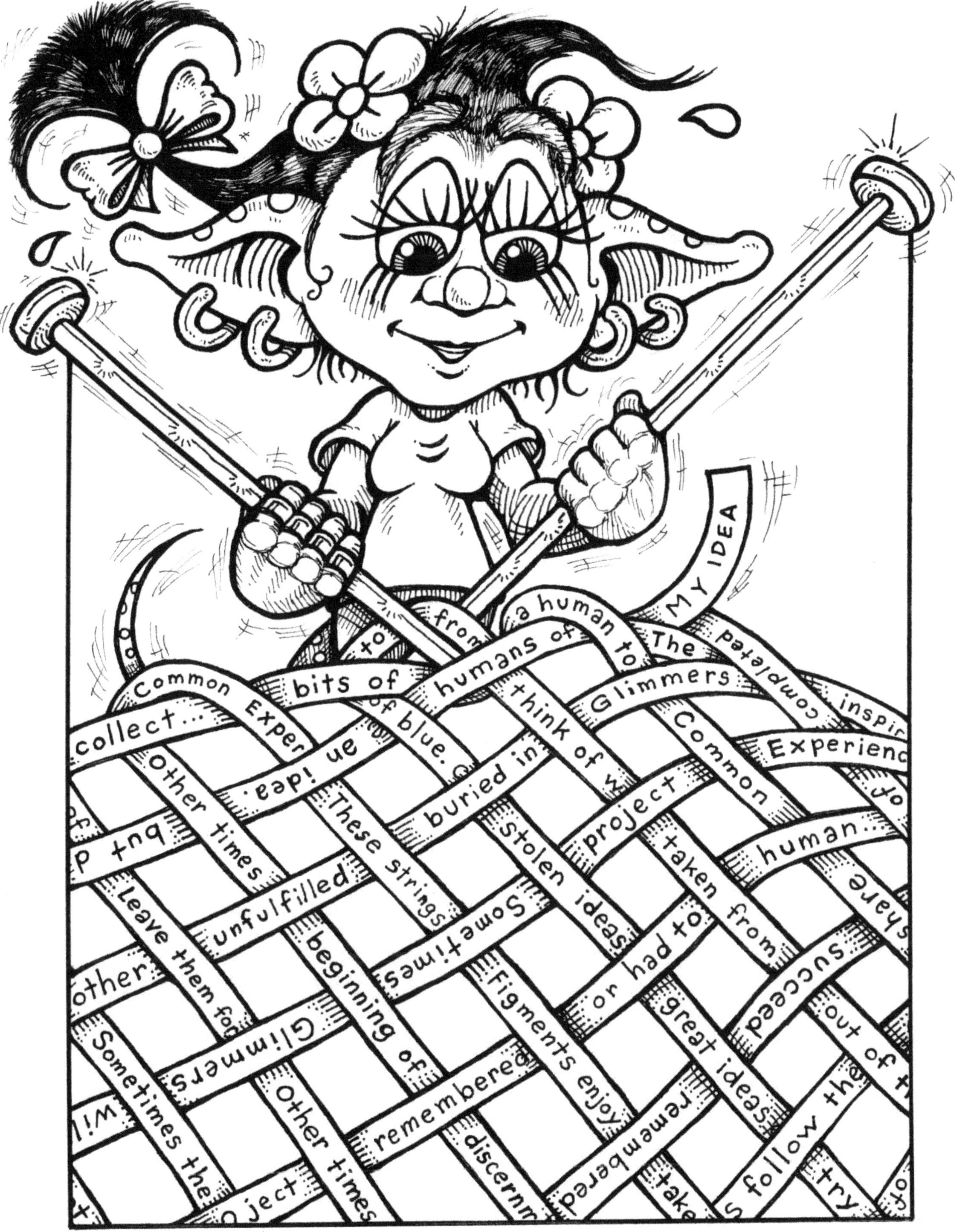

MY IDEA
Common Exper
collect...
Other times
but p
Leave them fo
Other
Sometimes the
Wil
Glimmers
Sometimes
beginning of
unfulfilled
These strings
leap!
bits of
of blue.
buried in
stolen ideas
think of
Glimmers
project
Common
taken from
human...
Experienc
The
inspir
Complicated
from
a human to
humans of
Figments enjoy
remembered
discernm
great ideas
or had to
Succeed
share
out of t
follow the
try
take

Critical Opinions

Platitudes: *As Figments go, these little ones collect and are too willing to share their version of high-minded moralistic views. Holding conflicting opinions doesn't matter to a Platitude. Spreading their entrenched viewpoint does. Facts are another issue that doesn't matter to a Platitude. Being heard for what they have to say is a definite need for a Platitudes. They revel in the human's uncertainty about any topic. That is not to say they lie; they may be so involved in making sure that they share their critical opinion that it is hard to imagine or find an actual stated point. The thing is that they NEED to share their views with all who will listen (or pause) in their general vicinity. Willing to hear might be too strong. Those not sure how to get away might be more accurate.*

(Emotions)

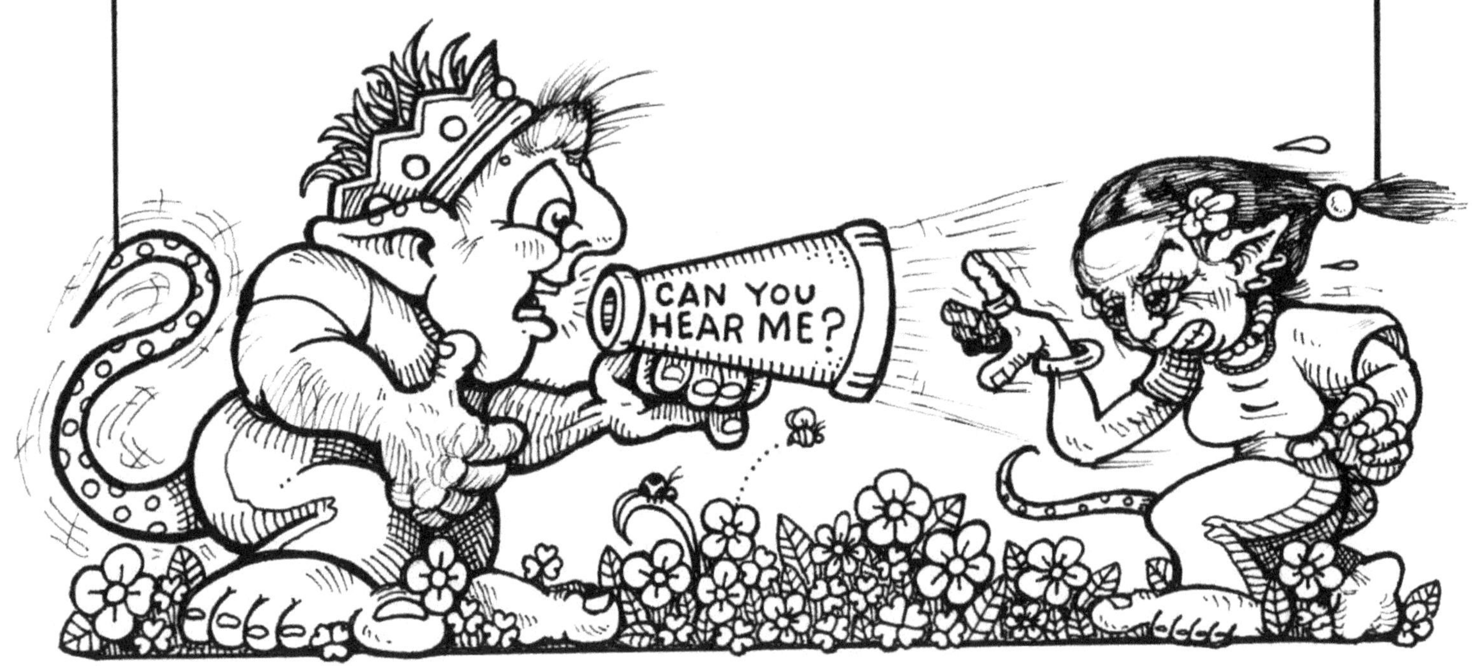

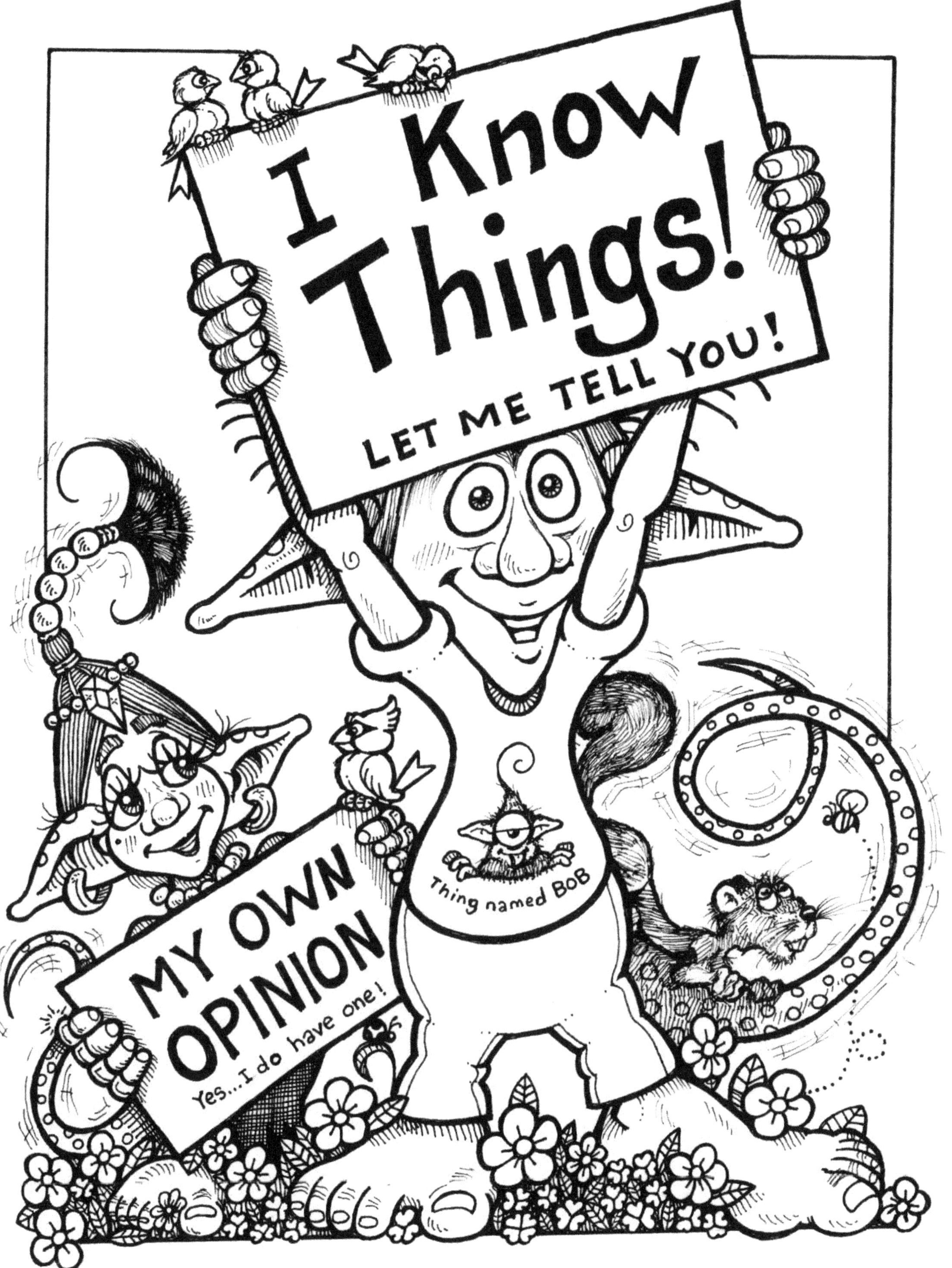

I Know Things!
LET ME TELL YOU!
MY OWN OPINION
Yes...I do have one!
Thing named BOB

Rather Obvious Point

Trites: Trites are Similar to Platitude Figments, and sometimes found with Platitudes, sometimes on their own. Trites love to collect and, as Platitudes, share, but in the case of Trites, it's usually a rather obvious point. However, they seem to have few convictions but will repeat and spout any remark, opinion, or idea they acquired somewhere else. They rarely have an original idea but substitute repetition for originality, believing that it could become both innovative and a purpose if the thought is repeated enough times. They are rarely correct but very persistent. They can be very insidious little Figments, wanting to share the unoriginal idea to be heard or seen.

(Emotions)

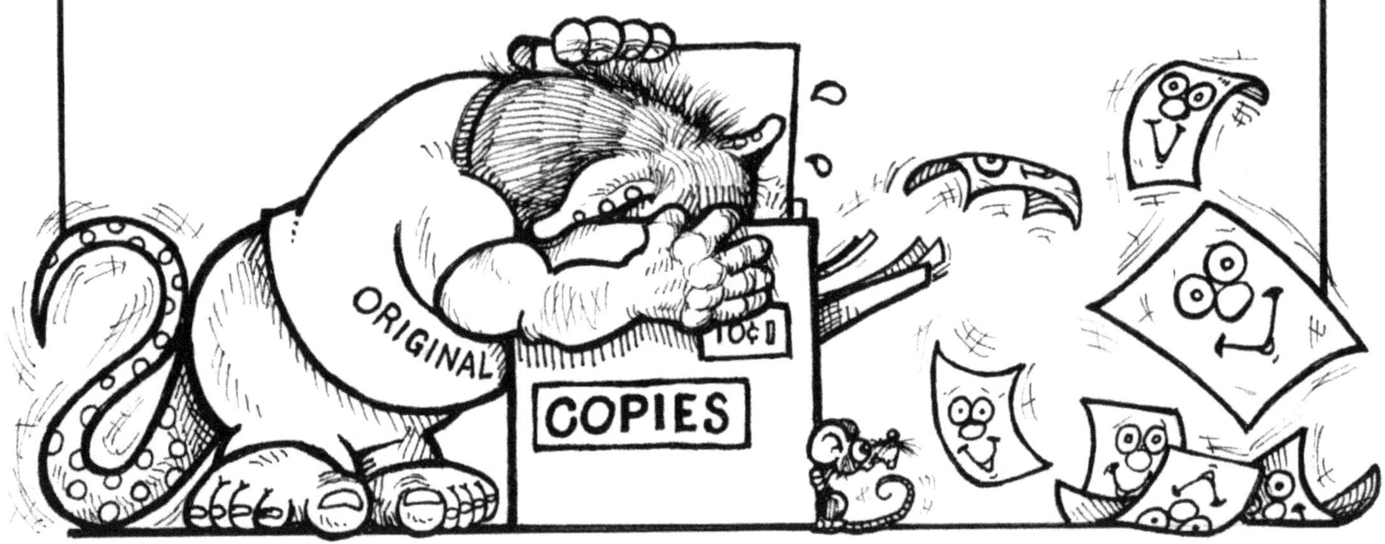

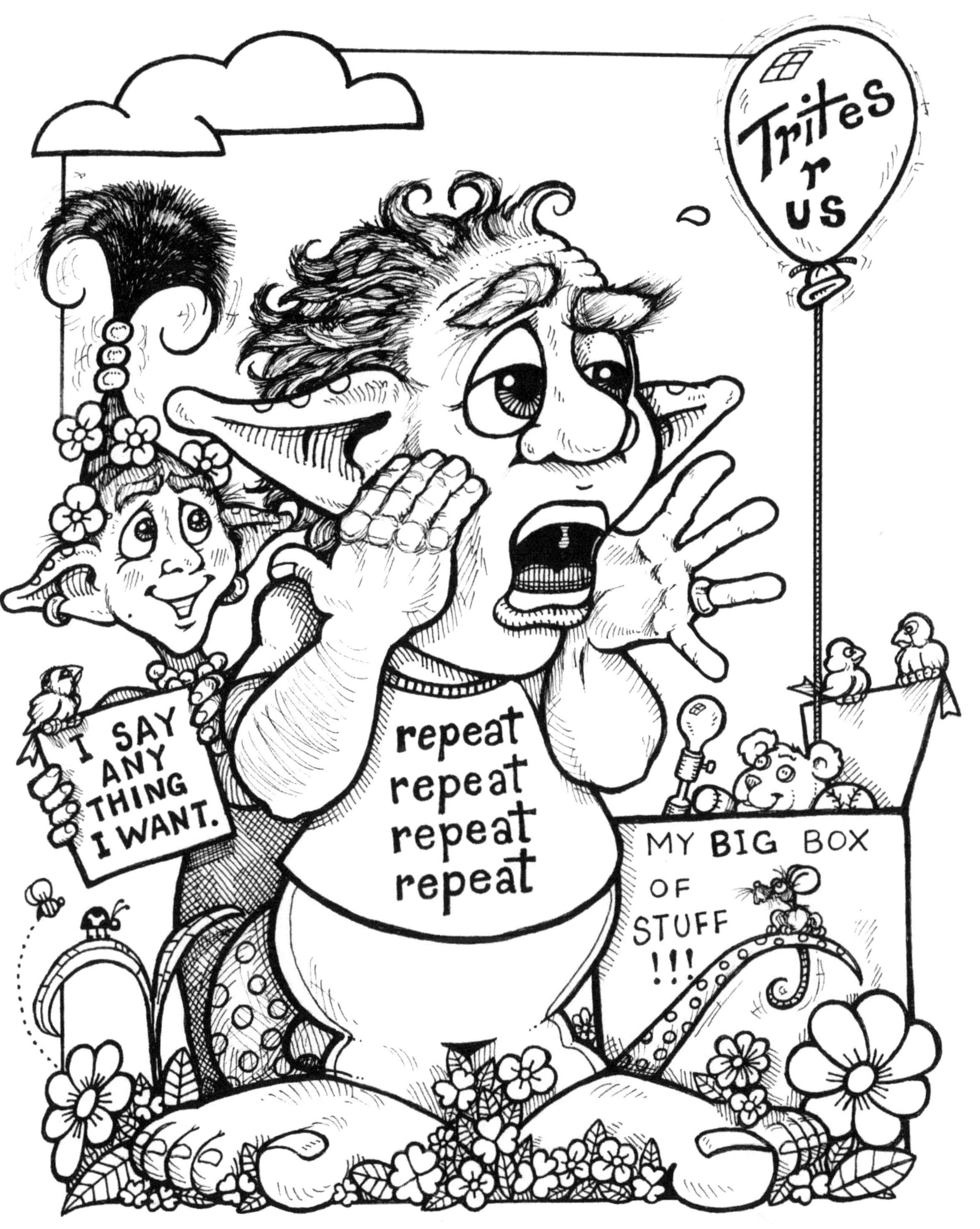

Trites
r
US
I SAY
ANY
THING
I WANT.
repeat
repeat
repeat
repeat
MY BIG BOX
OF
STUFF
!!!

Things to Collect

Rabbit Hole Figments: They like to collect things and put them in caches. If the stores remain undisturbed long enough, these Figments will begin to connect the caches like warrens. There can be hoards in the most unexpected places. Some are underground, some are on coffee tables, and some Rabbit Holes can exist on social media. You see, they can be actual or virtual caches. (Bit of background, Rabbit Hole Figments used to be called by a different name, but well, there was an "incident" involving the cousin of the Easter bunny, some fermented carrots, and a Curmudgeon who was sitting close enough to influence him... Well, that indeed is a long story for another time, suffice it to say, the cousin of the Easter bunny claimed responsibility for the caches, was overheard, someone fell down a hole, and today these Figments are now Rabbit Holes.) The former name has been lost in time and to Befuddles. Now Rabbit Holes retain their ability to keep people entranced for minutes or hours looking at the items within. If you fall into a Rabbit Hole's cache that leads to other collections, I hope you can find your way out before dawn.

(Common Experience)

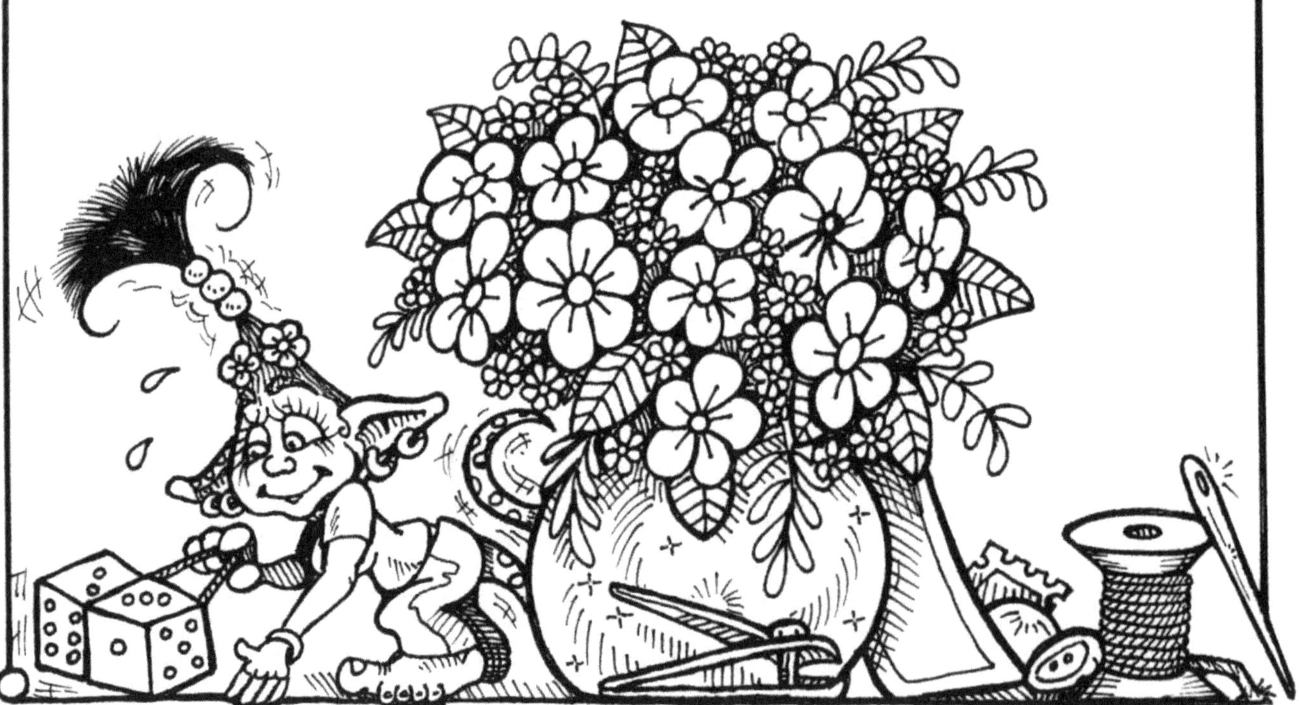

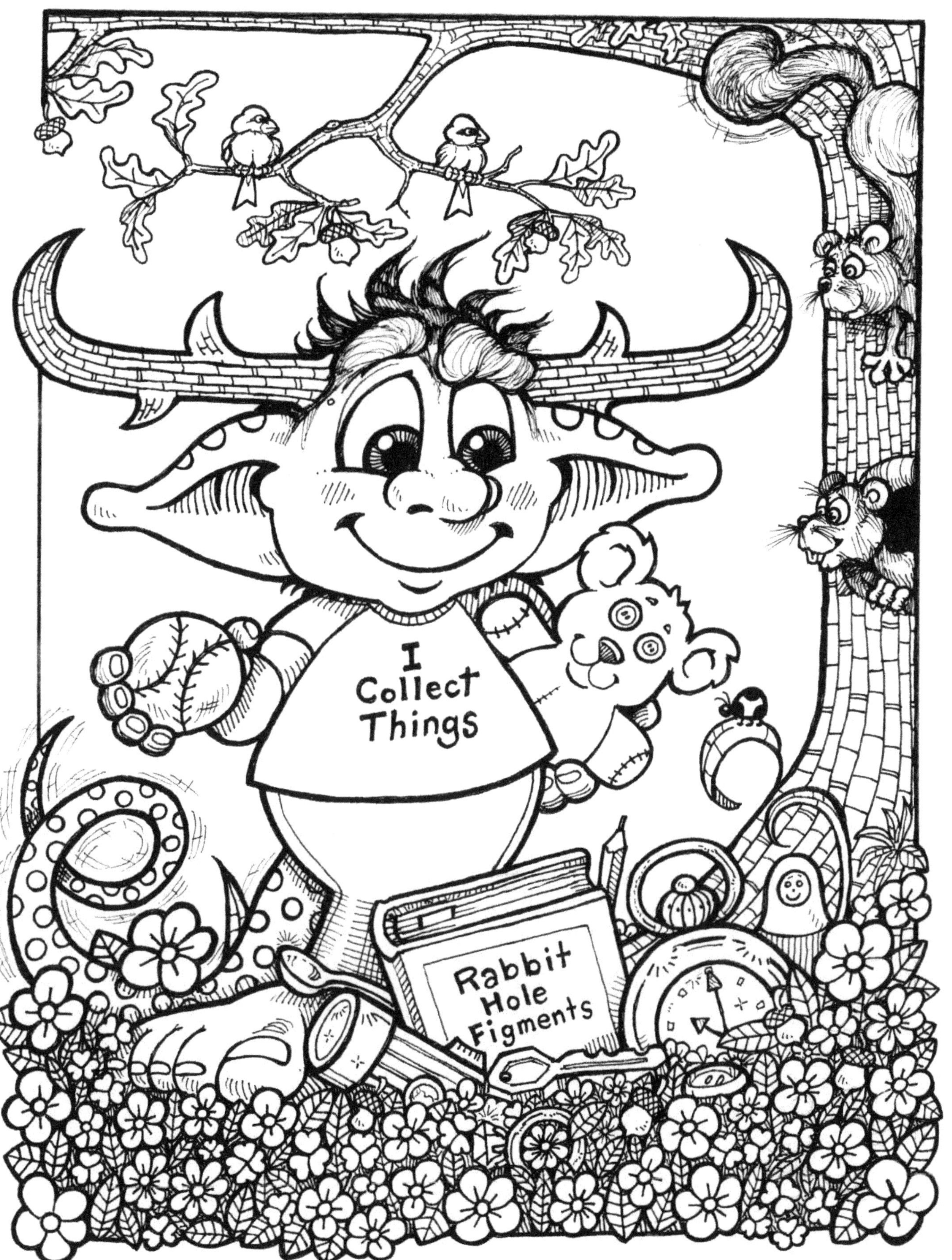

I Collect Things
Rabbit Hole Figments

Murphy's Law ★ bad Karma

Basket Case: Oddly enough, these Figments live in baskets; they feel comfortable there. Still, no matter what, they cannot get their act together. Whatever idea they are on, it falls apart. Basket Hole Figments believe it is through no fault of their own. They attract so-called lousy luck, Murphy's Law, or even bad Karma. In truth, it appears to a Basket Case Figments life is a series of minor disasters for which they take no control or responsibility. They mean no harm but always seem to be in the middle of things going awry. It is difficult to determine if they are trying hard or trying and making it complicated. Cute in a messy way, they are seemingly always in the center of chaos, whether tremendous or small. That chaos seems to transfer to any nearby human.   Unfortunately, they also apparently reduce the ability to make plans for dealing with any small disasters, thereby soon creating yet another.

(Common Experience)

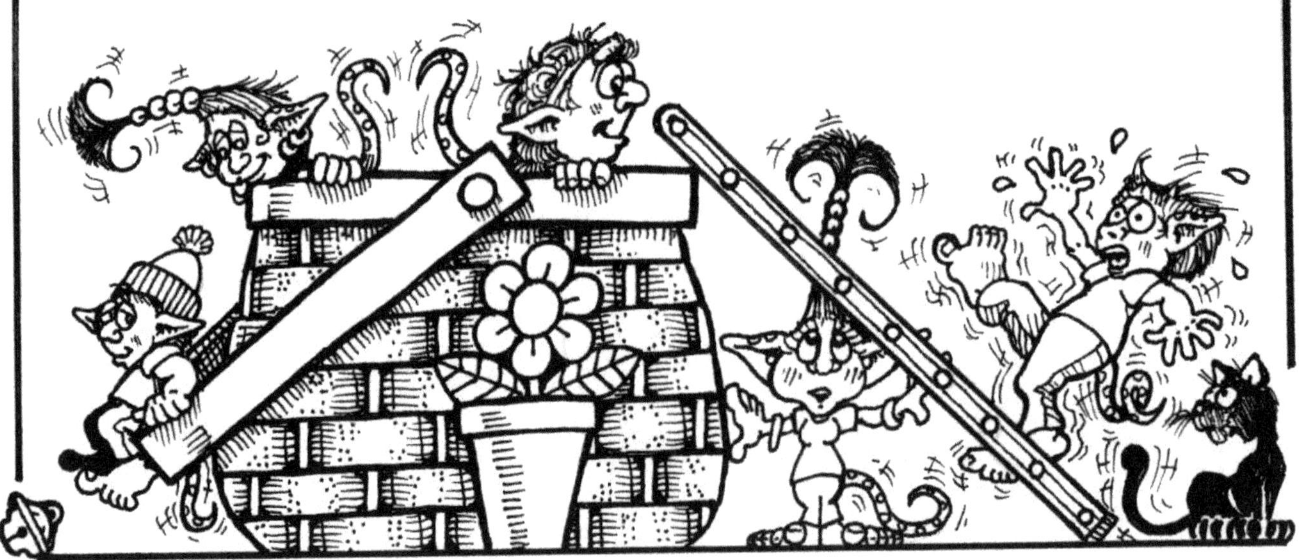

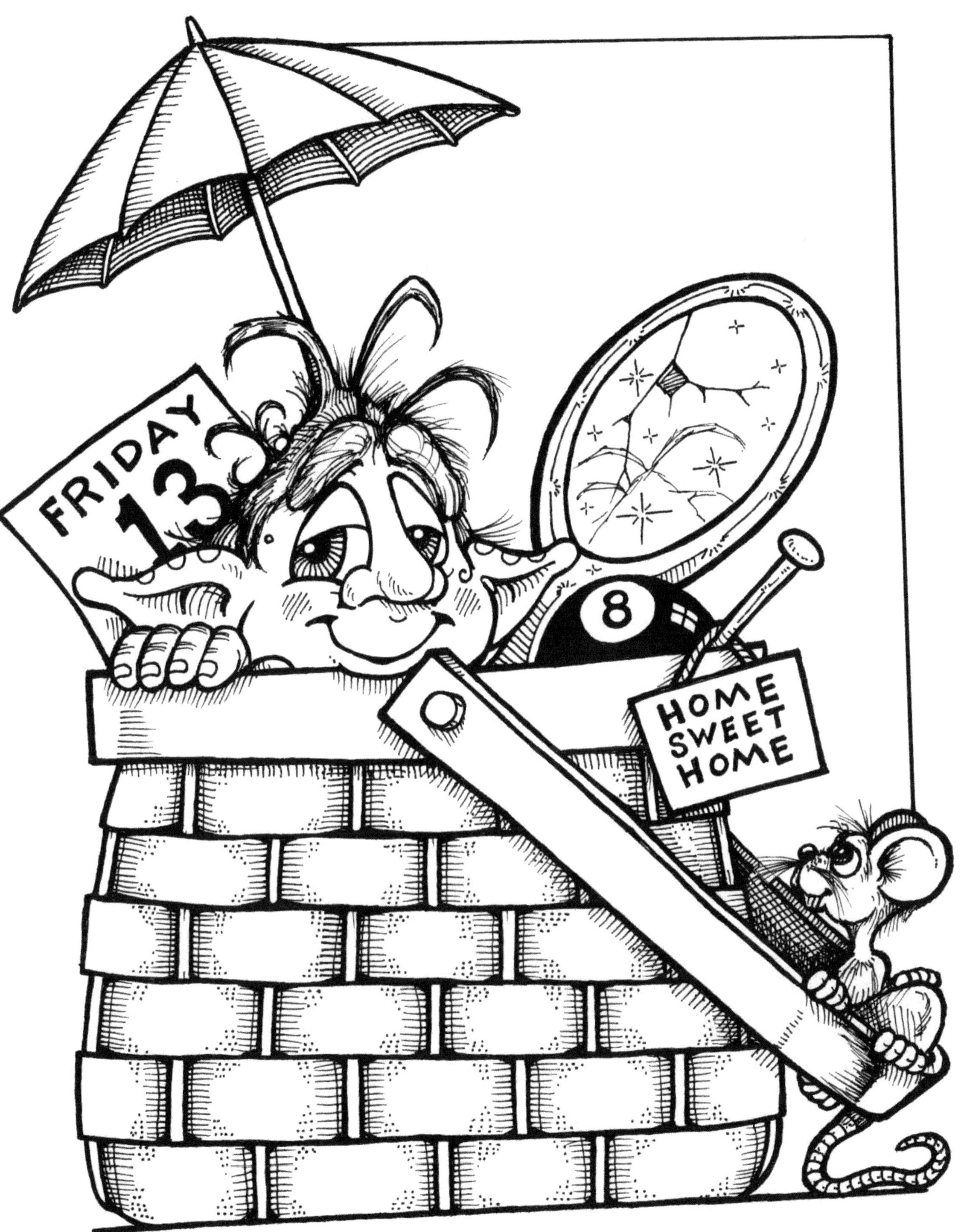

FRIDAY
13
8
HOME
SWEET
HOME

A need for Order...

Pigeonhole: These can be useful Figments as they love to put away things. They will find places for everything. They cannot stand disorder and adore labels. Everything and everyone they believe has an area needs to be in order and organized. It can be pretty disturbing if you have too many Pigeonhole Figments around; they can cause humans to have unusual reactions to anything they cannot categorize. They reflect the emotions of "need for order" quite precisely. They have a great need for order in all things. They will file things (whether the items should be filed away or not) and will affect some humans to do the same thing. Filing may be helpful to a human or not, as they may not put items in an order or a place, never to be seen again. They simply put things "away" where it is unseen. It will make sense to the Pigeonhole Figment but rarely to anyone else. If you can figure out this Figment's Logic, you may find your missing things. If not, Well, you might be looking for a while. But whatever is lost will be neat, probably rolled up or folded when you find it.

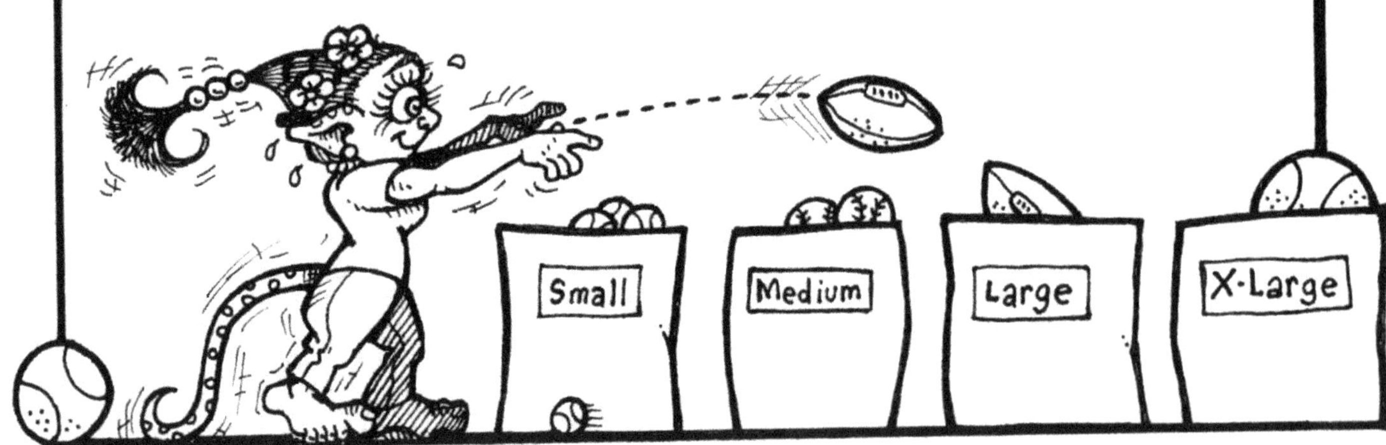

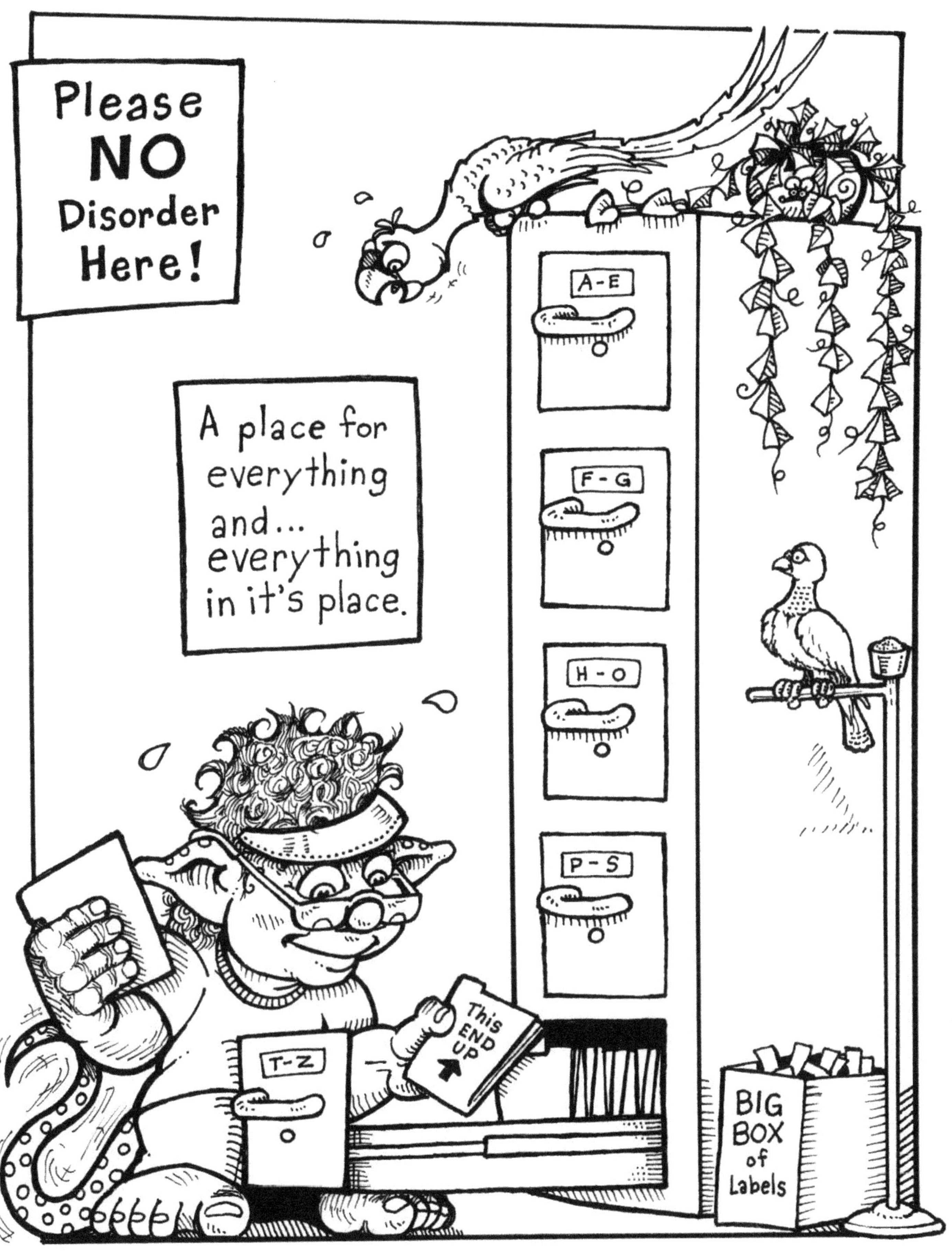

Please
NO
Disorder
Here!
A place for
everything
and...
everything
in it's place.
A - E
F - G
H - O
P - S
T - Z
This
END
UP
BIG
BOX
of
Labels

Shells, Sand, Leaves Oh My...

Floras. Flora Figments seem to need to be surrounded by nature. Live natural things are best, but good copies of essential items, whether dried or imitation such as silk, are OK substitutes. But they need to have plant-like things to be happy. Flora Figments will add nature items to everything. Including the environments of other Figments. They will inspire humans to keep old flowers that make them have memories, such as a boutonnière or corsage, flowers from a unique bouquet, or bits from nature collected from a memorable trip. Flora can extend to shells, sand, leaves, rocks, or other natural items. Some Figments will ask a Flora Figment to help decorate their environments, knowing the Flora might decorate asked or not.

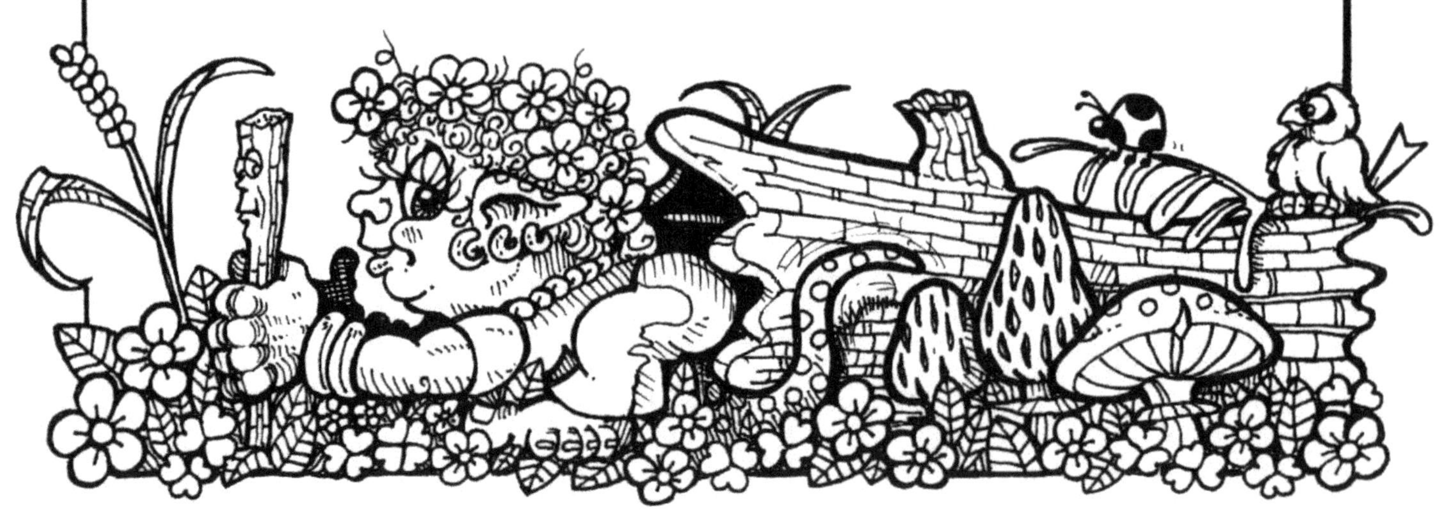

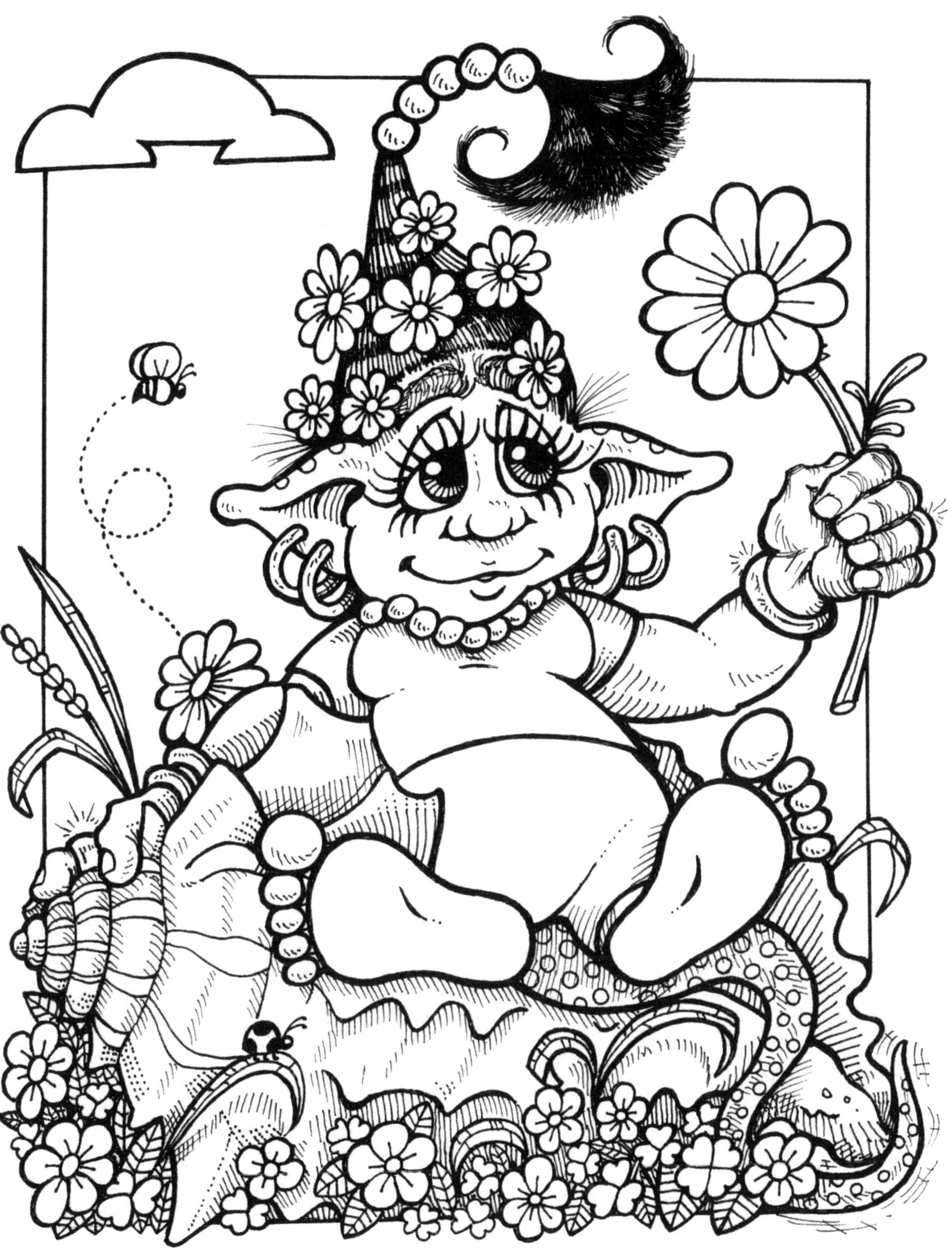

Go Willy Nilly away

Bestower: These Figments love to give things away. They seem to feed off the need to give items to others. They find collections of items sometimes collected by other Figments and will give everything away. When hanging around humans long, they will cause them to clean and purge the human environment right down to minimalist status. They give things away willy nilly. They will give items away that are useful or wanted by others, but often randomly with no apparent reason for the bestowment. They cannot stand to have objects around them in plain sight. So, they will give them away. If a human has a Bestower in their life, they will also feel compelled to give things away.

(Common Experience)

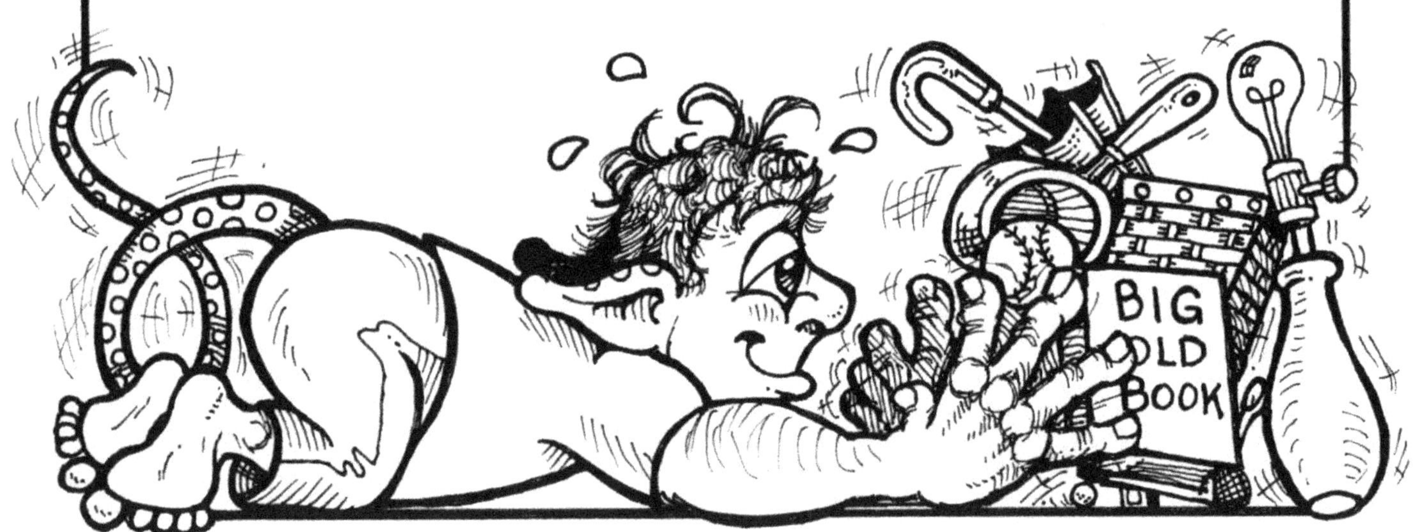

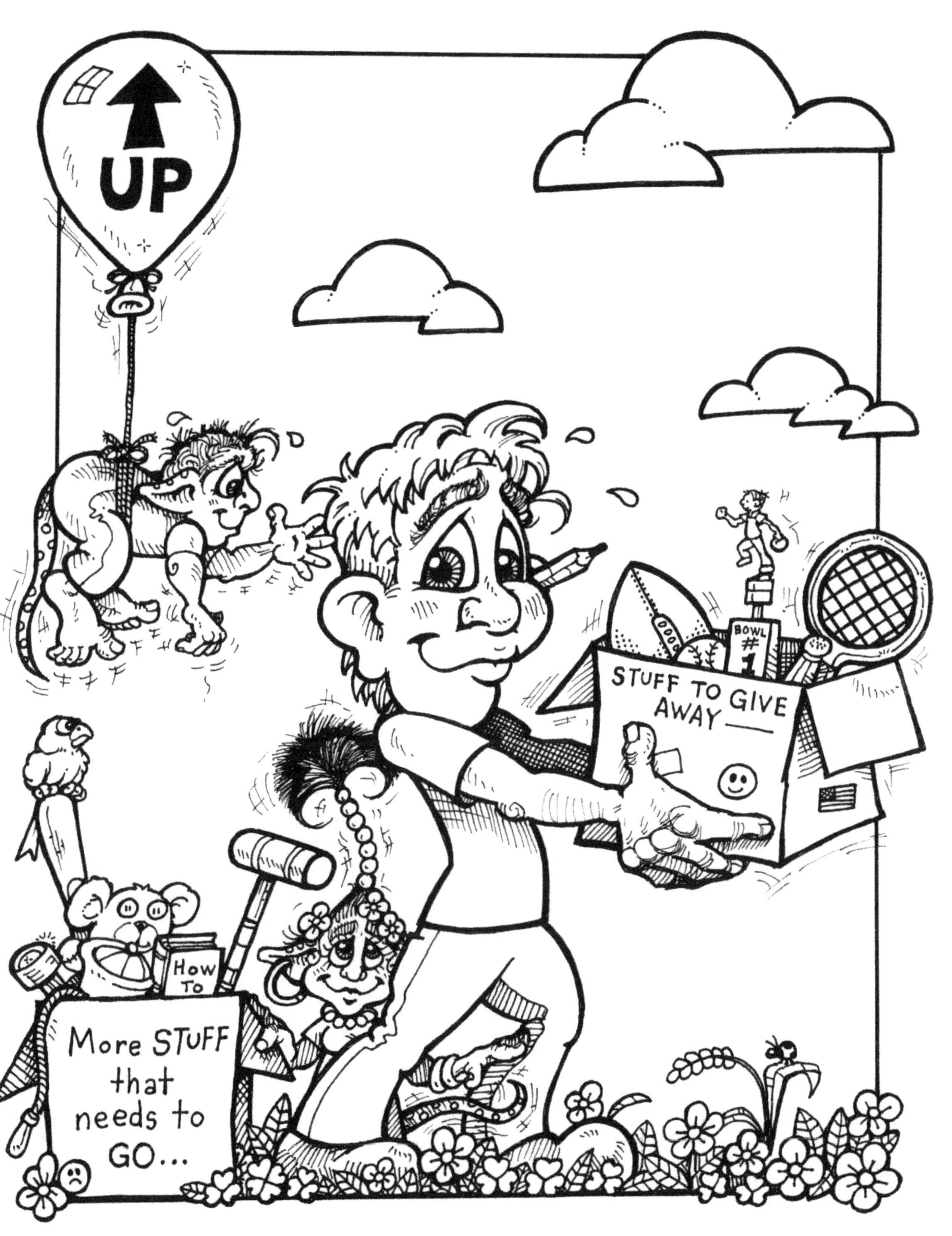

UP
STUFF TO GIVE AWAY
BOWL #1
How To
More STUFF that needs to GO...

Memory of the Nightmare

Qualms: Qualms often collect the bits of bad dreams that are gone almost upon waking. The feeling is left, but not the memory of the nightmare. They will sometimes give away a bit of a dream if they have too many of one kind in their collection. They love the negative feelings like dreams of falling, being later, or the fear of being unprepared. Qualms inspire these. Usually, subtle but quite insistent emotions arise in humans who have Qualms. They will hang onto and share their feelings throughout the day.

(Emotions)

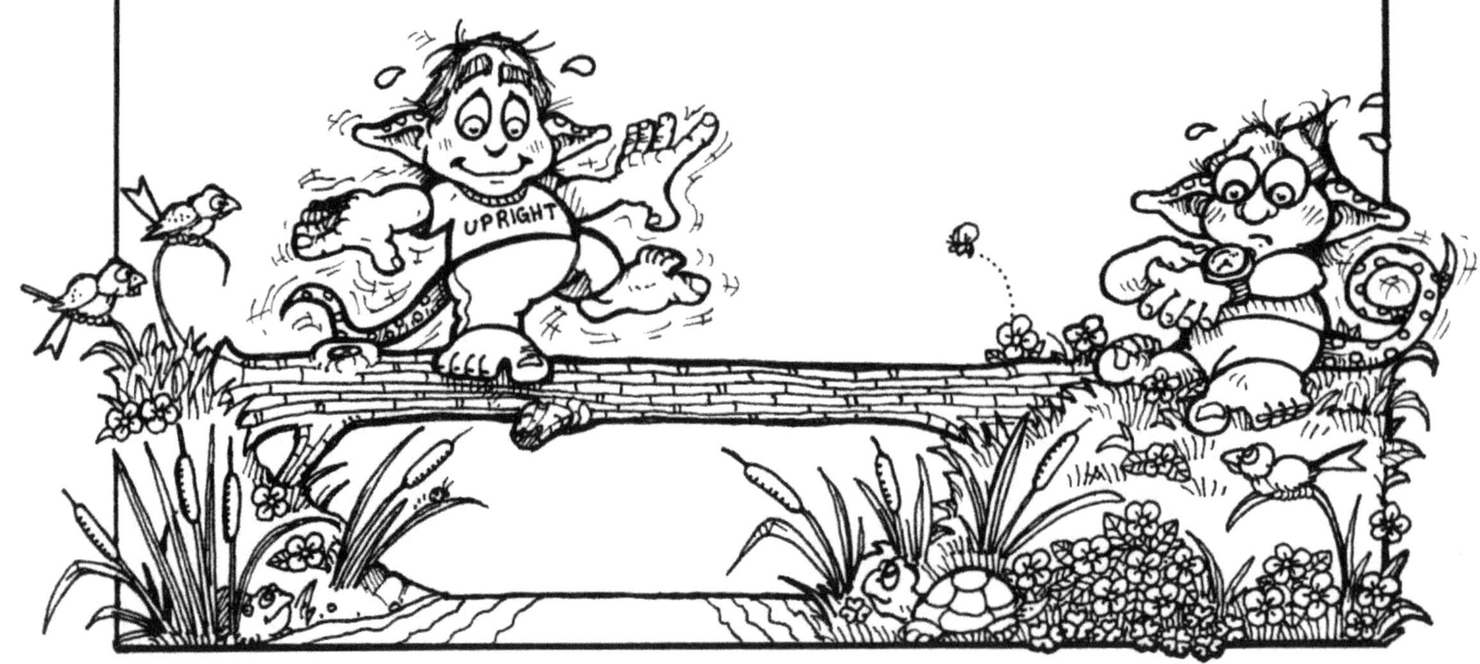

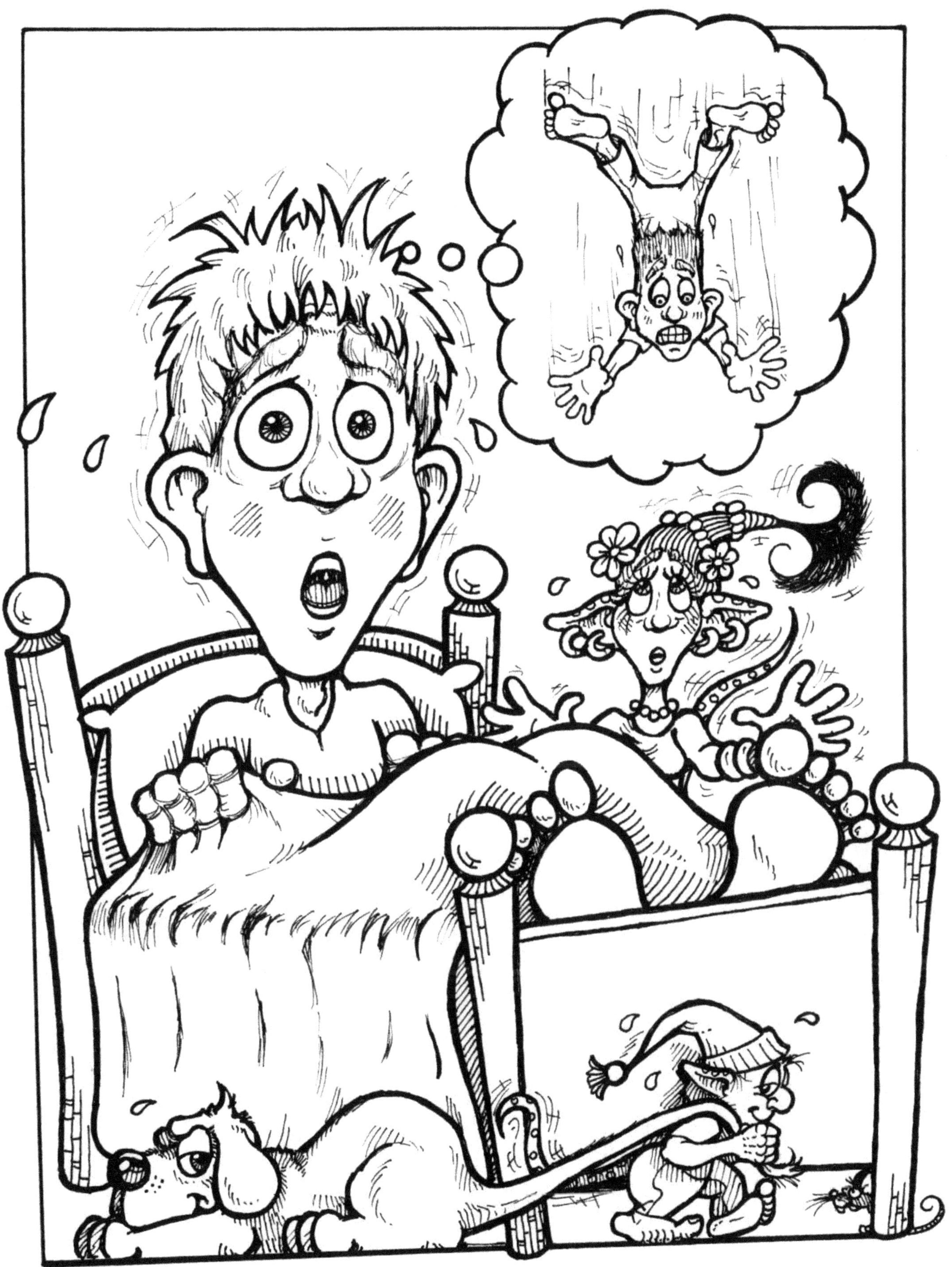

One thing for another...

Barterer. These Figments like to exchange one thing for another thing. Usually, a barter involves both parties agreeing to terms. These Figments find negotiating to

be too lengthy a process and dealing with humans quite messy, so they just skip that step. They will always exchange one thing for another. They believe they are changing in good Figment faith and want to keep the Barter even. The Barter may go awry because this Figment may have a different understanding of what an equitable trade means. Since Barterers do not know the human value, they may exchange one shiny object for another, such as foil for a bit of silver or a coin for a slice of carrot. They are both flat and round. It would be a good swap in their view. They often inspire those around them to want to do similar things, but it gets more complicated when humans try to play this game as, again, complications arise. Those complications further the belief that getting humans involved is unnecessary. The other, often frustrating thing is that they have little sense of time. They will always swap one thing for another. But in collecting one thing, they will return… eventually with the item to be exchanged. First, it might be challenging to determine that it is a swap since it might be seconds or months until they return with the item they are exchanging. Second, since they only realize it is a Barter, it might look like the item has disappeared. If a human loses a significant ring but finds a bread tie tied in a circle, they may have been in a Figment barter. Barterers have changed one small round loop for a different round loop. They have a very refined sense of responsibility and will ALWAYS make good on the trade, eventually. It's just that they might not return promptly to finish the exchange. Time has little meaning to many Figments.

(Common Experience)

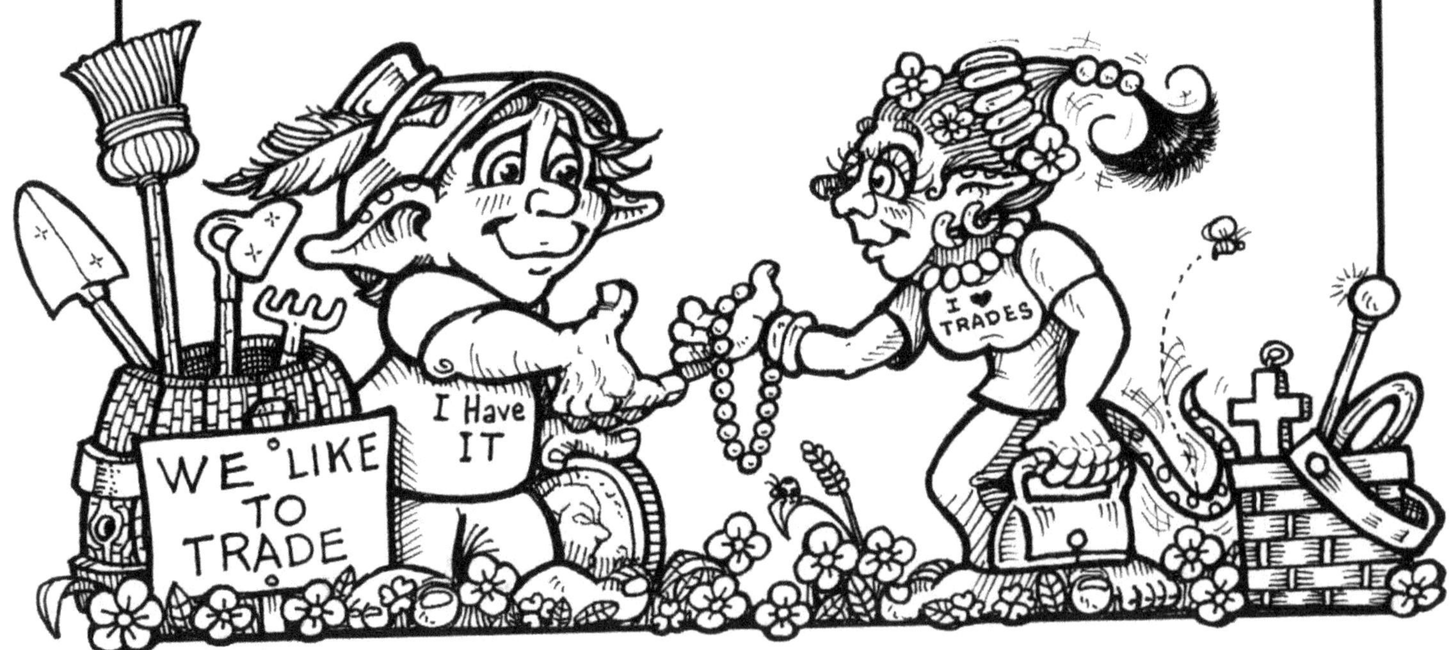

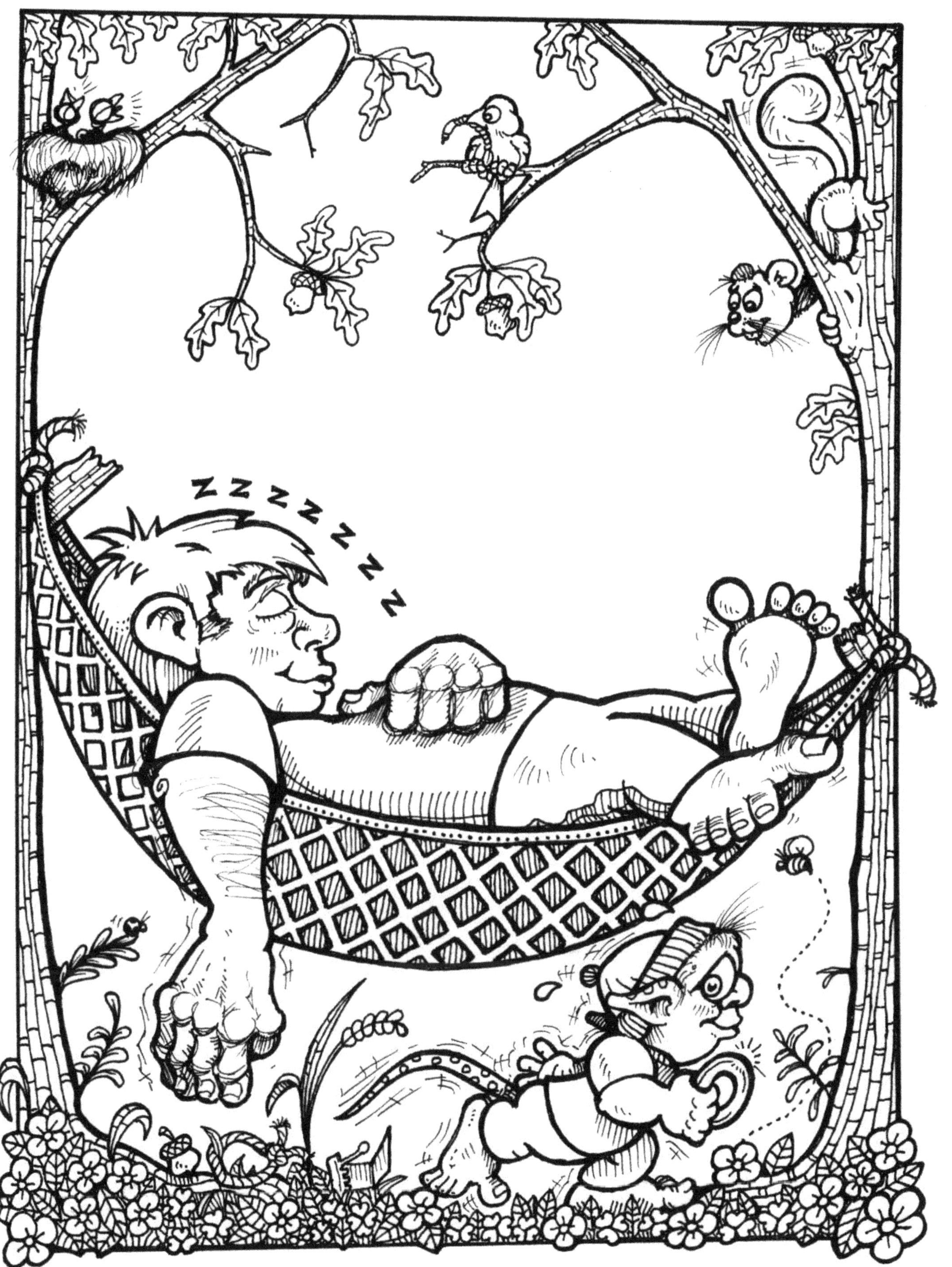
ZZZZZZZ

Develop a deep hatred...

Abhorrents: These Figments manifest from an absolute hatred for a specific inanimate item. Certain items will cause an Abhorrent. Humans will give reasons to explain their hatred of the inanimate object and will often believe that reason to be valid but not always. Once an Abhorrent has attached to a thing, it is nearly impossible to shake off. They multiply whenever more of the objects are found or sometimes even seen in pictures—often affecting previously unaffected humans that encounter another human with an Abhorrent. They also seem to develop a deep hatred for an object when it happens. It could be a specific type of thing or a category such as all glitter, bells, whistles, red hats, etc. Or the Abhorrent could so completely hate the purple cup in a cabinet. Like Peeves, people seem to cultivate their Abhorrents and embrace them, rarely attempting to give them up. They are less pet-like than Peeves as they are less cuddly; Abhorrents are usually kept close throughout a human's life and sometimes passed on. Abhorrents are typically found in enclosed places, and like Peeves, they are so similar in their attachment to a human. Once attached, they don't like to leave.

(Emotions)

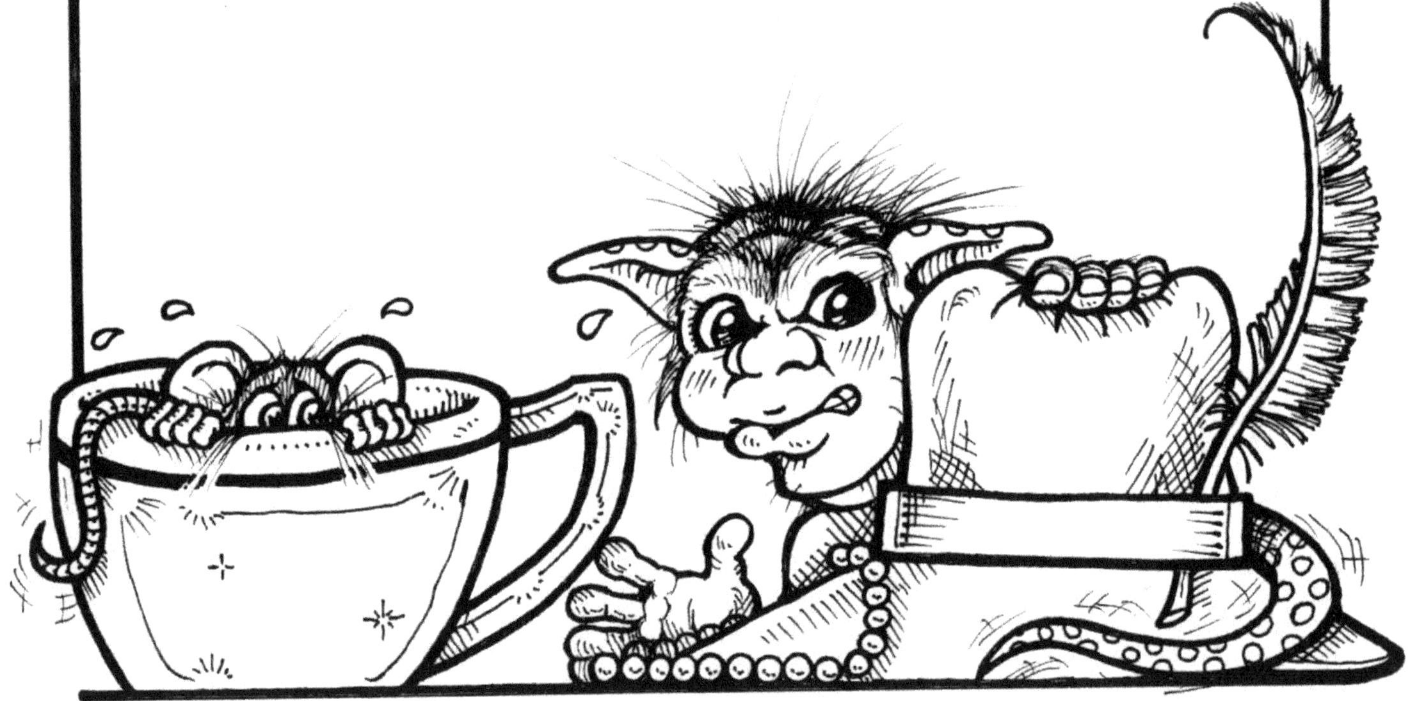

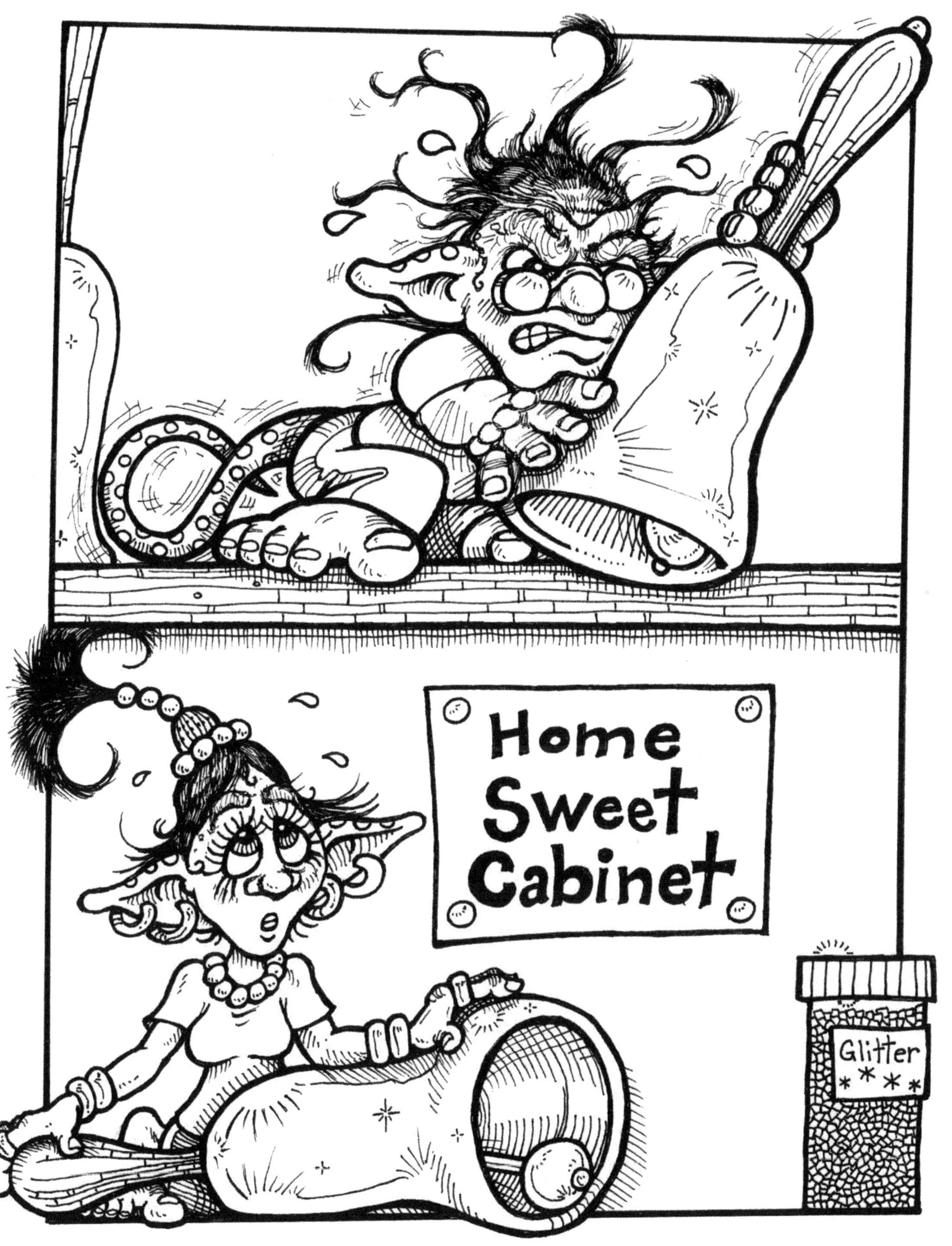

Home
Sweet
Cabinet
Glitter
***

Worrywarts
Please we do not have any WARTS!

Cerebral Tizzies: When you can't sleep, and your mind feels like it is on a wheel for a gerbil — too many thoughts. Your brain has been affected by a Cerebral Tizzy. They love lost sleep irritations as well as the smell of coffee beans. It seems as if they poke your mind just when you are ready to sleep and recharge. They have ideas, worries and cannot stop. If they can't stop worrying, why should you? Indeed, they were called worrywarts in times past, but they didn't like that. They have no warts.

(Emotions)

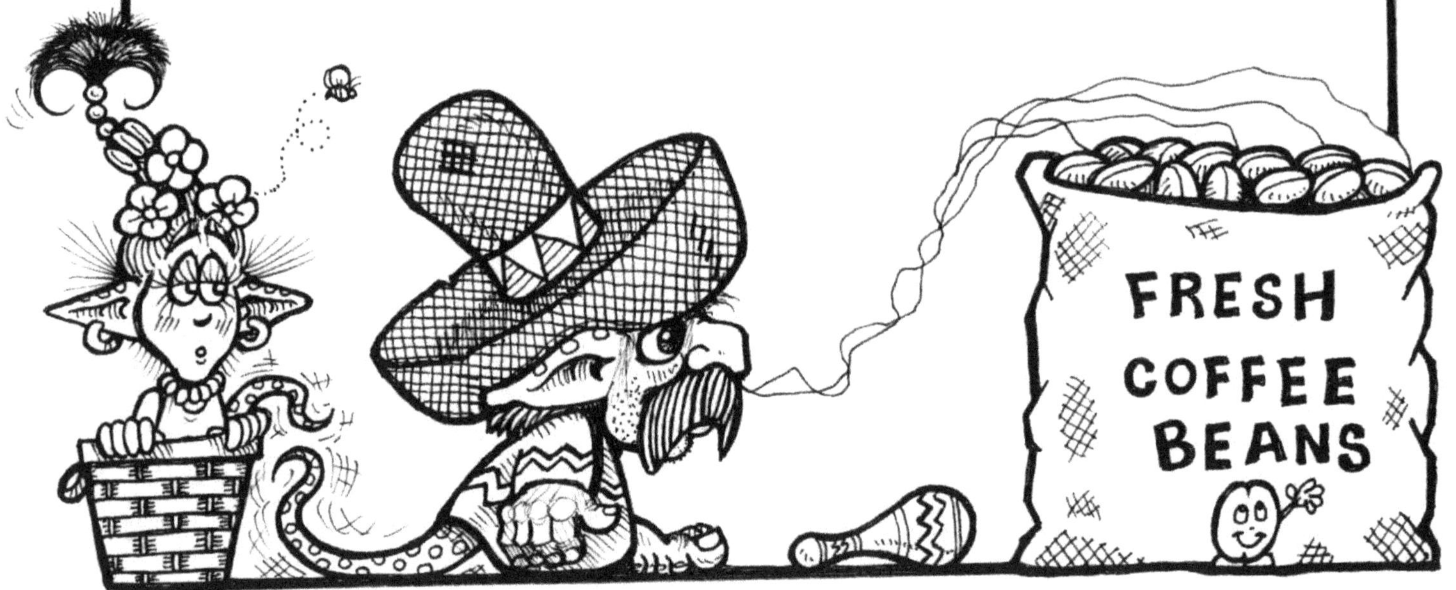

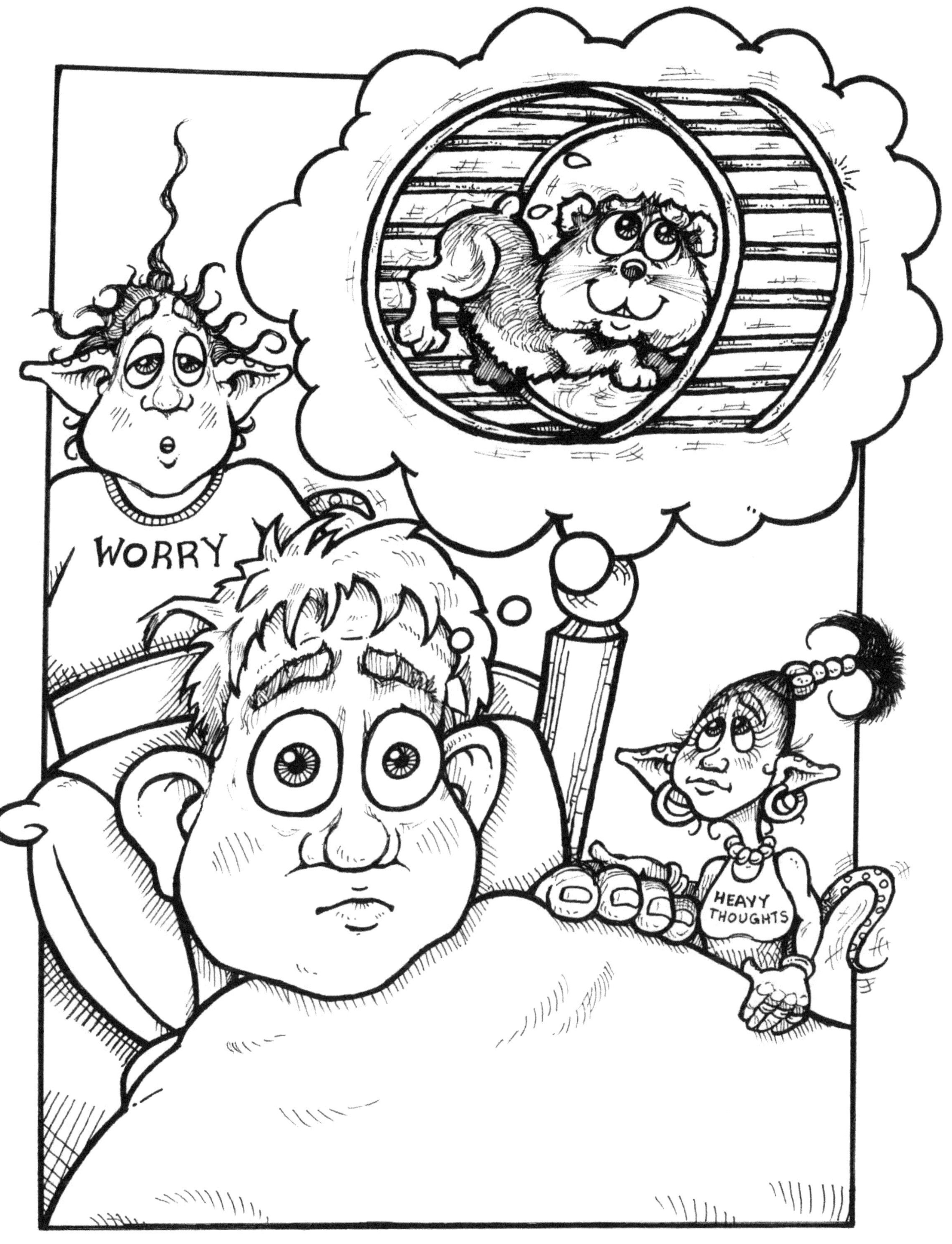

WORRY
HEAVY THOUGHTS

Be Happy & Feel Good

Serendipity: They are attracted to happy and good feelings. When you are walking down the beach or simply a sidewalk, and suddenly all seems right in the world, you have encountered a Serendipity. They don't tend to attach to one person and stay, and instead, they drift around spreading joy and warm, happy feelings. They randomly hang out in areas like parks, beaches, libraries for some, ice cream parlors, and others like older men. A Serendipity can occasionally be in hardware stores. Serendipities tend to like small groups of a few people but not so much large crowds.

(Emotions)

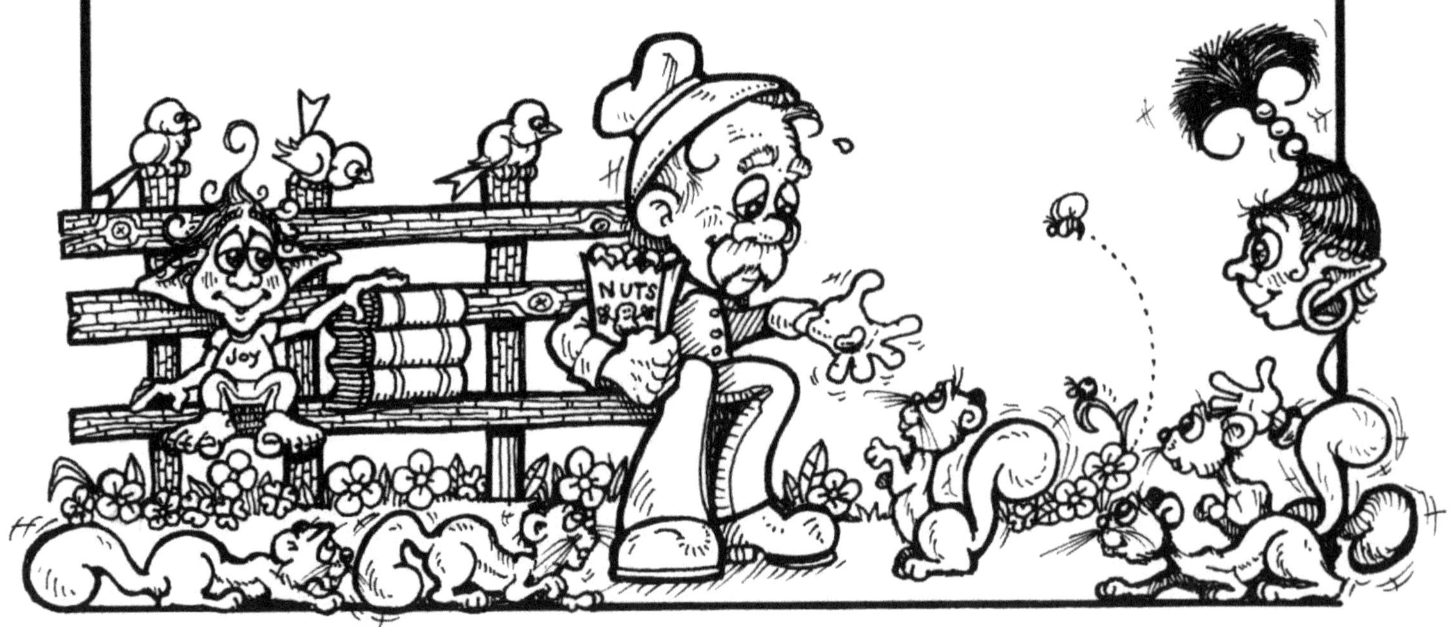

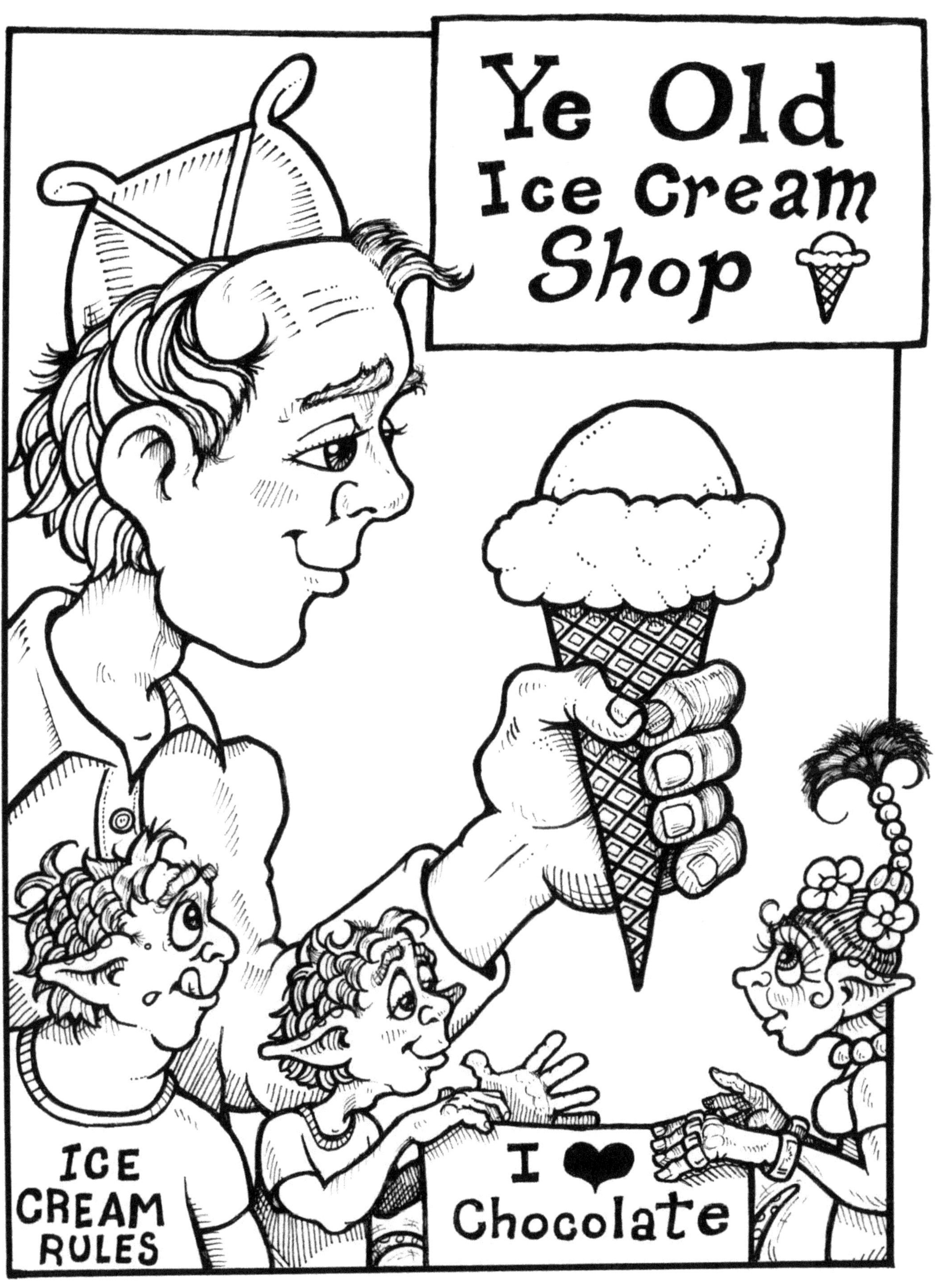

Ye Old
Ice Cream
Shop
ICE
CREAM
RULES
I ♥
Chocolate

Carelessly completing tasks...

Cursorys: They make decisions with little thought or basis. These Figments are almost related to Fripperies, but they have their own distinct. They are very carefree and are not the most profound thinking of Figments. They seem not to have enough regret about having uncomplicated feelings or actions — kind of a not very connected to anything, Figment. These Figments can be impatient, but more often, they are simply on to the next thing without enough consideration for the job they are currently doing. With too many Cursorys in your life, you will not complete tasks. You might be almost blindly carefree to the point of carelessly completing tasks. Cursory Figments are not mean or malicious but rather not inclined to follow through.

(Common Experience)

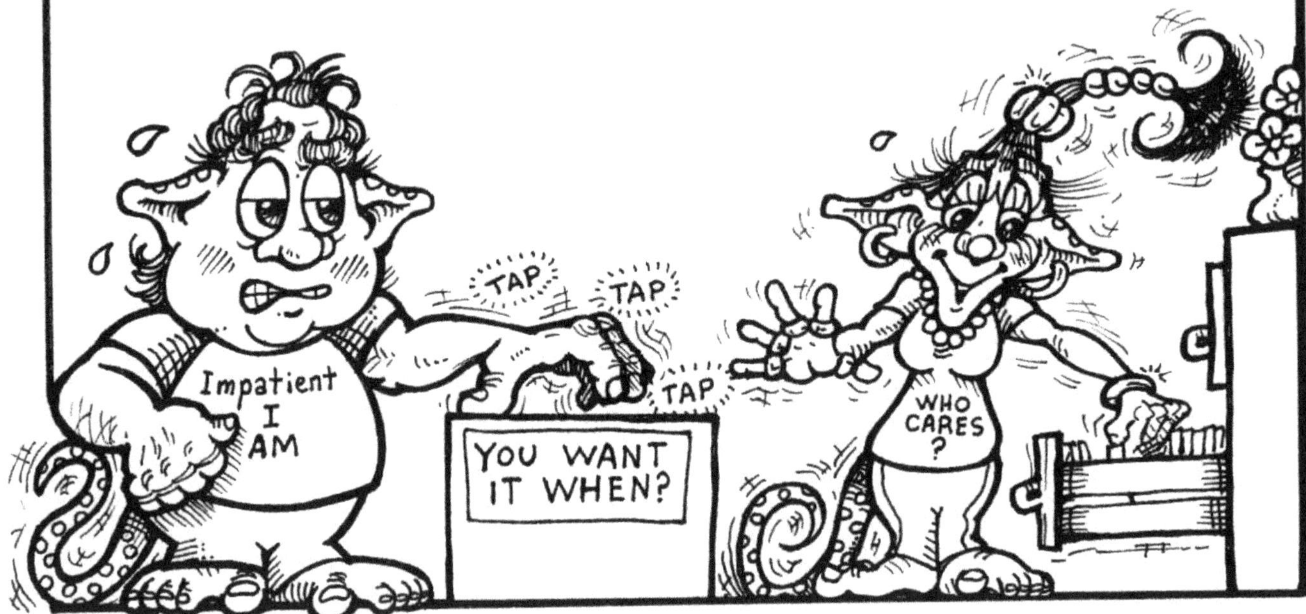

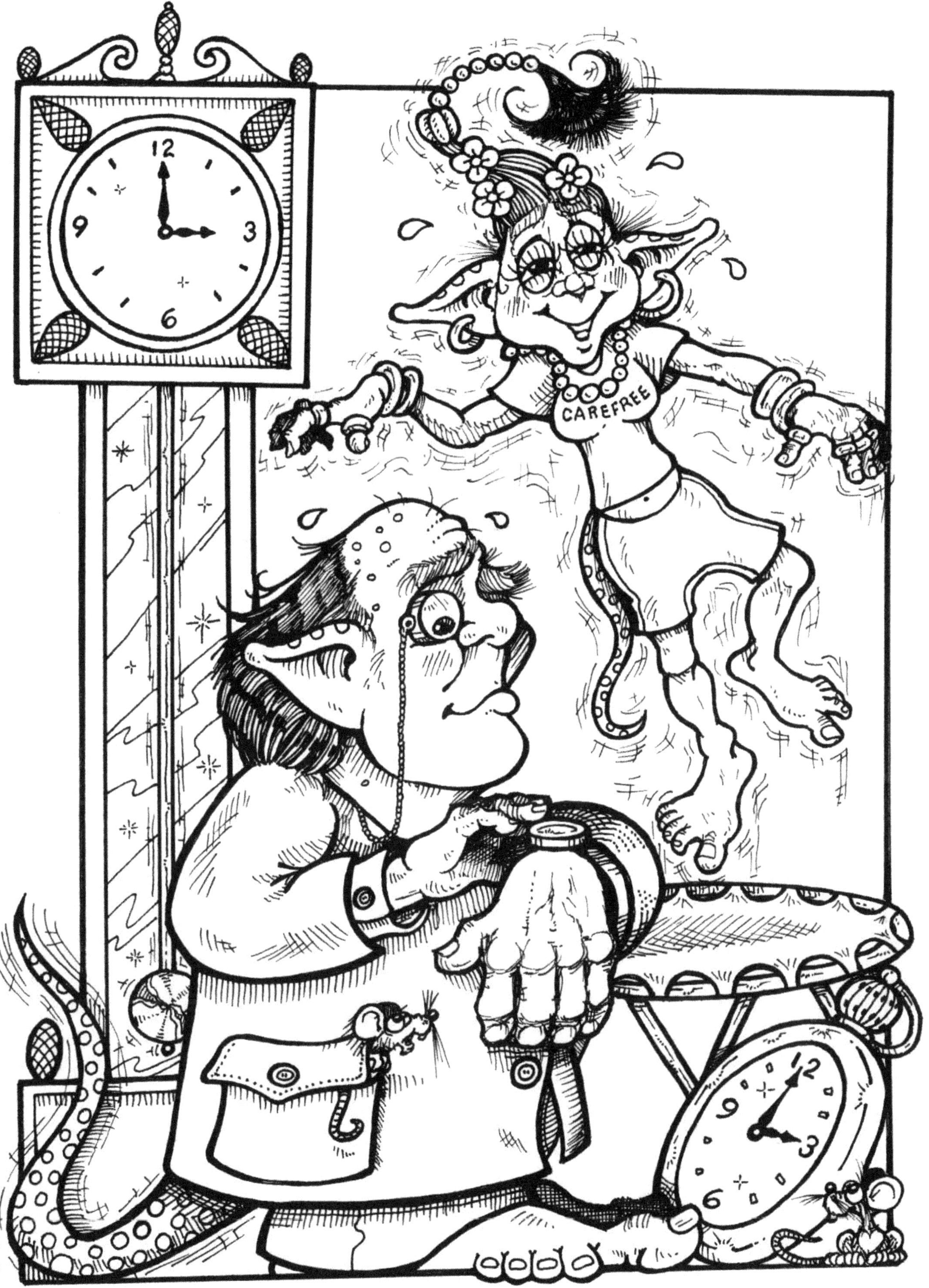

CAREFREE
12
9 3
6
12
9 3
6

Feeling stuck in a Loop...

Déjà Vu: This is a very complicated Figment. There are two sides to the emotions/feelings inspired by this Figment. Sometimes you feel as if you have done a thing before. While knowing that you have not, it is as if you have a memory of the event. You are almost creating a mirror of what you are currently doing.

Déjà Vus causes frustration, a vague feeling like everything has a short overlap. Almost like the world studdered. You might "know" you are not repeating an action or a thing, but the sense of repeating is there. You can feel stuck in a loop. It's often an uncomfortable feeling — the r for a moment. It has the resonance of familiarity, yet not accompanied by accurate recollection.

(Common Experience)

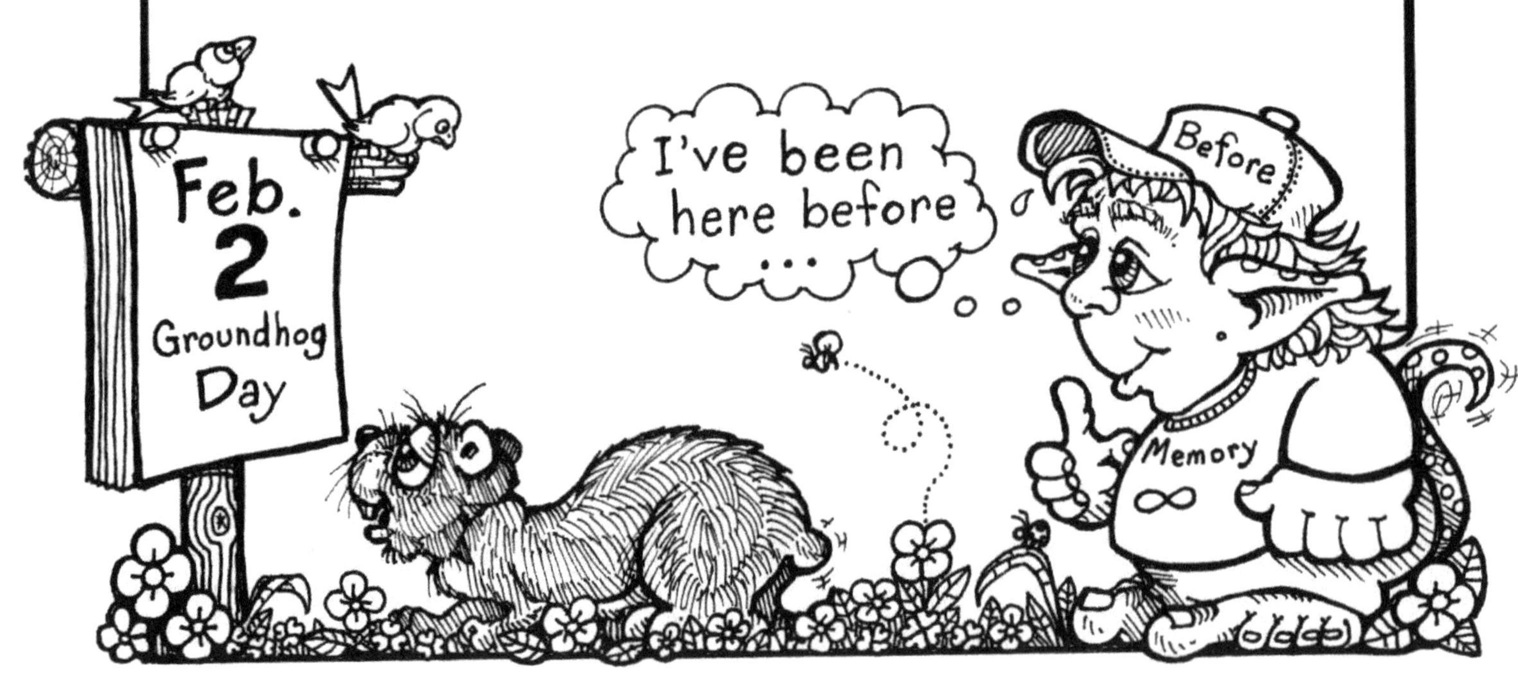

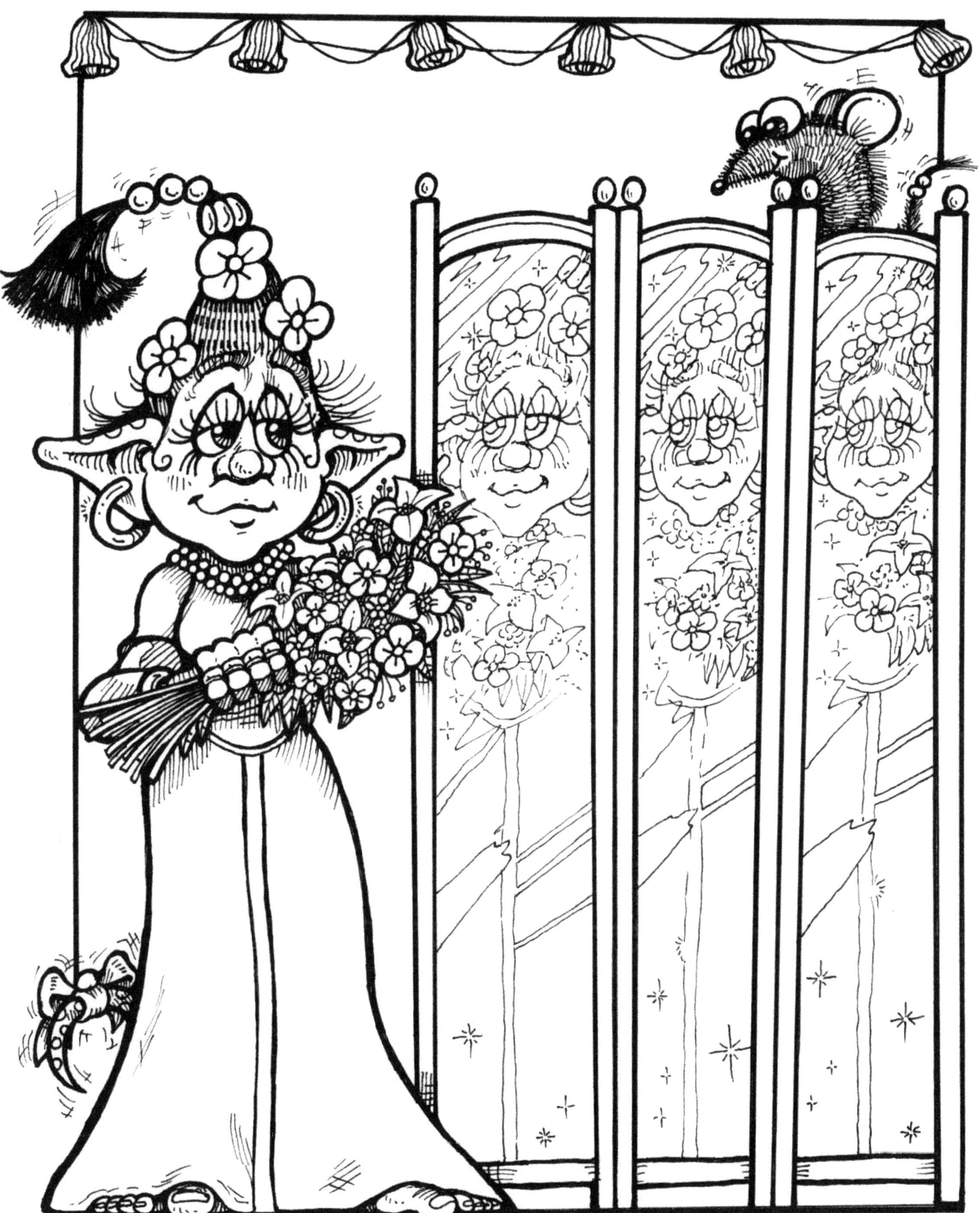

Feelings of Empathy...

Smidgeons: Smidgeons might be the smallest of the Figments. They adore tiny things. They will collect them and revel in them. Miniature food, miniaturized elements, something that generally comes in a much more considerable amount. Not a whole brownie, but a smidgeon. Not the more enormous teacup but a smidgeon of its average size for a tea party. Not a very precise Figment. They are a bit flighty. But they do cause feelings of empathy toward the smallest of things. Smidgeons adore any object that has become miniaturized.

(Common Experience)

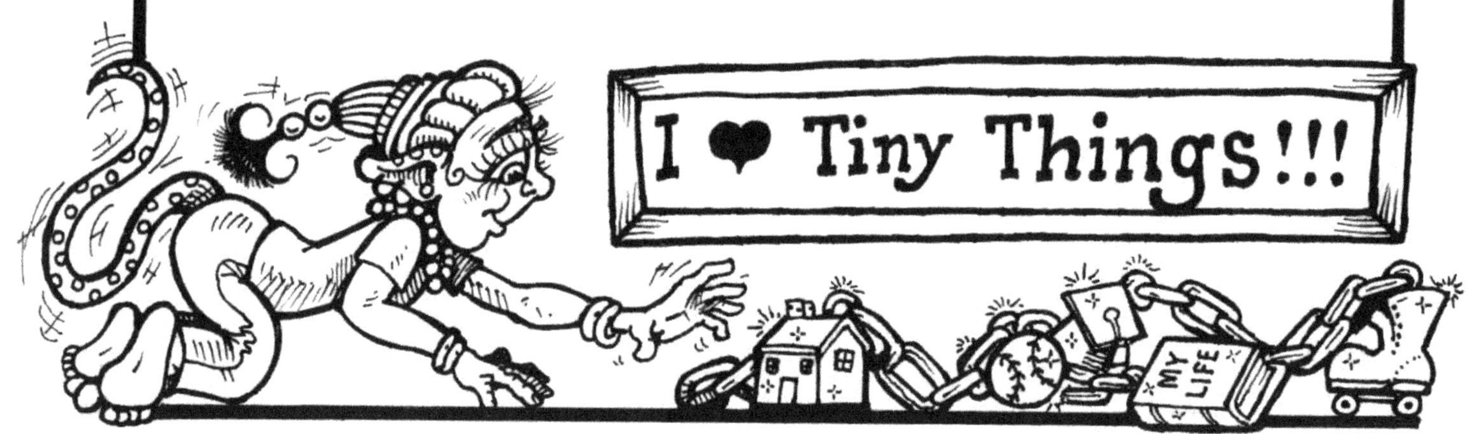

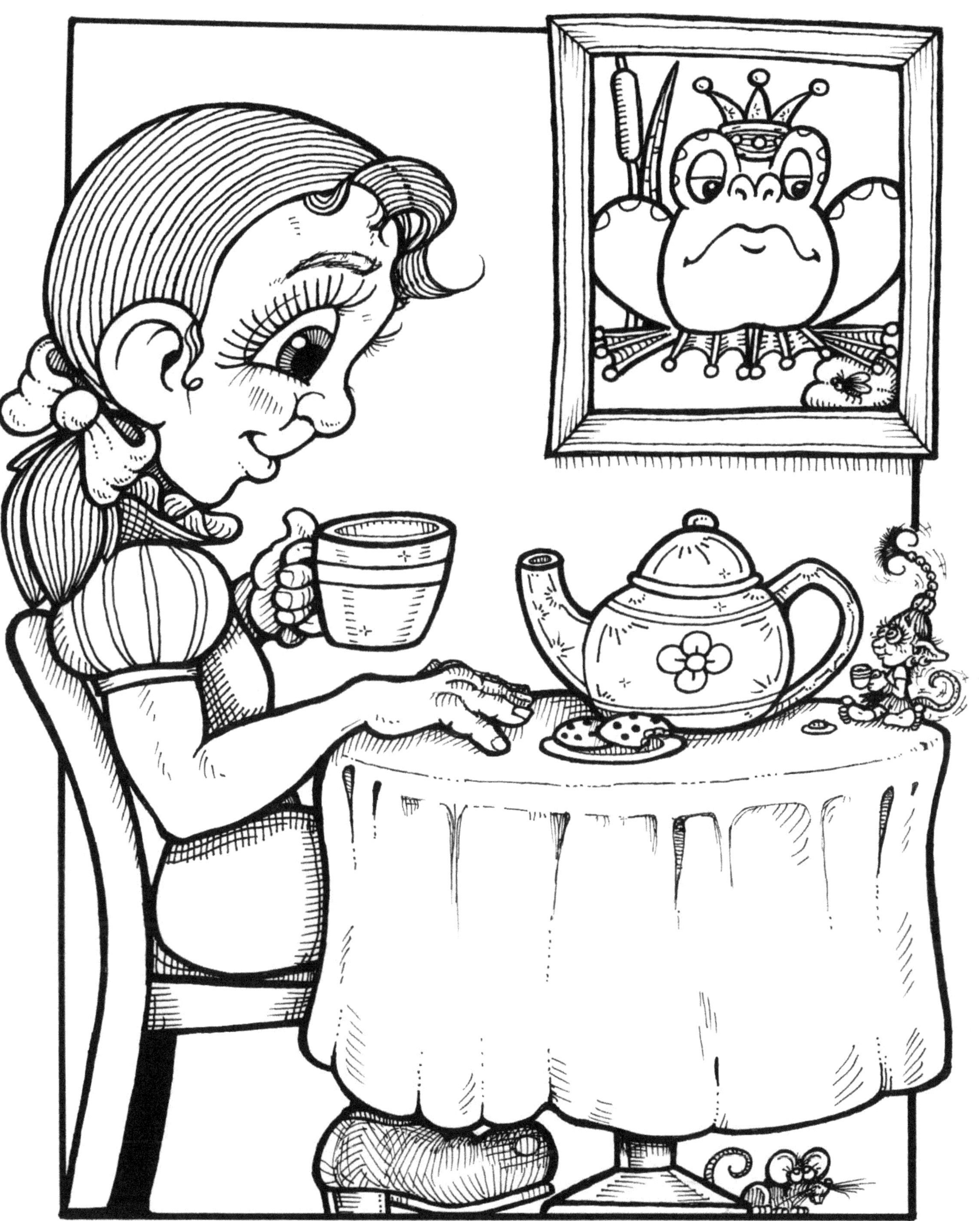

Misgivings & Nostalgia...

Regrets: They inspire songs and occasionally a change in human behavior, but they often are also quite dark in their sadness. They can cause bitterness, anguish, and heartache if too many Regrets gather together. Many, if not most, people have a few of them. They can sometimes overwhelm humans with their misgivings and nostalgia that goes way too far. Regrets can be OK when you learn from what caused their inception. In the sense of remorse, they can use the grief and sadness combined with doubts to generate future positive changes. Run amok. They are almost paralyzing in their effect.

(Emotions)

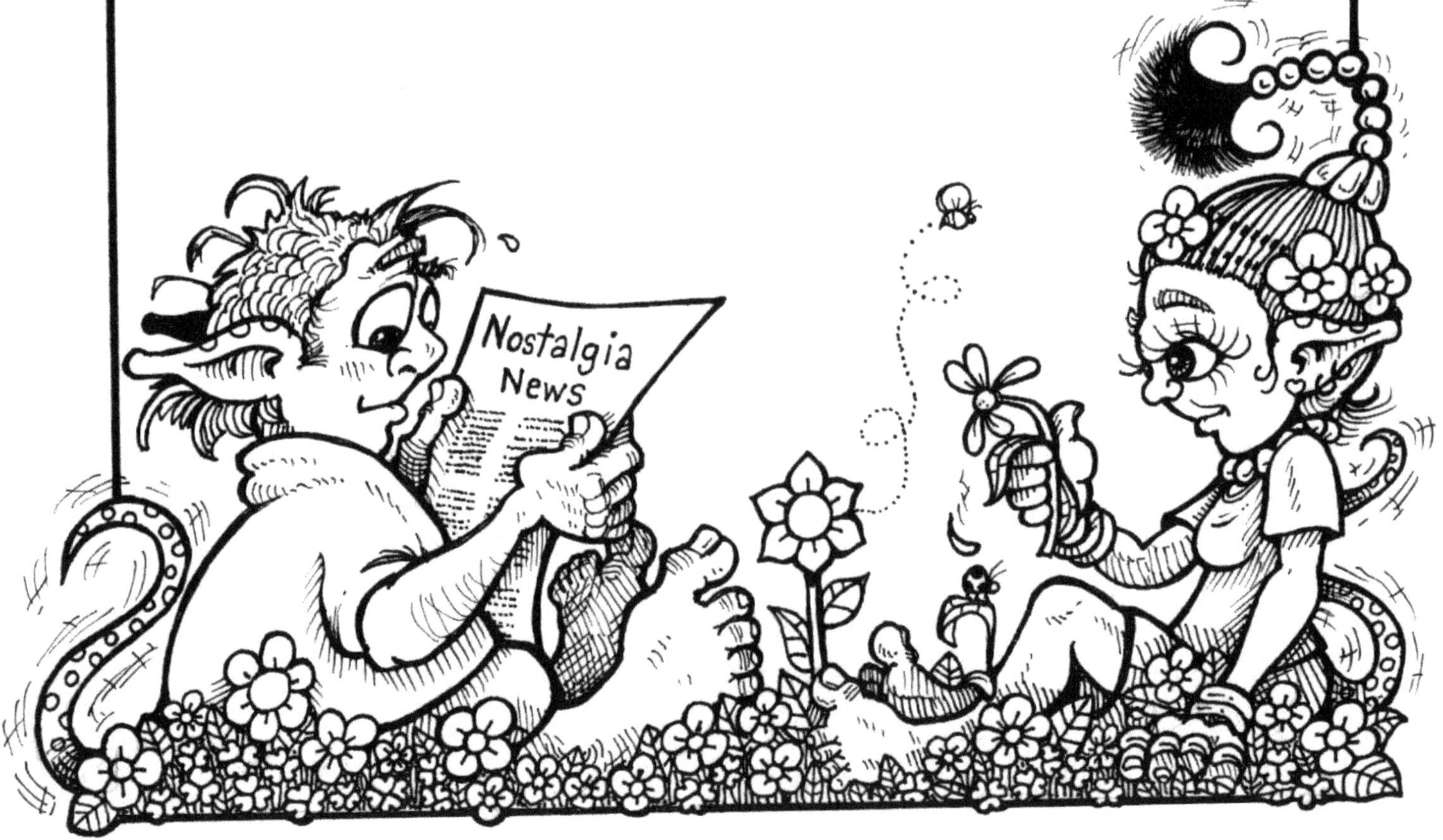

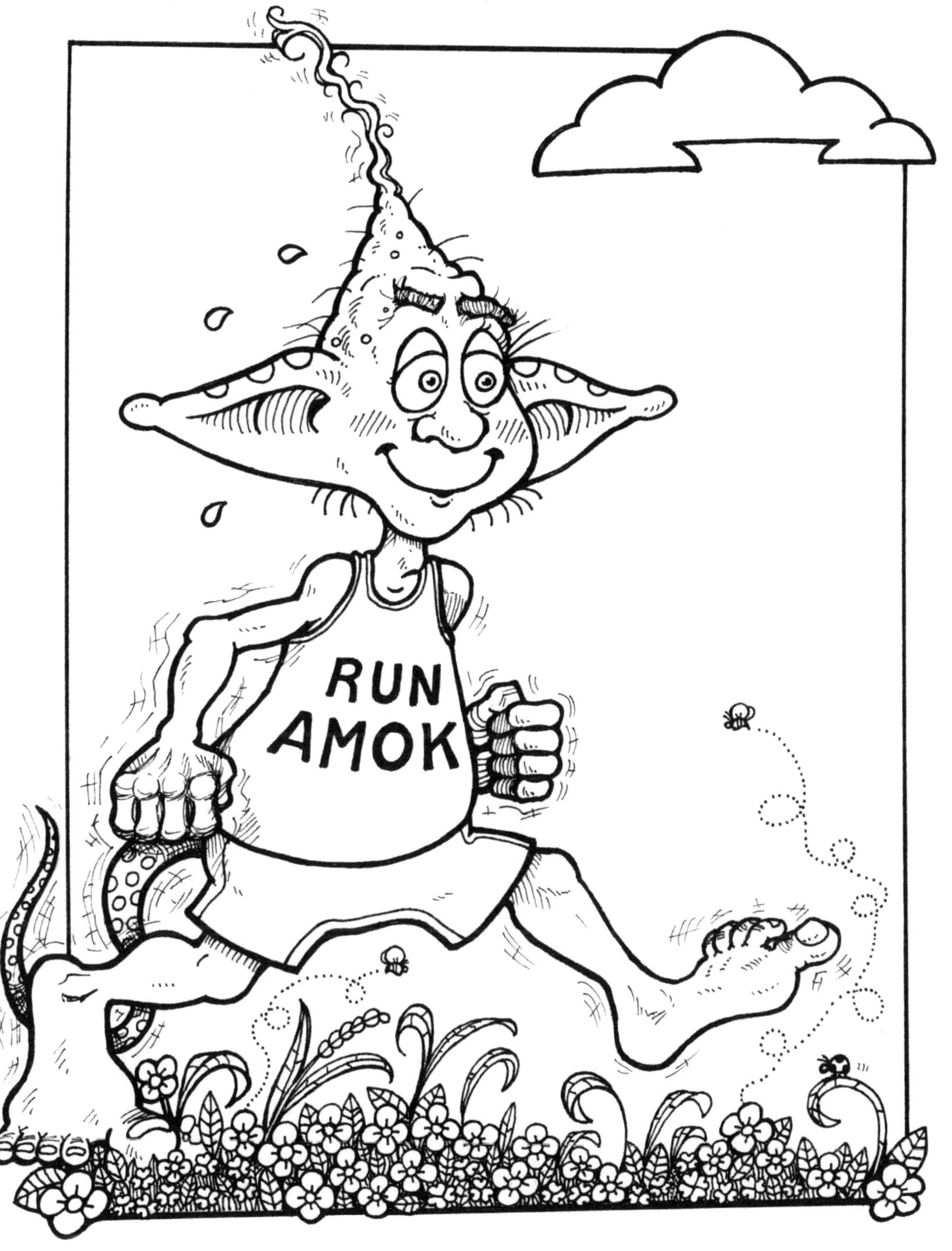
RUN
AMOK

Perceptions about things.

Perceptions: They filter and influence everything in how their humans receive input from the real world. They can help to define their human character and attitudes in life. They like to hang with Scruples that match their filters and the information they give to their humans. It tends to be quite a problem when Perception and Scruple Figments fail to bond together. Kindness, hate, love, and all other emotions originate from one's perceptions about things. Perception Figments help shape a human's goal and outlook on life.

(Emotions)

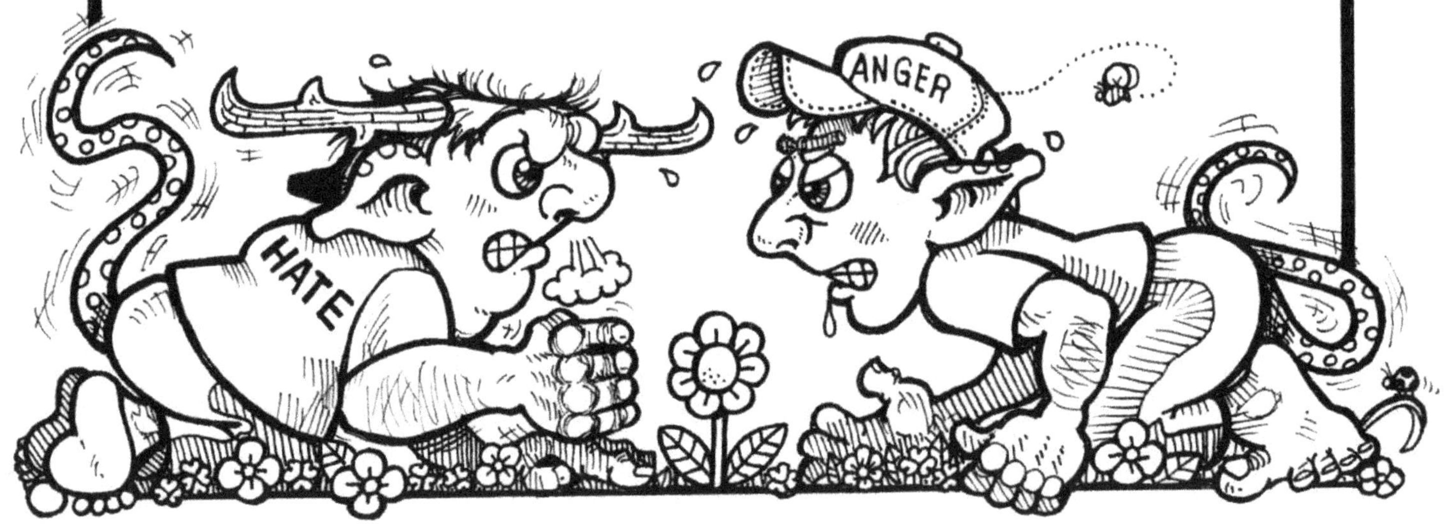

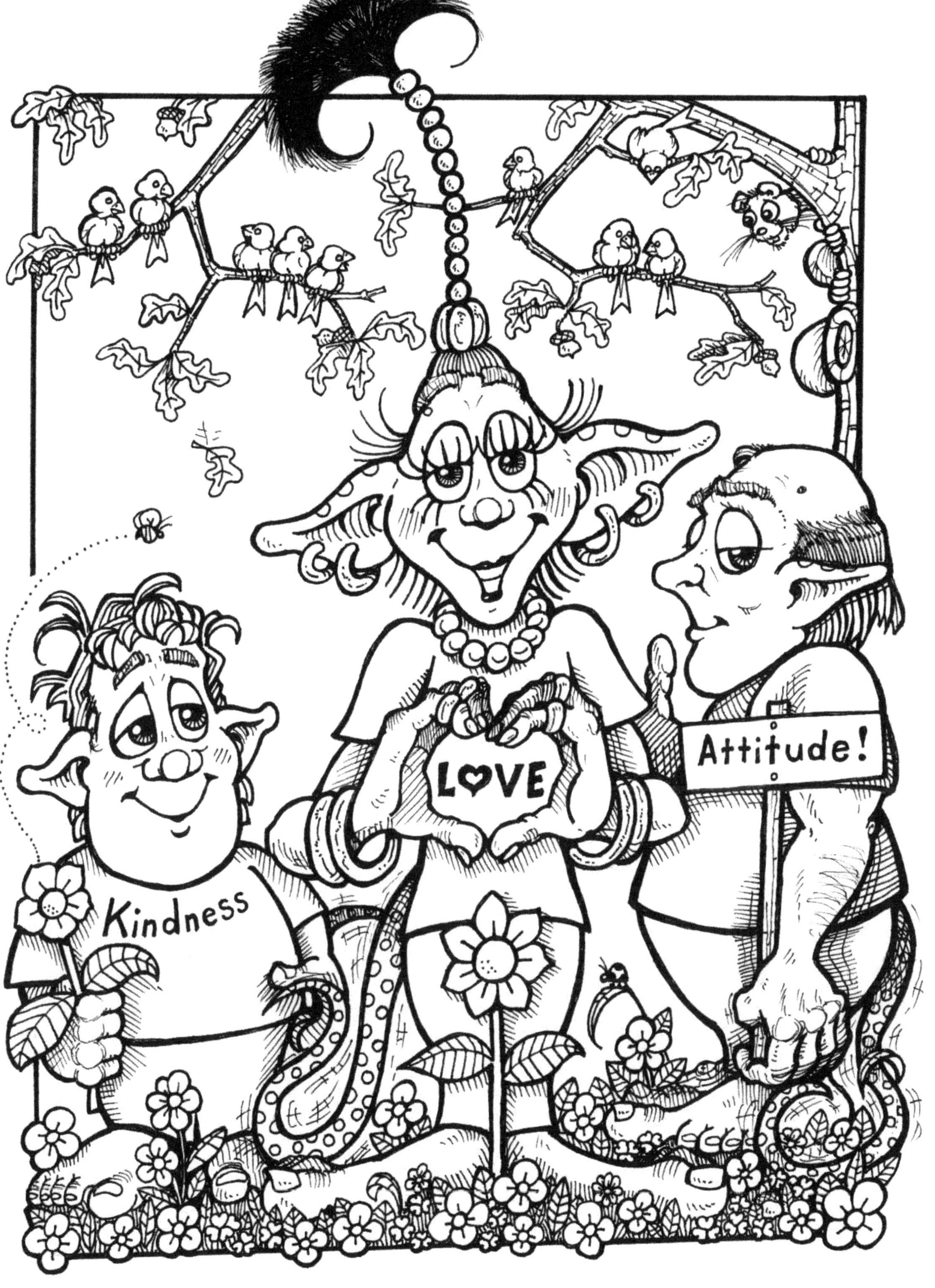

Kindness
LOVE
Attitude!

Make your Life easier...

Demeanors.

Demeanors influence your facial appearance or behavior as they reflect and intensify emotion. Your Demeanors mustn't overly influence what is going on in your head at times. They can get you in trouble. Playing poker with out-of-control demeanors will cost you money. Same thing if your Demeanors need to be in control on the job, or you cannot check your face at the appropriate times. That is not going to be good. If a lousy Demeanor influences your behavior, well. Disasters can happen. Demeanors tend to be singular; however, practicing controlling your Demeanor is essential — something to ever be diligent in doing. If you do not remain aware of your Demeanors, they can cause some havoc. On the other side, when they are working for you, they can smooth the way and make your life easier. Just be aware of them.

(Emotions)

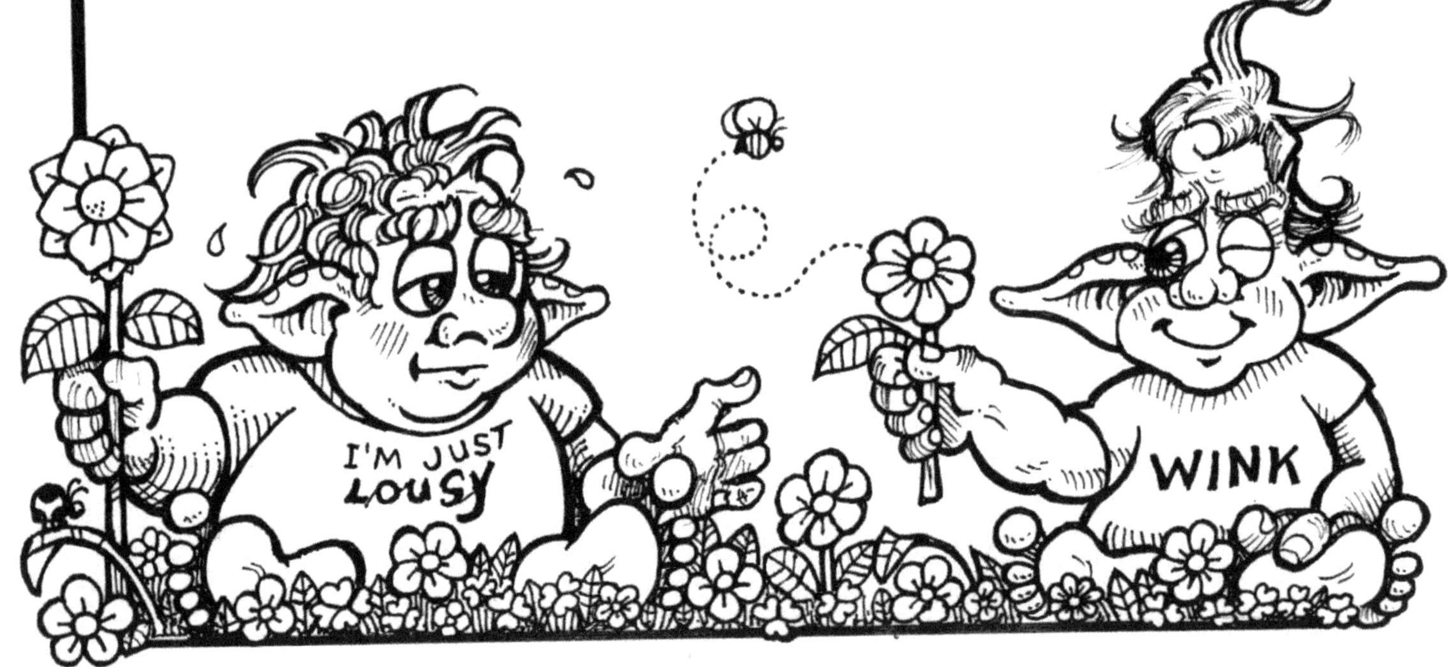

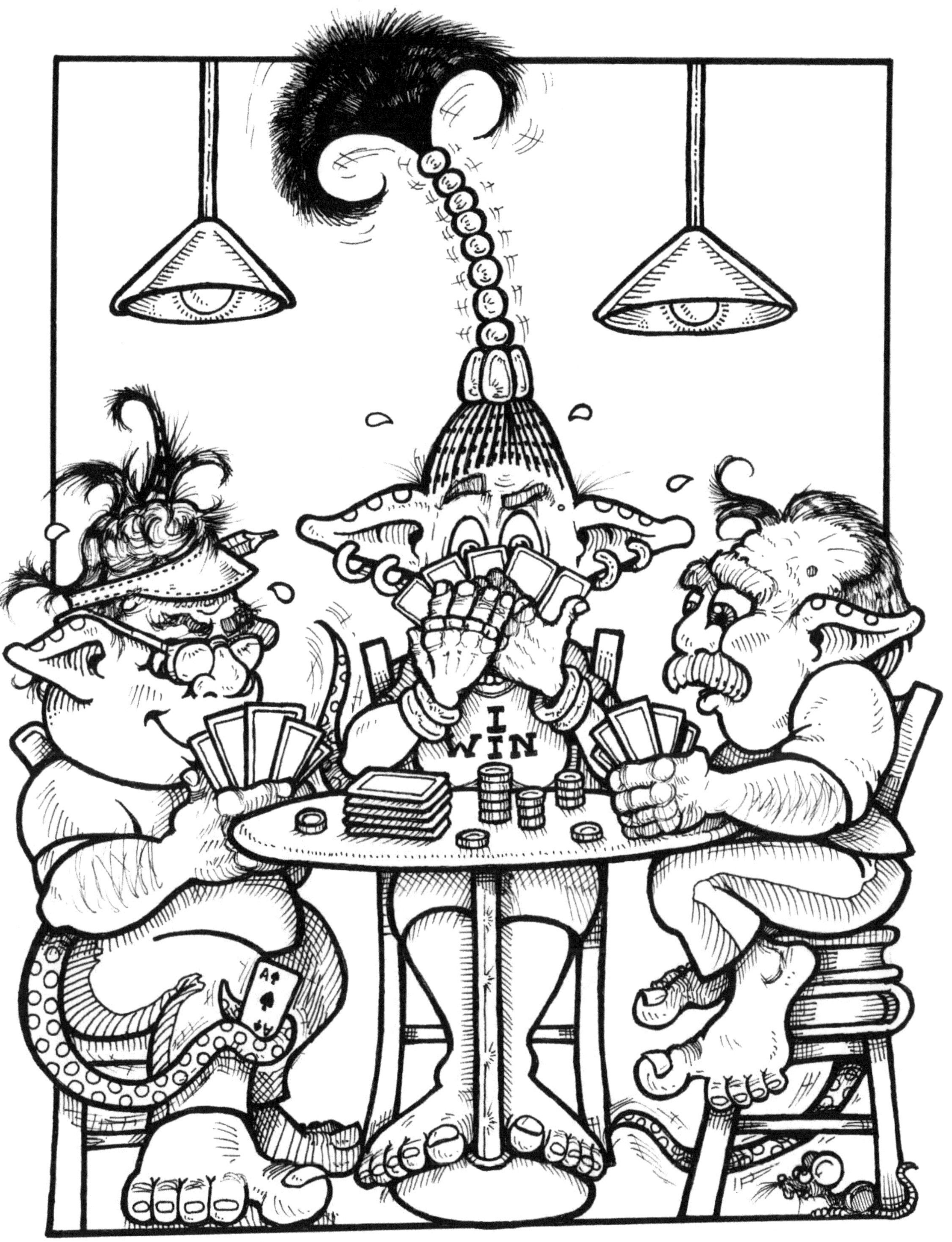

I
WIN

Be a beautiful thing...

Placids

If a person has Placids in their life,
it can be a beautiful thing. They can help you through some rough
times. Help you remember that the Sun will come up tomorrow, no
matter what chaos seems to be happening around you. And can help
you channel peace and tranquility in your world. As with other
Figments, too many can throw a human out of balance; that is a bad
thing. But beware: unmoving or lack of forwarding motion also keeps
many good things from happening.   Do not become so tranquil that
you are no longer living life.

(Emotions)

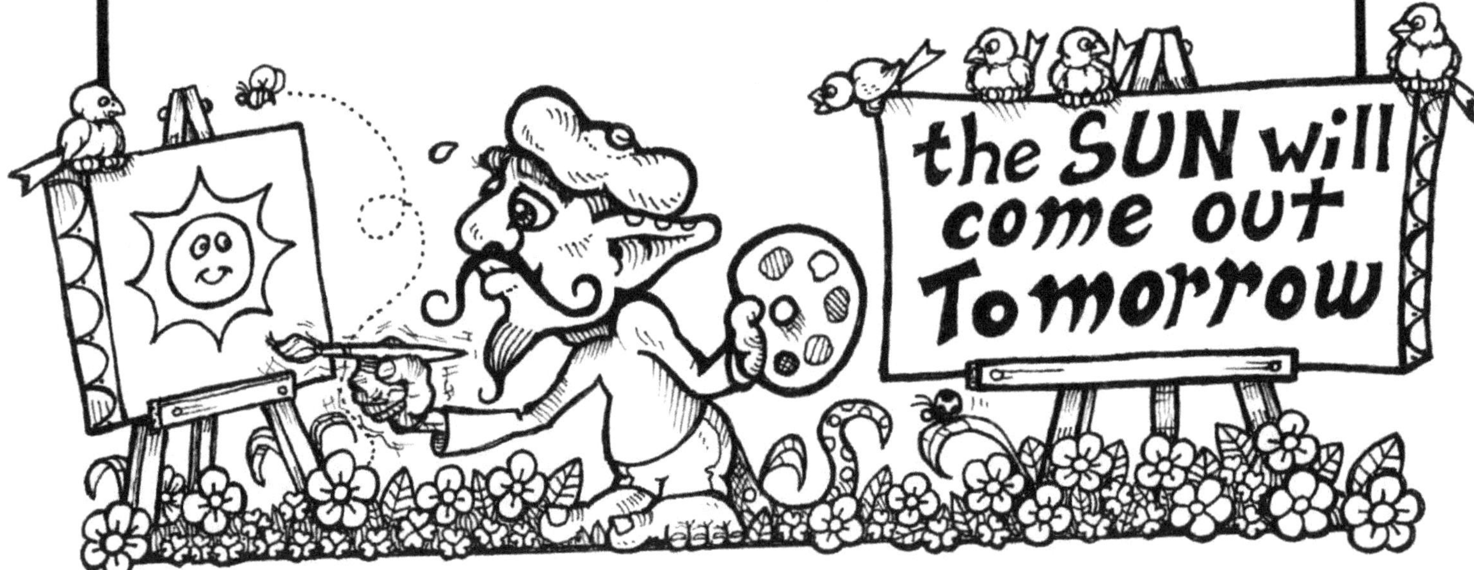

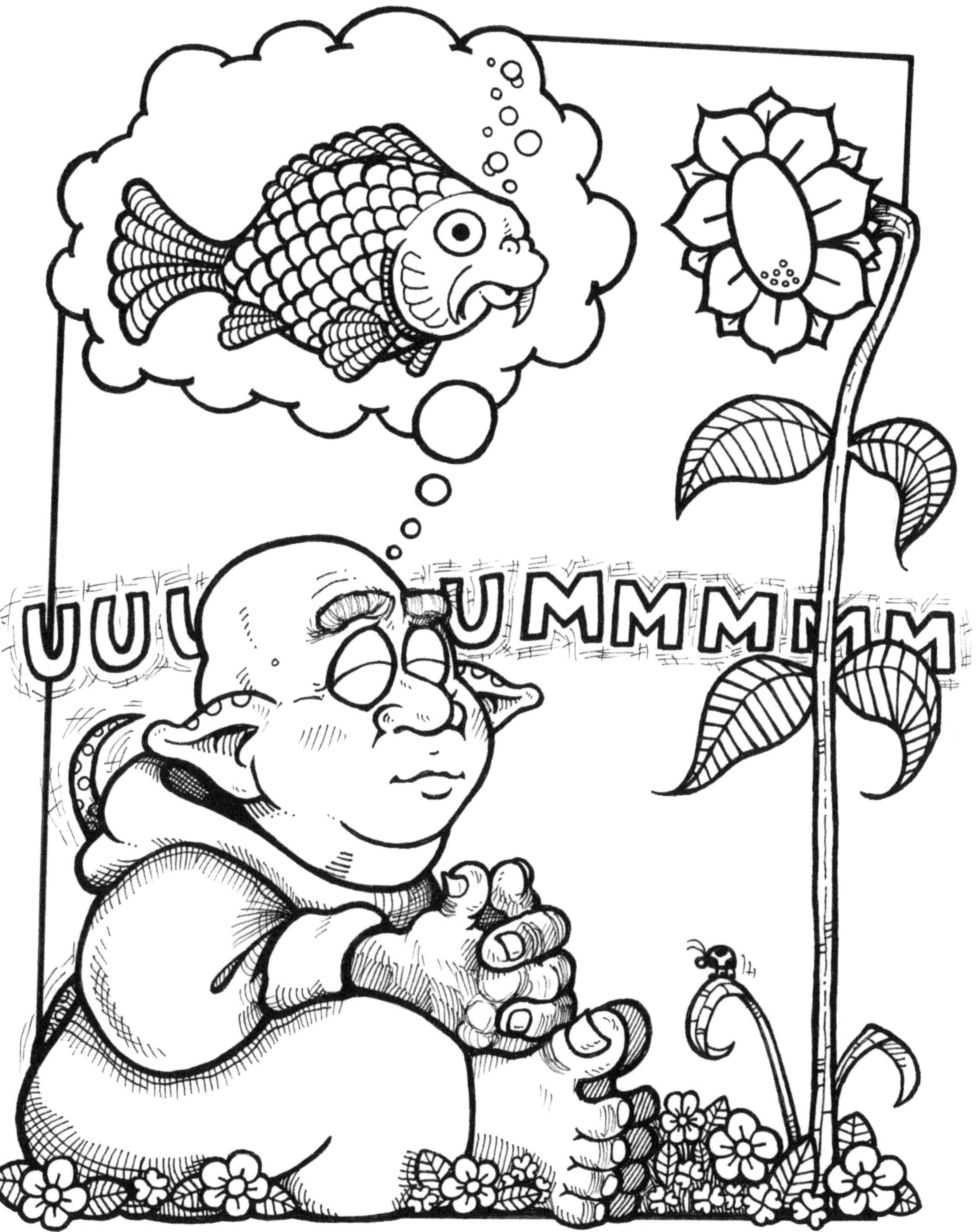

UUUUUUMMMMM

Keep the recollections...

Retrospect:

The Figment of past phrases. They keep memories alive of the things our parents or caregivers used to say and make you relive and use them yourself. When you hear yourself say something that your mother, father, or family members used to say, it keeps the family connection strong. Retrospects might also keep memories of phrases and gestures of the family of choice. They keep the recollections of our past connected to traditions and family history.

(Common Experience)

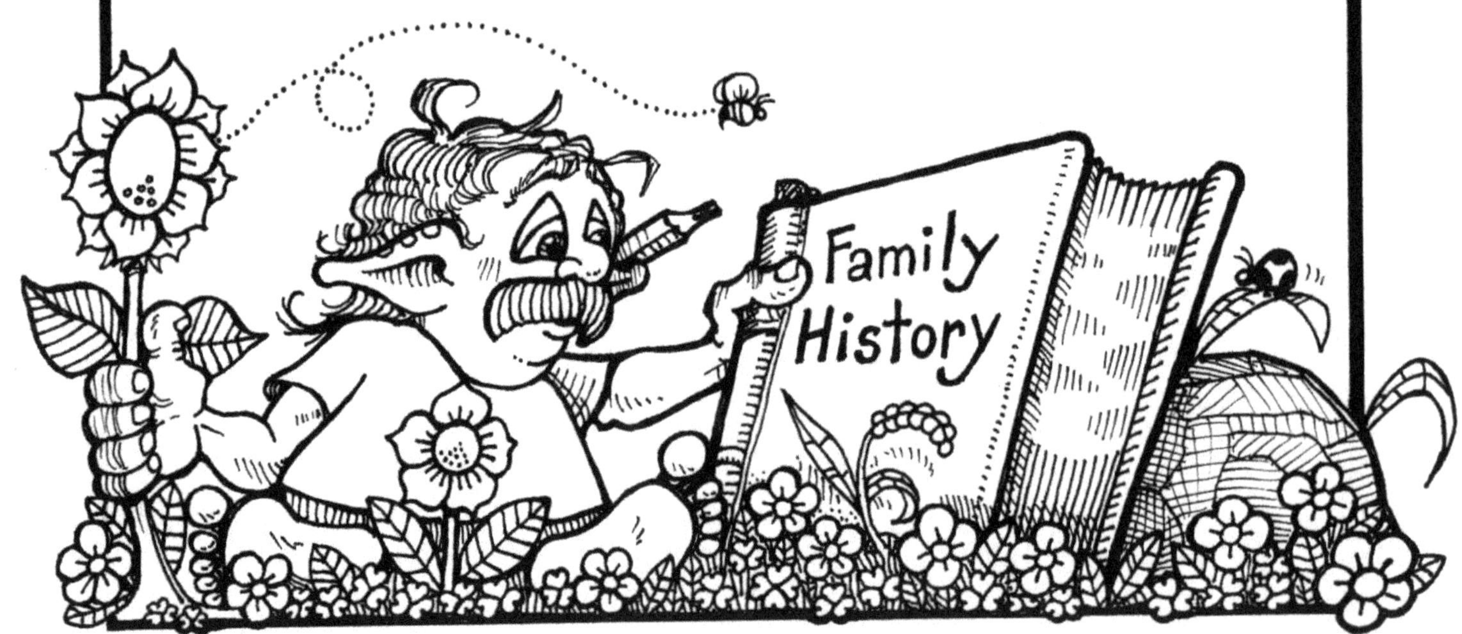

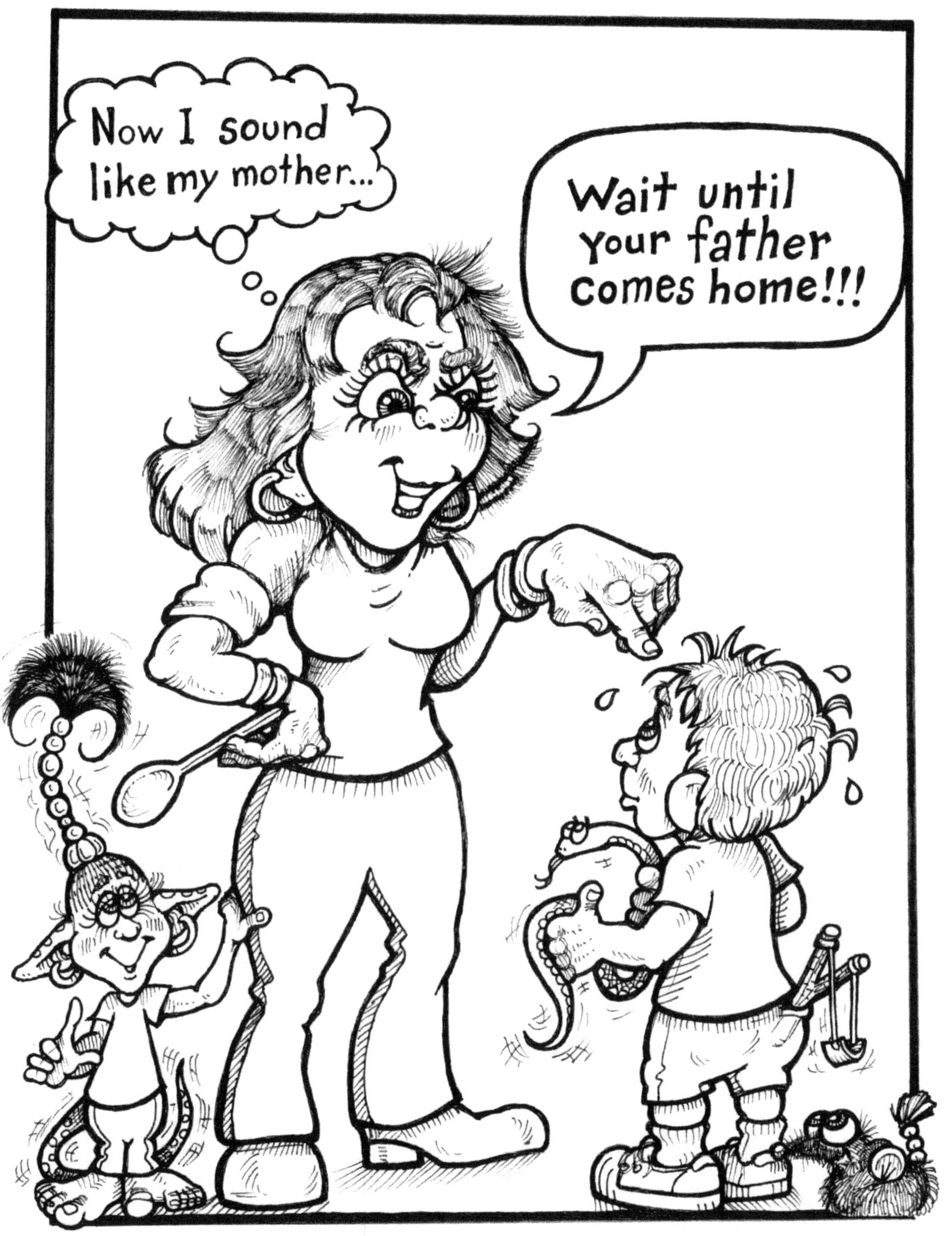

Now I sound like my mother...
Wait until your father comes home!!!

Burst of Imagination... POW

Ennui's:

Figments of extreme boredom. In some cases, having an Ennui can cause bursts of imagination. In other humans, they produce just great perceived angst.   Although passing through or by other humans, they congregate around teenagers, and older folk can cause boredom for a few minutes. The best way to chase away an Ennui is to remain engaged in something. Reading, sports, whatever it is that interests you. Engagement does not have to be active movement, just keen mental interests. Ennui Figments are allowed by those they come from. Those who seem to have little interest in anything and less ability to become engaged. This Figment does seem to enlarge the feelings and help a human wallow in them.

(Common Experience)

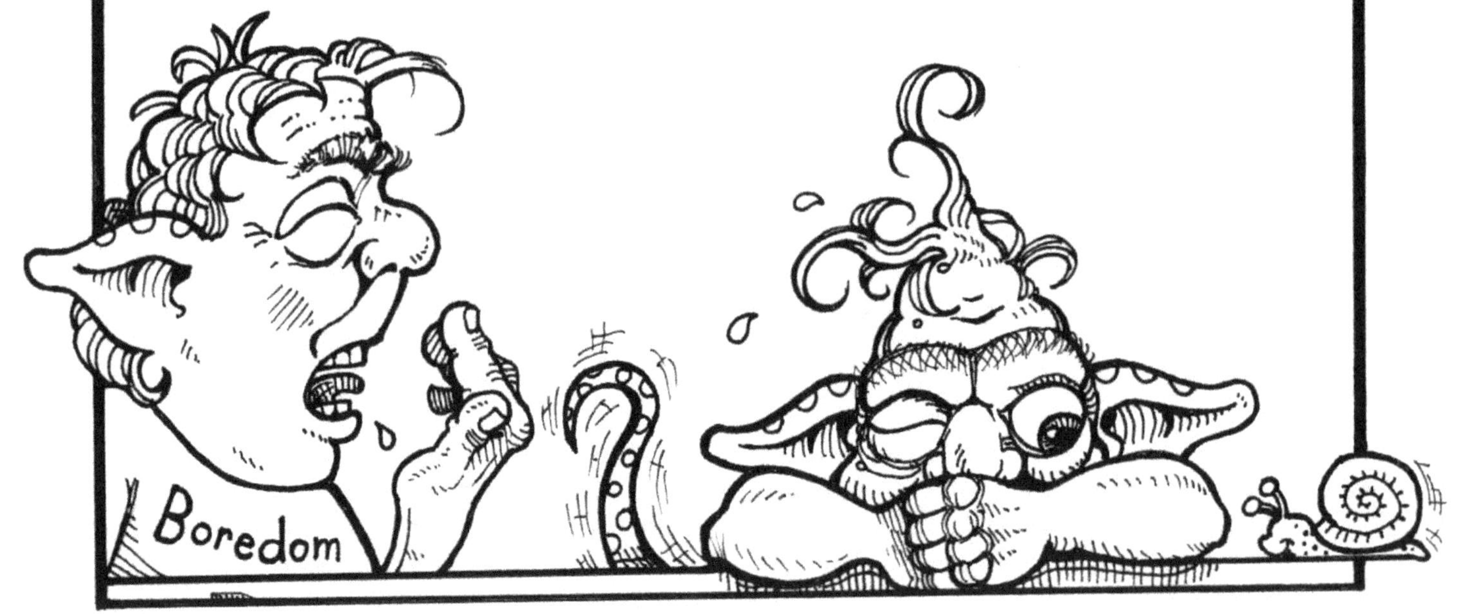

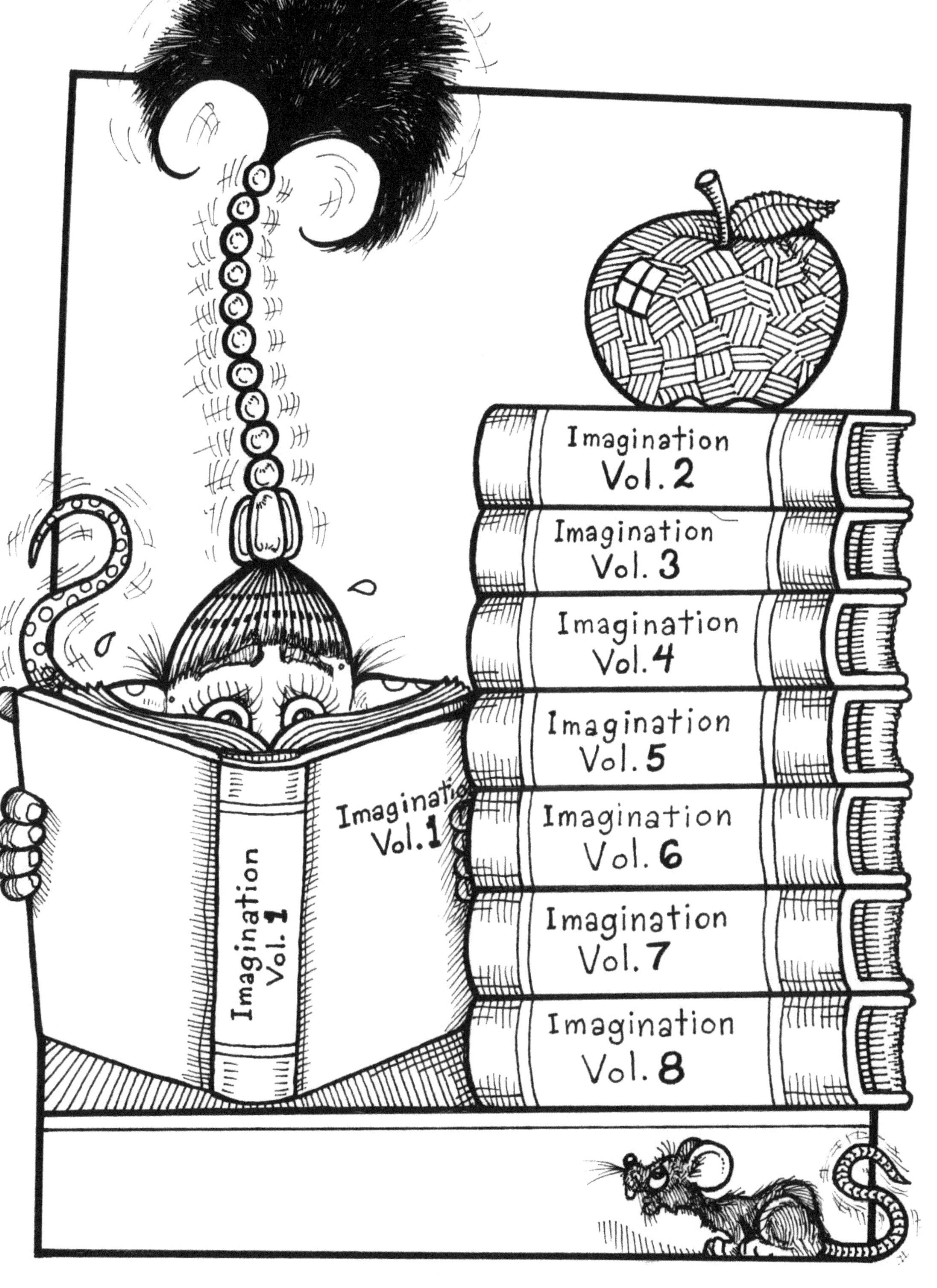

Imagination
Vol. 2
Imagination
Vol. 3
Imagination
Vol. 4
Imagination
Vol. 5
Imagination
Vol. 6
Imagination
Vol. 7
Imagination
Vol. 8
Imagination
Vol. 1
Imagination
Vol. 1

Putting things off...

Deferments:

Figments that keep putting things off. Putting things off can cause significant stress later when those things are pile up waiting to happen. They love to cause procrastination. Some humans affected by too many Deferments will attempt to put the tasks or blame everywhere but on their procrastination. Sometimes, however, putting things off may be caused by prolific Deferments. Deferments are found in many places but like to congregate on college campuses.

(Common Experience)

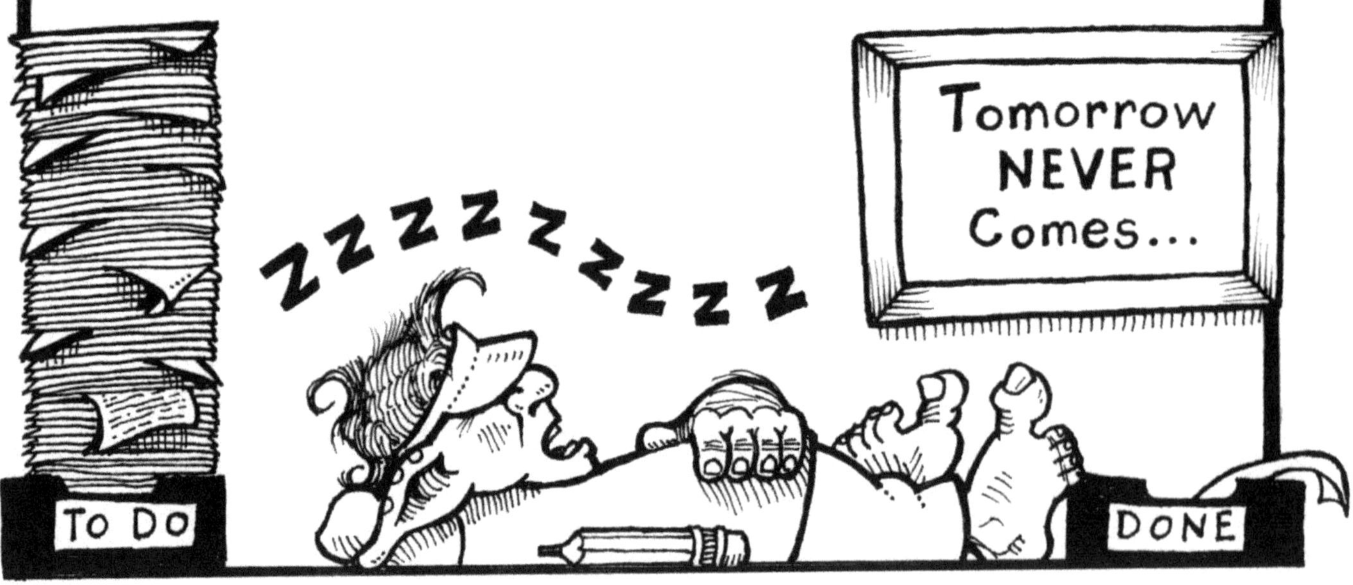

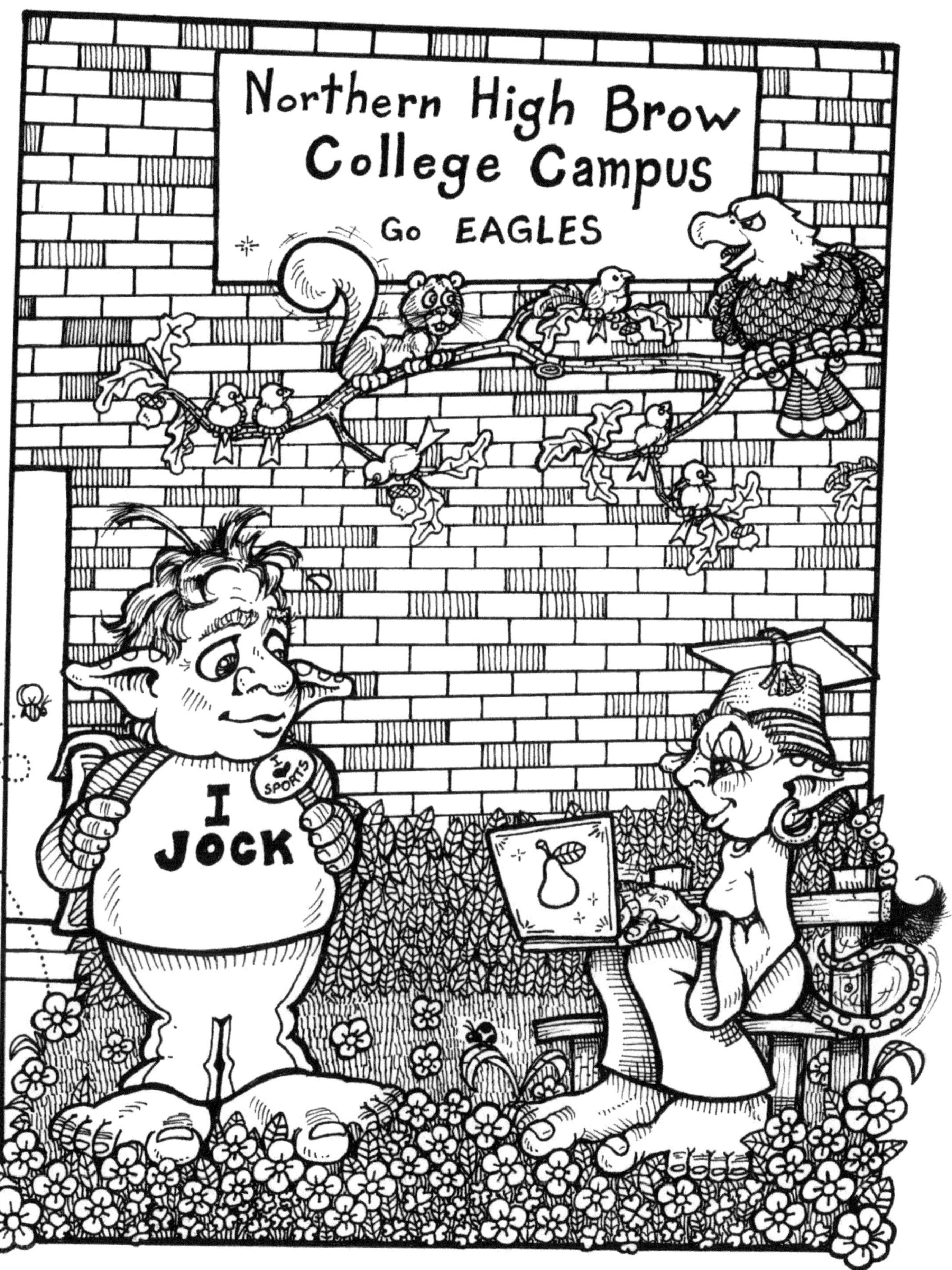

Northern High Brow
College Campus
Go EAGLES
I SPORTS
I JOCK

Stick in the Mud...

Dawdlers:

This Figment is so laid back it is a laggard or putterer.

They are even lackadaisical in their actions.

They can dawdle through any task to become the stick in the mud or loafer. If a human has a Dawdler, they are often the last in line, the slowest to do a task, every time, the one who is the last out to do, well, pretty much anything at all. Their human is not lacking motion, just speed or Energy.

(Common Experience)

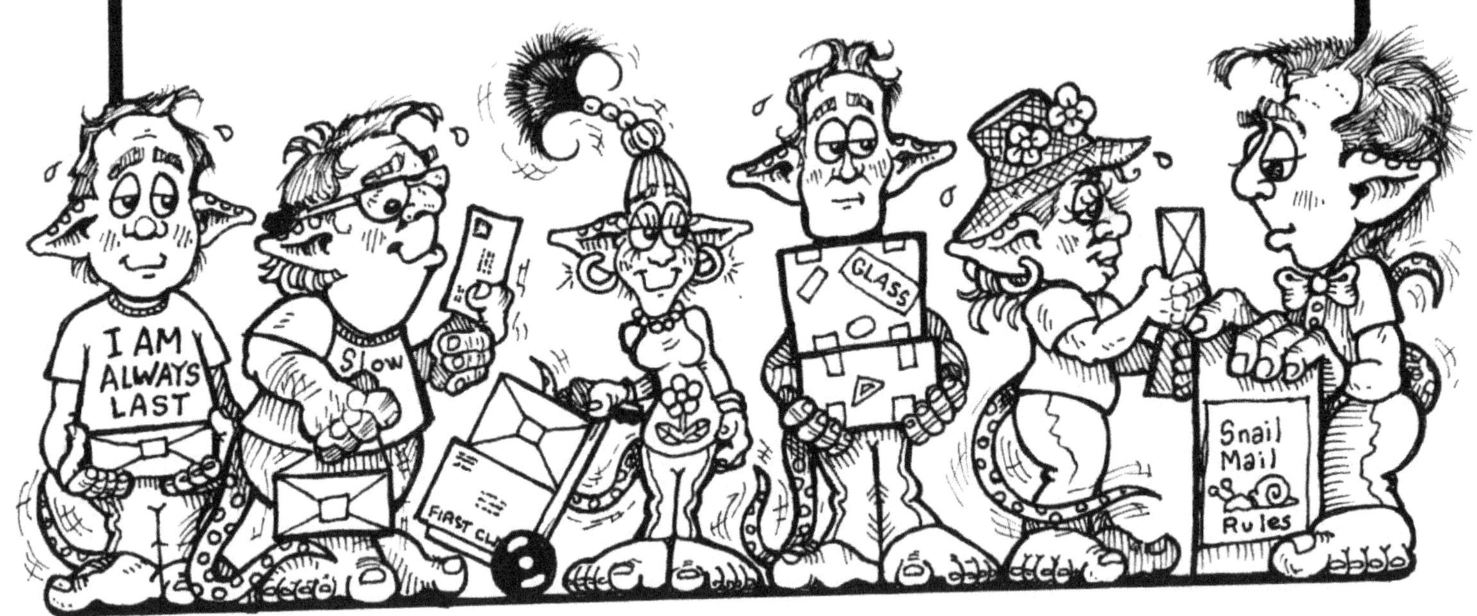

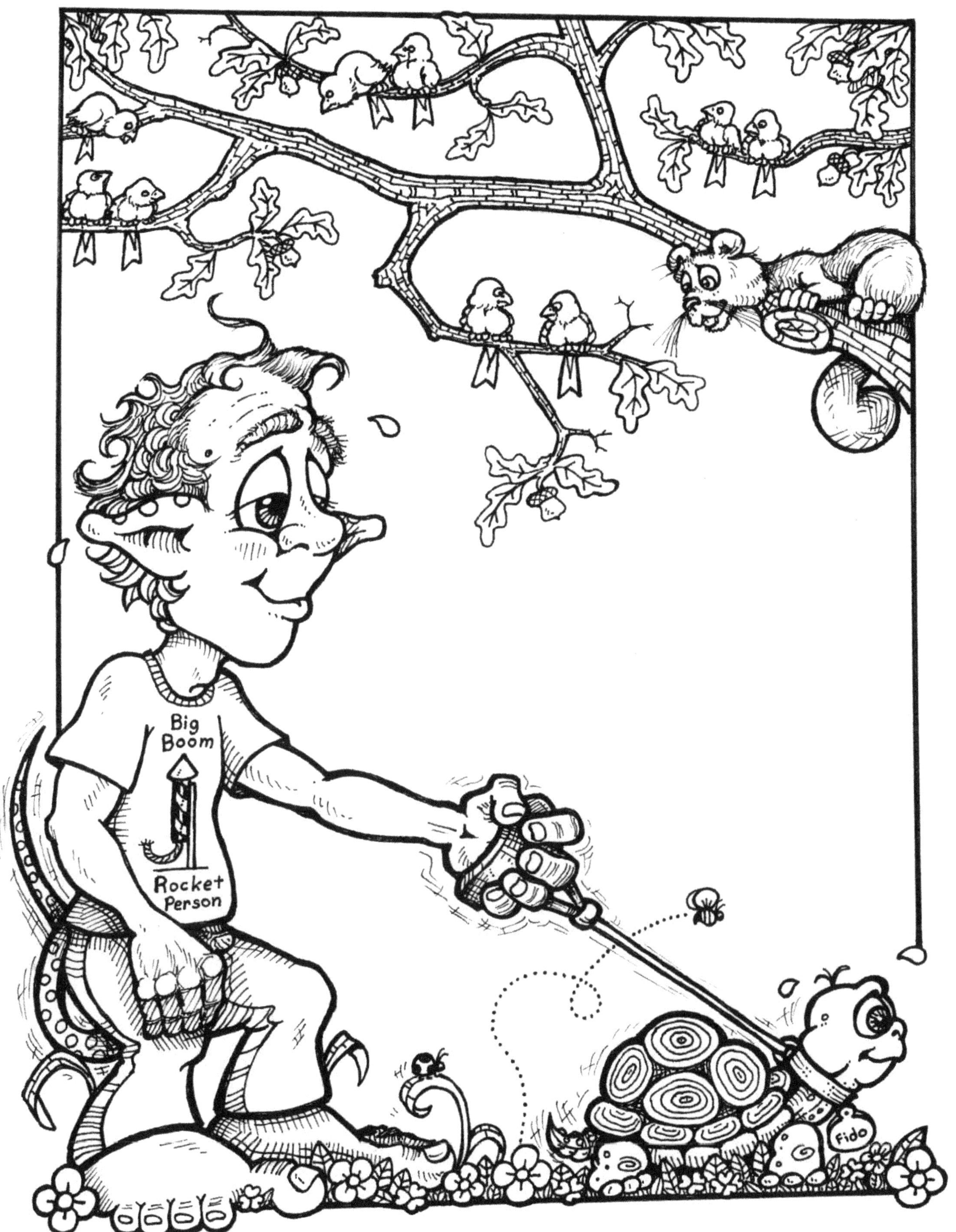

Big
Boom
Rocket
Person
Fido

Some are self-imposed...

Obligations:

Many people have Obligations. Some are self-imposed, others are given or compelled by others, but they are weighty Figments. They can be in slightly different forms, those of a moral type and those of a more legal variety.

Whether chosen or imposed, obligations are hard to put aside once obtained. Sometimes we want the Obligation; other times, they can feel a bit like an albatross. If you acquire too many of this Figment, you can seemingly drown in Obligations. If not careful, they can hold us back from accomplishments. Often you are merely under obligations. They often connect us to those we love, which is good.

(Common Experience)

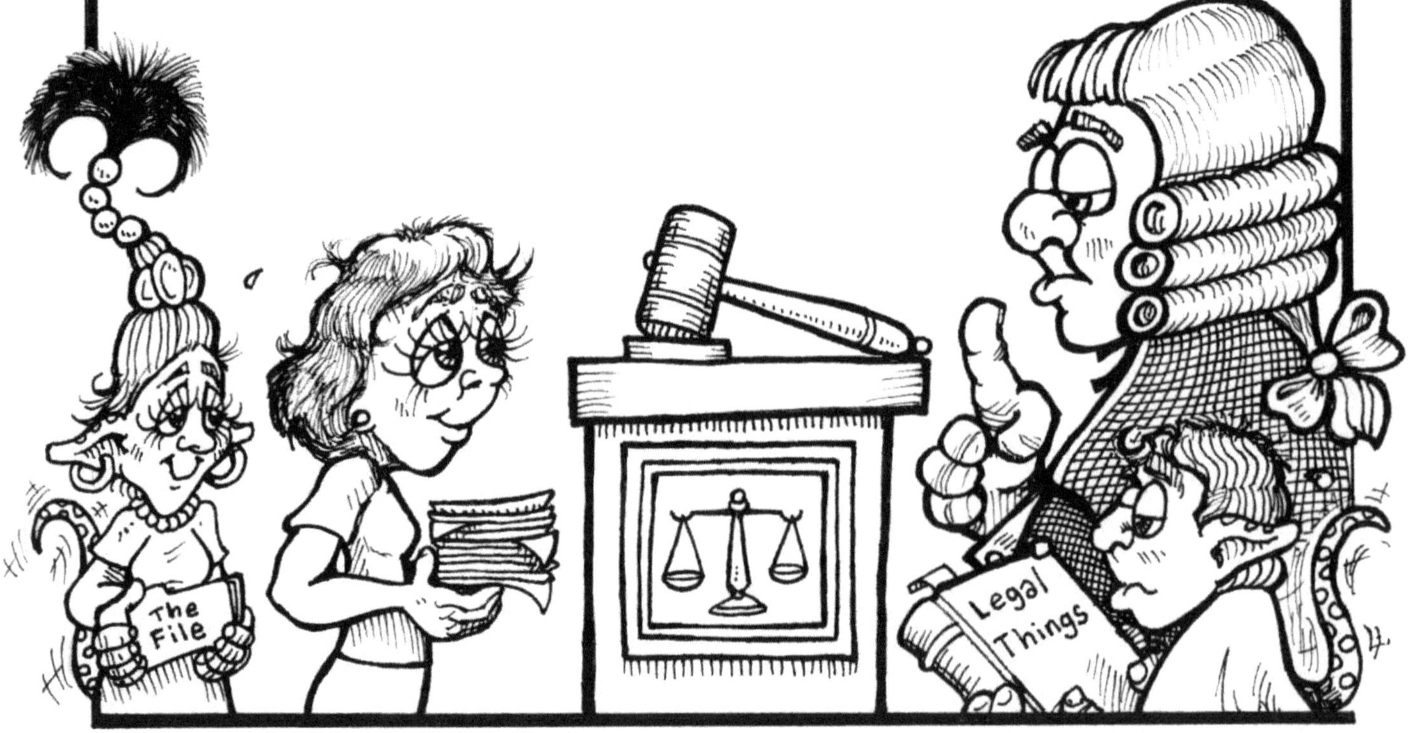

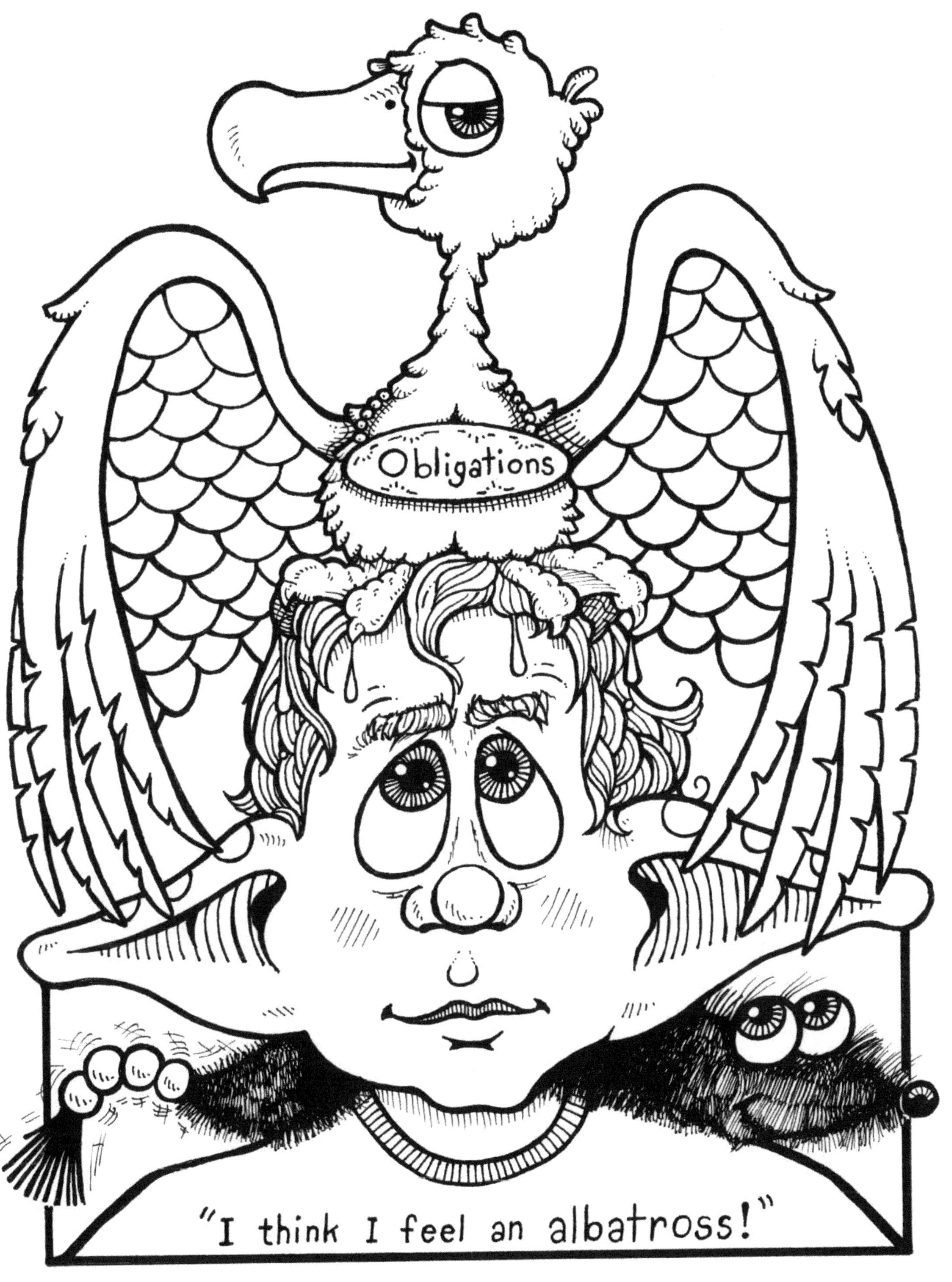

Obligations
"I think I feel an albatross!"

Large public gatherings... 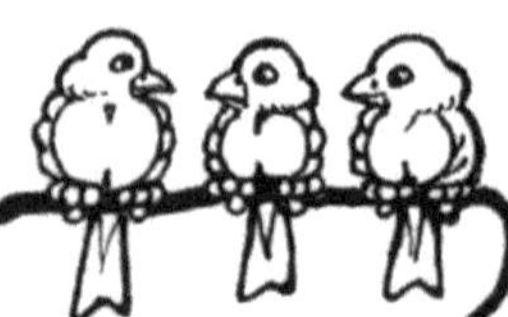

One of the few Figments that comes from collective emotions. Their inception is the undercurrents running through a crowd of people, that feeling of potential power. The understanding is that it would only take a touchstone to set off the collective behavior and often not in a positive way. The feelings shared in a crowd are associated with mass hysteria or mob behavior. Often a conglomeration of emotions. Seethe Figments sometimes are found in crowds that gather for a variety of reasons, sporting events, concerts, parades, and other large public gatherings. All too often, young humans are susceptible to their influence, but Seethes are pretty influential to those who have indulged in liquid spirits. These Figments do not appear often, but humans do not exhibit their most exemplary behavior when they are present.

(Common Experience)

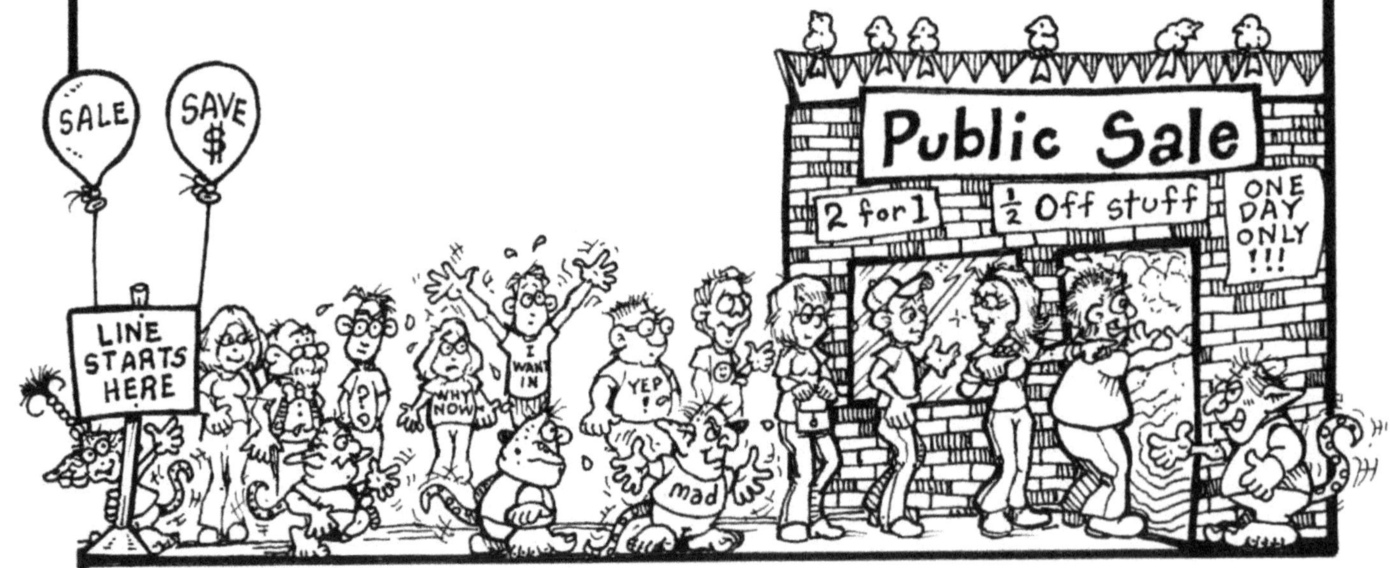

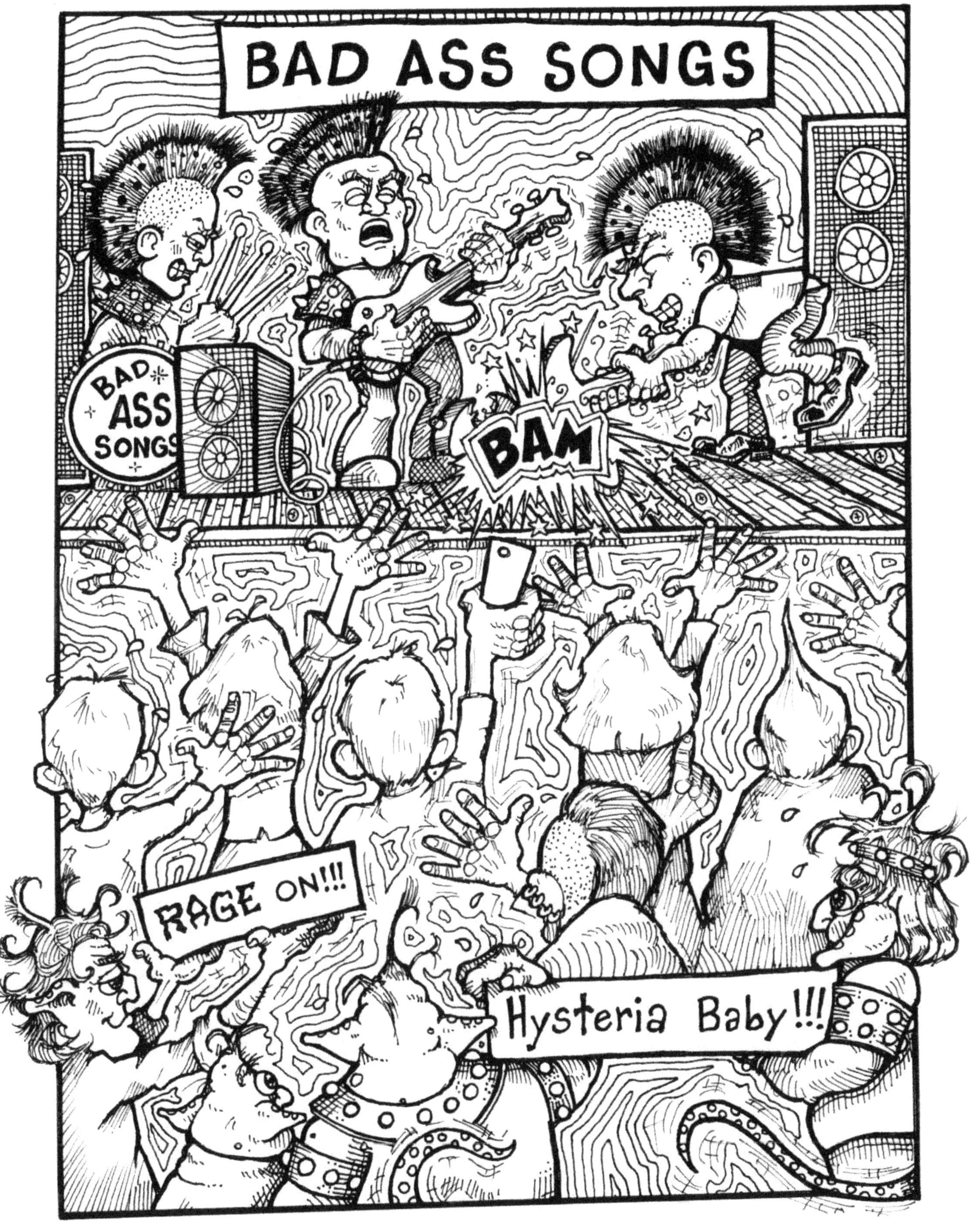

BAD ASS SONGS
BAD ASS SONGS
BAM
RAGE ON!!!
Hysteria Baby!!!

Burst of emotion...

Peeves:

People take irritations in bursts of emotion and hold onto them, manifesting them as Figment Peeves. They grasp, store, and revel in those Peeves, even sometimes bragging about them.

Until a time when they have become so familiar, the Peeves become pets. Different Peeves seem to appeal to other people, and some people have many Pet Peeves, almost as if they were collecting them.

(Emotions)

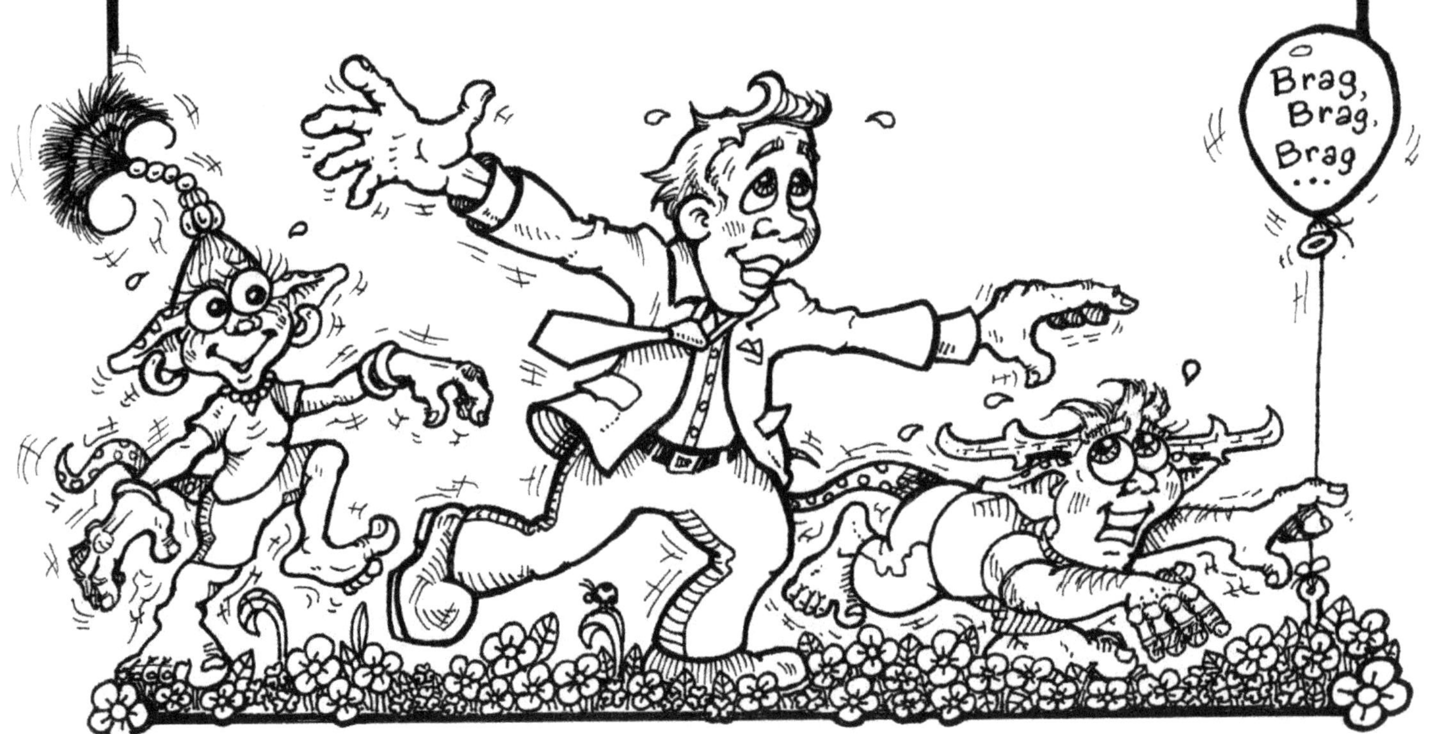

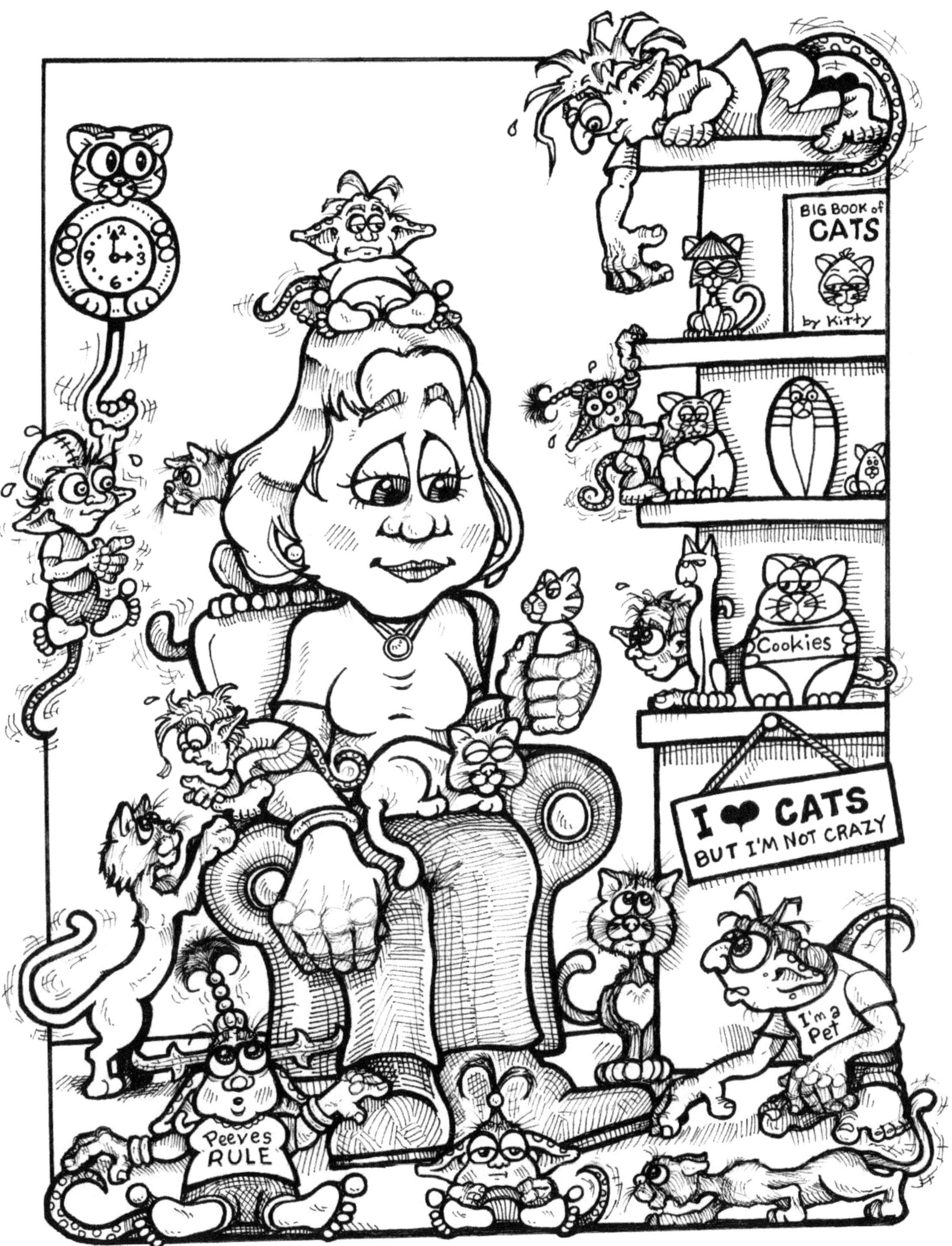
BIG BOOK of CATS
by Kitty
Cookies
I ♥ CATS
BUT I'M NOT CRAZY
I'm a Pet
Peeves RULE
12
9   3
6

Humans tend to latch onto and hold onto some things, even if those things are very

annoying. Peeves have startling eyes that catch your attention and stay with you. They

are unusual Figments and often irritating or will agitate a situation with humans;

perhaps that originally was small. They want to be with you all the time. While they

tend to be ugly, Figment's people can't help but collect them.

Peeves can be found in traffic situations,

as well as in many places in everyday life.

(Emoticons)

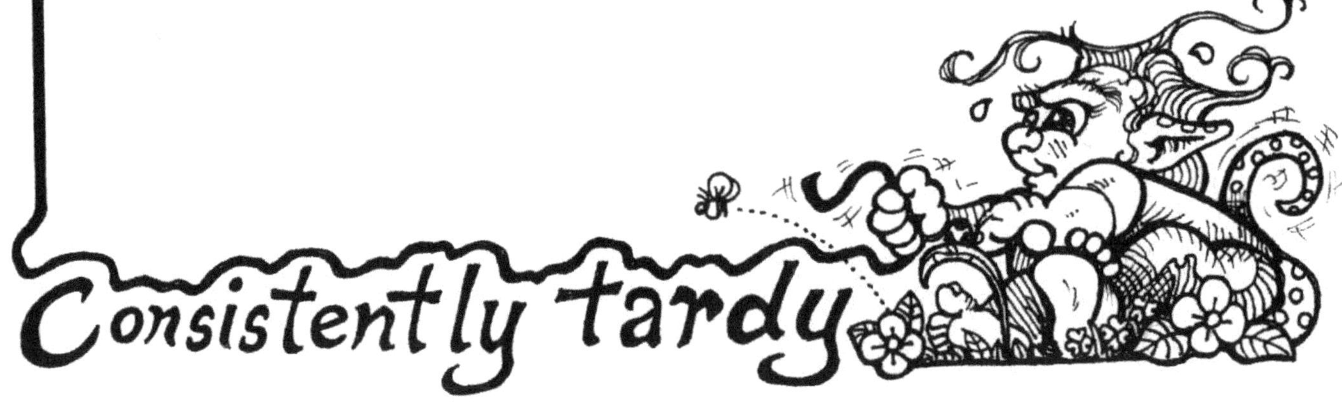

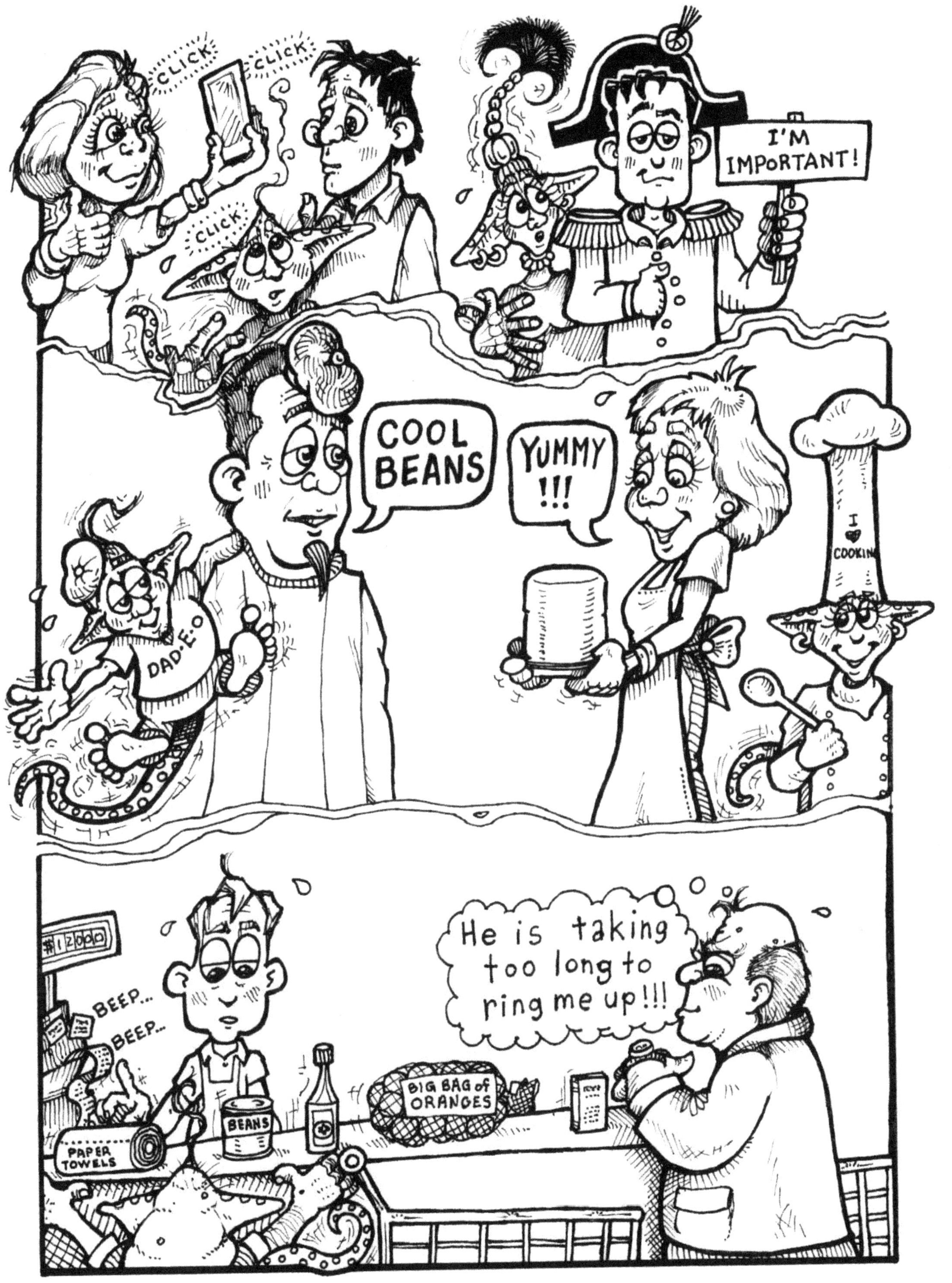

CLICK
CLICK
CLICK
I'M IMPORTANT!
COOL BEANS
YUMMY !!!
DAD-E-O
I ♥ COOKING
$12000
BEEP...
BEEP...
PAPER TOWELS
BEANS
BIG BAG of ORANGES
He is taking too long to ring me up!!!

Talking through the movie...

Really,

have you made pets

of many peeves?

Block the path...

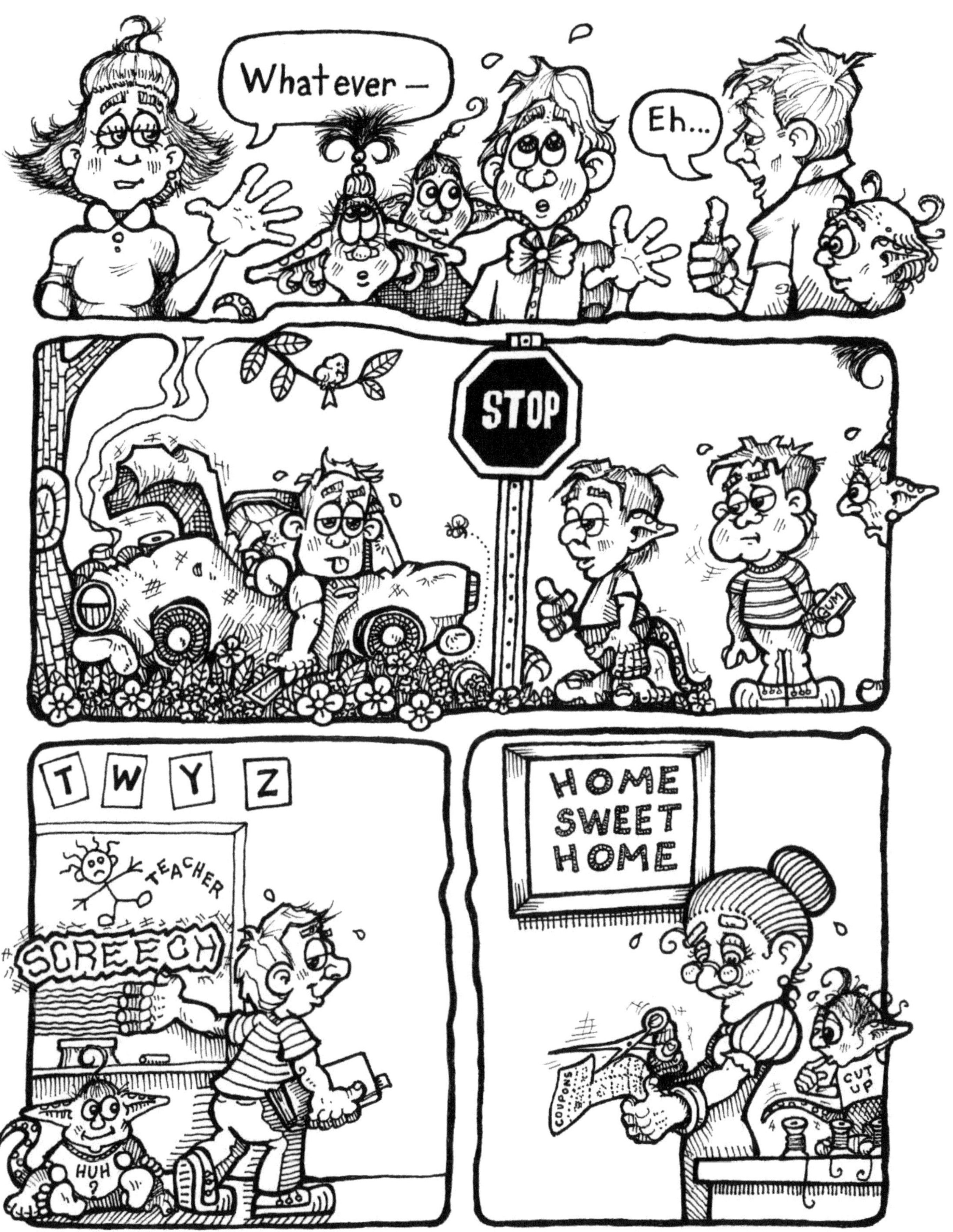
Whatever —
Eh...
STOP
T W Y Z
TEACHER
SCREECH
HUH ?
HOME SWEET HOME
COUPONS
CUT UP
GUM

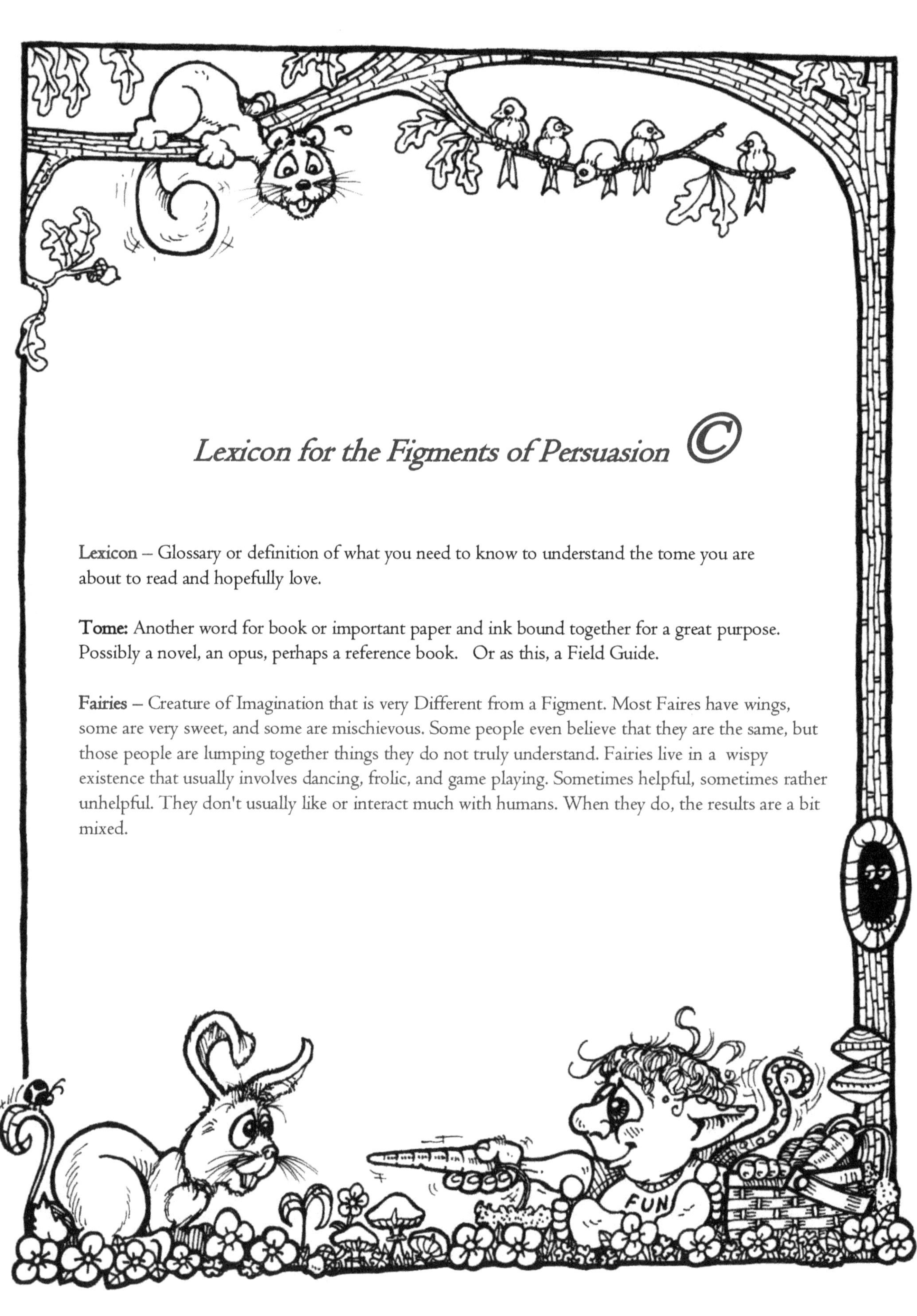

Lexicon for the Figments of Persuasion ©

Lexicon – Glossary or definition of what you need to know to understand the tome you are about to read and hopefully love.

Tome: Another word for book or important paper and ink bound together for a great purpose. Possibly a novel, an opus, perhaps a reference book.   Or as this, a Field Guide.

Fairies – Creature of Imagination that is very Different from a Figment. Most Faires have wings, some are very sweet, and some are mischievous. Some people even believe that they are the same, but those people are lumping together things they do not truly understand. Fairies live in a wispy existence that usually involves dancing, frolic, and game playing. Sometimes helpful, sometimes rather unhelpful. They don't usually like or interact much with humans. When they do, the results are a bit mixed.

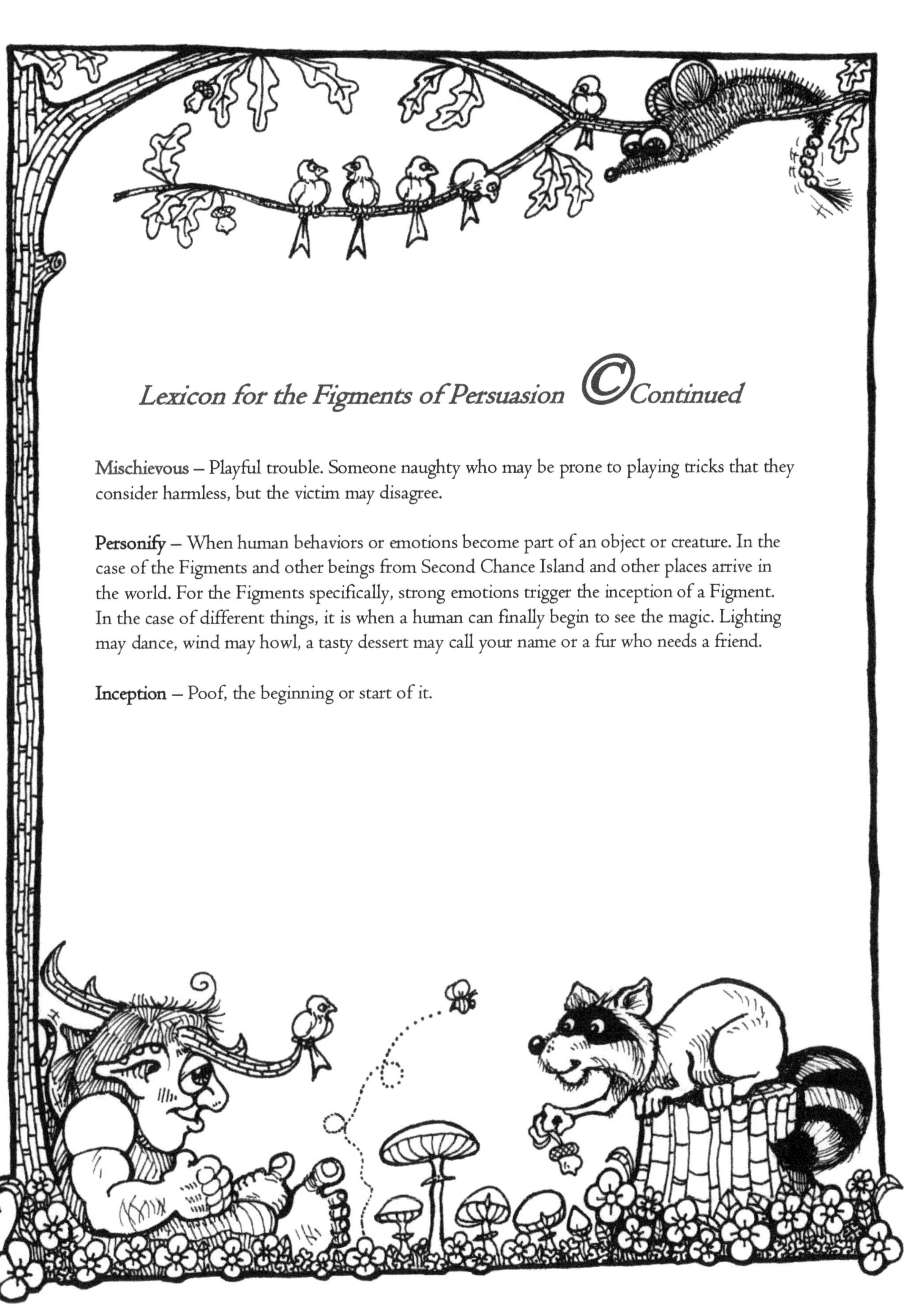

Lexicon for the Figments of Persuasion **C** *Continued*

Mischievous – Playful trouble. Someone naughty who may be prone to playing tricks that they consider harmless, but the victim may disagree.

Personify – When human behaviors or emotions become part of an object or creature. In the case of the Figments and other beings from Second Chance Island and other places arrive in the world. For the Figments specifically, strong emotions trigger the inception of a Figment. In the case of different things, it is when a human can finally begin to see the magic. Lighting may dance, wind may howl, a tasty dessert may call your name or a fur who needs a friend.

Inception – Poof, the beginning or start of it.

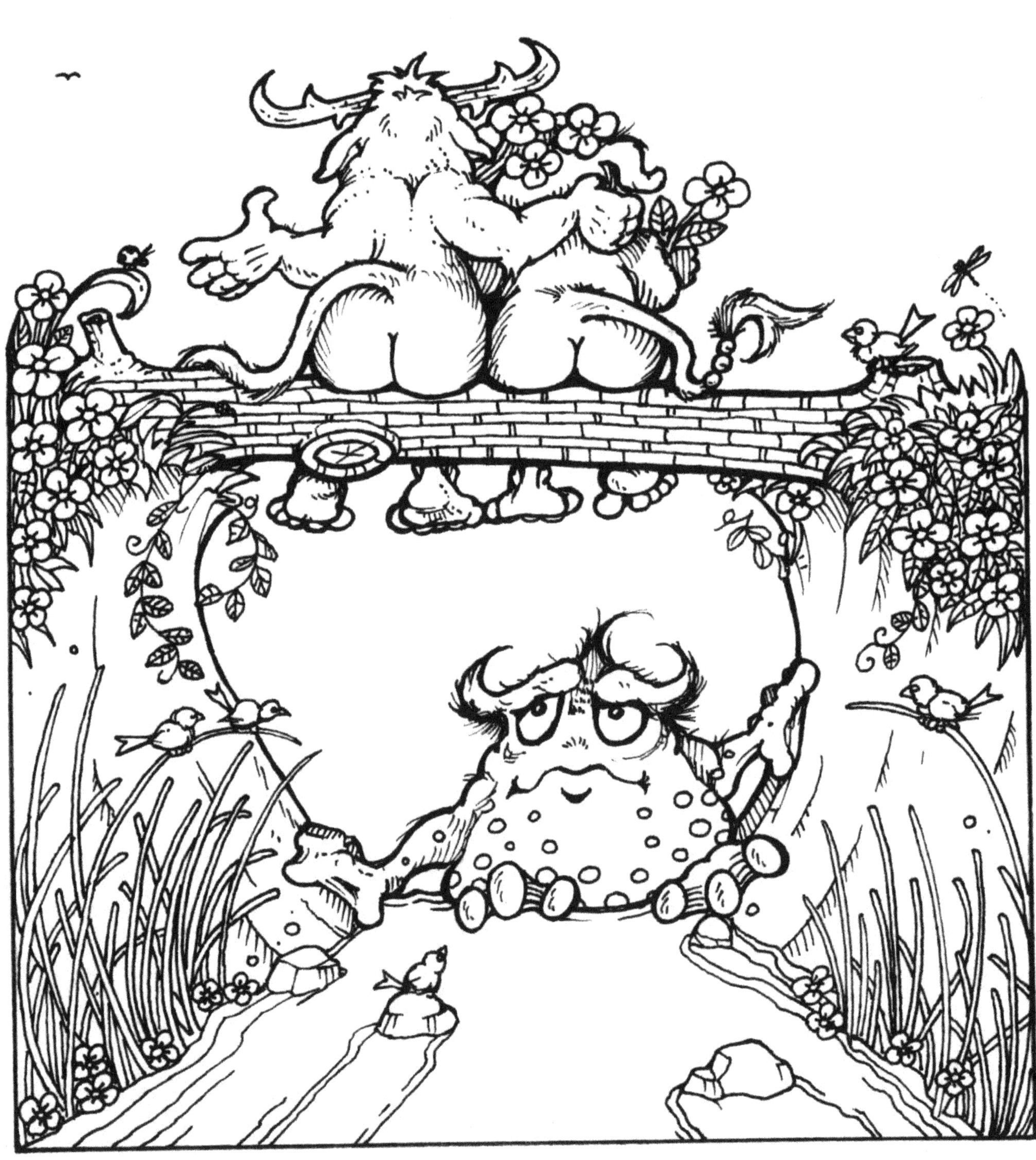
the End ?